RUFF GUIDE

to the UNITED STATES

RUFF GUIDE

to the UNITED STATES

INTRODUCTION

Since launching in 2006, BringFido.com has helped more than 10 million people bring their dogs on vacation. But it all started with just one—Rocco. Three years earlier, an animal control officer found him wandering the streets of Hartford on a snowy Christmas morning. He wasn't wearing any ID tags, but she was sure the little pup's owners would claim him as soon as they returned home from the holidays. No one came for Rocco on Monday morning, or the following week, or the week after that. Lots of people who wandered into the shelter asked if he was available for adoption, but for some reason, the officer kept saying no. She was waiting for someone special.

I had recently graduated from college and was living in Boston. I wanted a dog desperately and combed the pages of Petfinder.com on a daily basis, but for some reason, I hadn't been ready to pull the trigger. I questioned whether it was fair to have a dog in such a tiny apartment. And what would I do with a dog when I flew home to California or went on a business trip? But when I stumbled across Rocco's mug shot online, all bets were off. That was my dog! He looked just like the Rottweiler I'd grown up with as a kid, but weighed only 14 pounds. Surely, he'd be comfortable in my pint-sized apartment! I immediately pointed my car toward Connecticut and was happily making the return trip with Rocco in the passenger seat a few hours later.

From that day on, Rocco was always right beside me. I wouldn't even go down the street to Starbucks without him, so putting him in a kennel when I traveled was out of the question. Being a traveler by nature, it wasn't unusual for me to get out of town several times a month. However, I quickly became frustrated by the process of finding hotels that welcomed my canine companion. The big travel websites all had a 'pet friendly' icon, but their information was wrong more often than not. And when I finally found a hotel that did allow pets, I might also find a 'surprise' pet fee on my bill at check-out. That didn't seem very friendly to me.

I didn't think it should be so much work to go on vacation, and I knew there must be lots of other dog owners out there who shared my frustration. So, I decided to do us all a favor! With the help of my brother, and a dozen of our friends, we called nearly 50,000 hotels and built a robust database of hotel pet policies. We spent months quizzing front desk workers about whether their hotel allowed pets. And when we found one that did, we gathered detailed information about its pet fee, weight limit, the number of pets allowed per room, and any other 'intel' that might be helpful to dog owners.

When BringFido.com launched in 2006, it was the world's first travel agency for pets. We gave dog owners the scoop on more than 10,000 pet friendly hotels, and enabled them to book rooms online at a guaranteed low rate. All of our information was backed by a 'pet fee guarantee' and we even had a Canine Concierge on staff who made sure our customers were assigned to a pet friendly room, so there wouldn't be any unpleasant surprises at check-in. Two years later, we expanded to include international hotels and vacation rentals. And a year after that, we began adding outdoor restaurants, dog parks, events, and other animal attractions. By 2011, there were more than 100,000 pet friendly places listed on BringFido.com.

During those first five years, Rocco and I traveled all over the country together to promote BringFido.com. He marched in the 'Barkus Pet Parade' during Mardi Gras in New Orleans, threw out the first bone at the Atlanta Braves 'Paws in the Park' game, and was the only non-Pug invited on the 'Pug Crawl' in Chicago. It was a ruff life, but someone had to do it! My personal life was equally busy. I met my husband, Jason, got married (at one of the hotels in this book, nonetheless), and started a 'blended' family with his three cats. A year later, we added to it with the birth of our first (human) child, Jack.

Rocco sat watch on my belly the entire time I was pregnant, but his health declined rapidly during those nine months. After multiple trips to the veterinarian, he was diagnosed with an inoperable tumor, and I had to say goodbye to my travel buddy in the summer of 2011. My feelings of grief turned into shock less than a month later when I too was diagnosed with cancer. It was a tough pill to swallow, but when I finished radiation therapy, I knew it was time to get back on the road. I just needed a new co-pilot.

Even though Rocco was a small dog, he left some really big shoes to fill. So, when I saw the huge paws on a black lab mix named Ace at our local animal shelter, I knew I'd found the right dog for the job! Ace's first assignment as the new BringFido.com mascot was a 25,000-mile cross-country adventure. We made it our mission to visit as many of the places that had been rated '5 bones' by BringFido.com members as possible, and stopped at hundreds of dog friendly hotels and attractions. I'm not just talking about the local dog parks either—we took surfing lessons in San Diego, hiked Dog Mountain in the Columbia Gorge, slept in a safari tent in Yellowstone National Park, and rode a rollercoaster in Pennsylvania. Okay, it was a kiddie rollercoaster, but still, can your dog say he's done that? Probably not yet, but I hope he will soon!

Ace and I had a wonderful time on the road trip, but as we zigzagged across the country, I couldn't help wishing Rocco had been able to scratch a couple more items off his bucket list too. He would have loved visiting a dude ranch in Colorado! Or riding a dune buggy in Oregon! Inside this book, you'll find information on 365 of the best places to play and stay with your dog in all 50 states. As you flip through the pages, I encourage you to keep a 'bucket list' of the places you'd like to visit with your dog (and to make that a little easier, we've even included a blank one on the next page).

Whether your dog prefers to 'ruff it' on a hiking adventure or sit in the lap of luxury at a five-star resort, the assortment of trips in this book is sure to leave him (and you) begging for a vacation. I hope *Ruff Guide to the United States* inspires you to share some unforgettable adventures with your pooch, and I'd love to hear about them. If you discover any incredible new places to bring Fido during your travels, please email me at melissa@bringfido.com. Ace and I will meet you there!

Happy travels,

Melissa Halliburton

Melissa Halliburton
Founder, BringFido.com

FIDO'S BUCKET LIST

- [ ] _____
- [ ] _____
- [ ] _____
- [ ] _____
- [ ] _____
- [ ] _____
- [ ] _____
- [ ] _____
- [ ] _____
- [ ] _____
- [ ] _____
- [ ] _____
- [ ] _____
- [ ] _____
- [ ] _____
- [ ] _____
- [ ] _____
- [ ] _____
- [ ] _____

TABLE OF CONTENTS

Russell Cave National Monument

Take a prehistoric journey with Fido to the **Russell Cave National Monument** in Bridgeport. This 314-acre park welcomes leashed dogs to explore grounds inhabited by Native Americans more than 10,000 years ago. You and your leashed pup can take a guided tour of the cave shelter, which housed countless humans throughout the Paleo, Archaic, Woodland, and Mississippian archeological periods. Visit the picturesque wildflower meadow, hike along a portion of the North Alabama Birding Trail, or enjoy a picnic on this historic site. Ranger-led demonstrations of primitive tools and weapons provide a glimpse into the daily life of prehistoric humans. Well-behaved dogs are welcome throughout the grounds, including the cave shelter and the hiking trails. Dogs are not permitted in any park building. Russell Cave National Monument is open daily from 8:00 am to 4:30 pm, with the exception of New Year's Day, Thanksgiving, and Christmas. There is no admission fee.

Russell Cave National Monument
3729 County Road 98
Bridgeport, AL 35740
(256) 495-2672
www.nps.gov/ruca

Where to Stay:

Located on the scenic Nickajack Lake, the **Hales Bar Marina Floating Cabins** feature one, two, and three bedroom furnished accommodations with kitchenettes that are well-suited for the adventurous traveler. Fish from the dock or visit the adjacent Hales Bar Resort, where you can play a round of miniature golf, take a dip in the outdoor swimming pool, and shop for supplies at the Ship Store. Dogs of any size are welcome for an additional fee of $25 per pet.

Hales Bar Marina Floating Cabins
1265 Hales Bar Road
Guild, TN 37340
(423) 942-9000
www.halesbarmarina.com
Rates from $84/night

Where to Stay:

Following a day on the water, you can relax with your pooch at the **Staybridge Suites Gulf Shores**. This all-suite property features full kitchens in each guest room. Other amenities include a complimentary hot breakfast buffet, business center, outdoor pool, and fitness center. The hotel also provides guests with access to patio grills. Dogs up to 80 lbs are welcome for an additional fee of $75 (for stays up to six nights) or $150 (for stays of seven nights or longer).

Staybridge Suites Gulf Shores
3947 State Highway 59
Gulf Shores, AL 36542
(251) 975-1030
www.tinyurl.com/ruff01
Rates from $118/night

Hudson Marina

When the weather heats up, pack your pup's life jacket and head to the Alabama Gulf Coast for a relaxing weekend of water fun with Fido. Cruise the bay and do some fishing around Gulf Shores in a pet-friendly pontoon boat rental from **Hudson Marina at Skull Harbor** in Orange Beach. The crew at Hudson Marina will outfit you with the right equipment to make your day on the water one to remember. Pontoons range in size from 19-foot standard boats to 30-foot double-decker boats with slides. Prices vary from $195 for standard half-day rentals to $525 for deluxe full-day rentals. If your pup is up for a real thrill, the marina also offers Jet Ski rentals starting at $65 for half-hour rentals. Whatever option you choose, be sure to make your reservation in advance for the best selection and to ensure that a vessel is available for you.

Hudson Marina at Skull Harbor
4575 S Wilson Boulevard
Orange Beach, AL 36561
(251) 981-4127
www.hudsonmarina.net

3 Dog Night Hostel

Treat your canine companion to an Alaskan wilderness adventure with a visit to the **3 Dog Night Hostel** near Fairbanks. Owners Mike and Donna Ostler will introduce you to the recreational sport of sled dog mushing at their working sled dog facility, which also features a bed and breakfast and hostel for overnight guests. During the summer months, you and your pup can tour the grounds and choose from numerous moderate to difficult hiking trails that offer amazing views of the Salcha River Valley. If your dog loves the water, rent a canoe and paddle around Chena or Birch Lake. Anglers will want to bring their gear for some great rainbow trout, salmon, and char fishing. Utilize the free pick-up and drop-off service to Piledriver Slough, where you and your pup can spot moose, beavers, and a variety of birds on a scenic float down the waterway.

3 Dog Night Hostel
5972 Richardson Highway
Fairbanks, AK 99714
(907) 590-8207
www.3dognighthostel.com

Where to Stay:

After a long day of hiking, canoeing and fishing, you and your pooch can relax in the rustic Trapper's Cabin or the more elaborate Deluxe Cabin at **3 Dog Night Hostel**. The Trapper's Cabin provides a table, chairs, camping stove and teapot, but you will need to bring your own bedding. The Deluxe Cabin offers a furnished living area, full kitchen, heat, and running water. Guests are advised to book far in advance, and dogs are welcome for no additional fee.

3 Dog Night Hostel
5972 Richardson Highway
Fairbanks, AK 99714
(907) 590-8207
www.3dognighthostel.com
Rates from $60/night

Where to Stay:

Wahweap Marina allows dogs of any size on their deluxe and economy houseboats for a fee of $10 per pet, per night. If you want to experience the lake, but aren't comfortable driving a 46-foot houseboat, you can rent a small powerboat and stay at the **Lake Powell Resort** instead. The hotel allows dogs for an additional fee of $20 per pet, per night. Guests are also required to pay $15 per vehicle for entrance to the Glen Canyon National Recreation Area.

Lake Powell Resort & Marina
100 Lake Shore Drive
Page, AZ 86040
(928) 645-2433
www.lakepowell.com
Rates from $80/night

Lake Powell Resort & Marina

Located on the border of Arizona and Utah, Lake Powell is best known for two things—houseboating and the spectacular scenery of the **Glen Canyon National Recreation Area**. With a pet-friendly houseboat rental from **Lake Powell Resort & Marina** in Page, you can easily enjoy both with man's best friend! After a brief introduction to houseboating at the full-service Wahweap Marina, set off on an adventure to Rainbow Bridge National Monument or explore the lake's 1,800 miles of shoreline. Lounge on the deck and soak up some sun as your home on the water floats through one of the scenic slot canyons. See the sun rise from the outer deck, drop a line over the side for an afternoon of fishing, and enjoy dinner under the stars with your canine companion. Rental rates vary depending on the season and vessel selected, and rentals are subject to a three-night minimum throughout the year.

Lake Powell Resort & Marina
Wahweap Marina
100 Lake Shore Drive
Page, AZ 86040
(928) 645-2433
www.lakepowell.com/houseboating

McDowell Sonoran Preserve

The pet-friendly **McDowell Sonoran Preserve** is a 27,000-acre desert oasis featuring more than 100 miles of hiking trails in the heart of Scottsdale. Start at the Gateway Trailhead, where you'll find plenty of parking, a doggie water fountain, and visitor's center. Hit the 4.5-mile Gateway Loop Trail to see impressive wildflower displays and lush cacti forests. Trailhead hosts are available on weekends and most weekday mornings to assist you with route planning. Ask them about the 'Paws in the Preserve' program, which offers activities for dog owners and helpful information on hiking with your pup in the desert. Admission is free, and dogs must remain leashed at all times. After exploring the preserve, bring your pooch to the **McCormick-Stillman Railroad Park**, which features an antique carousel, train rides, shops, museums, and picnic areas. Dogs of any size are welcome, and small dogs can even ride the train with you!

McDowell Sonoran Preserve
18333 N Thompson Peak Parkway
Scottsdale, AZ 85259
(480) 998-7971
www.mcdowellsonoran.org

Where to Stay:

For a luxurious stay in the Arizona desert, look no further than Kimpton's **FireSky Resort & Spa** in Scottsdale. Relax in the shade by the hotel's inviting lagoon, rejuvenate your body with a treatment at the full-service spa, and enjoy s'mores around the firepit. Pet beds and bowls are provided at check-in, and Fido is welcome to accompany you during the complimentary wine reception each evening. Dogs of any size stay in patio and courtyard rooms for no additional fee.

FireSky Resort & Spa
4925 N Scottsdale Road
Scottsdale, AZ 85251
(480) 945-7666
www.fireskyresort.com
Rates from $132/night

Where to Stay:

After a day of adventure on the red rocks, luxury awaits at the **El Portal Sedona**. This AAA Four Diamond boutique property features 11 dog-friendly guest suites, several of which have enclosed private patios for their canine guests. Dogs of any size are welcome for no additional fee, and treats and other pet amenities are provided at check-in. Many restaurants with outdoor seating are within walking distance, including **Ken's Creekside Restaurant**, which features steak tartar on the doggie menu.

El Portal Sedona
95 Portal Lane
Sedona, AZ 86336
(800) 313-0017
www.elportalsedona.com
Rates from $199/night

A Day in the West Jeep Tours

No trip to Sedona would be complete without an off-road adventure in one of the town's ubiquitous four-wheel drive Jeeps. Fortunately for Fido, **A Day in the West** offers you and your dog the chance to explore the area's canyons and natural rock formations on your own off-road adventure. The family-owned company offers a number of guided tours in and around the Coconino National Forest, including the Mogollon Rim Tour, which features breathtaking panoramic views courtesy of an exhilarating ascent to an elevation of 7,500 feet. If you want to see a particular site or attraction, customized tours are available for you and your pup. A Day in the West operates daily, with tours ranging from 90 minutes to three hours. Prices start at $49 per person. Lap dogs are welcome for no additional fee; larger dogs ride for the price of a child's ticket ($37 and up). Advance reservations are recommended.

A Day in the West
252 N Highway 89-A
Sedona, AZ 86336
(928) 282-4320
www.adayinthewest.com

Garvan Woodland Gardens

Dog lovers with a green thumb shouldn't pass up the chance to bring Fido to **Garvan Woodland Gardens** in Hot Springs. Pick up a self-guided tour map and roam the 210-acre meticulously manicured grounds. Your dog is welcome to explore all areas of the park except the ponds. The park is open daily from 9:00 am to 6:00 pm. Admission is $10 for adults and $5 for dogs. After your garden tour, take a short drive to Lake Hamilton for a cruise aboard the **Belle of Hot Springs Riverboat** with your furry friend. While you savor gorgeous views of the Ouachita Mountains, mansions and natural islands, the Belle's captain will entertain you with engaging stories, revealing the history of the area and sharing colorful anecdotes as he narrates the 15-mile sightseeing cruise. Cruises are offered at least once daily throughout the year. Adult fares are $18, and dogs ride for free.

Garvan Woodland Gardens
550 Arkridge Road
Hot Springs, AR 71913
(501) 262-9300
www.garvangardens.org

Where to Stay:

Beautiful views of Lake Hamilton await your arrival at the serene **Lookout Point Lakeside Inn** in Hot Springs. All of the inn's pet-friendly rooms feature a porch with access to the property's lush garden. When you aren't relaxing in your luxurious guest room, you can take Fido for a swim or canoe trip in the lake. Dogs of any size are welcome for an additional fee of $25 per pet, per night, and each pup receives a welcome treat upon arrival.

Lookout Point Lakeside Inn
104 Lookout Circle
Hot Springs, AR 71913
(501) 525-6155
www.lookoutpointinn.com
Rates from $159/night

Where to Stay:

Bungee jumping is a once-in-a-lifetime experience for most people, so it's only fitting to sleep in a one-of-a-kind motel after you make the leap. The **Wigwam Motel** is a historic Route 66 icon where you can sleep in a giant stucco tipi. Each of the 19 wigwams is equipped with modern amenities like indoor plumbing, air conditioning, internet, and TV. They share a kidney-shaped pool, barbecue grill, and grassy area for playing fetch. Dogs are welcome for an additional fee of $15 each.

Wigwam Motel
2728 Foothill Boulevard
San Bernardino, CA 92410
(909) 875-3005
www.wigwammotel.com
Rates from $70/night

Bungee America

Serious thrill-seekers are sure to find excitement with a **Bungee America** jump off the Bridge to Nowhere in Asuza. This isn't your average jump; it's an all-day, unforgettable adventure. Beginning with a 30-minute drive into the gorgeous San Gabriel Canyon, the day continues with a five-mile hike to the **Bridge to Nowhere** in the Angeles National Forest. Dogs are welcome to trek along with you and watch your feat of bravery, but this is no walk in the woods. The hike takes you over rugged terrain and crosses several creeks. For your pup's safety, he must have significant backcountry hiking experience and be comfortable swimming in a swift current. Single jumps start at $79, and one spectator can come along with each jumper for free (additional spectators are $10 each). Bungee America has trips scheduled every Saturday and Sunday morning year-round. Midweek jumps are available by special arrangement.

Bungee America
Bridge to Nowhere Trailhead
Camp Bonita Road
Azusa, CA 91702
(310) 322-8892
www.bungeeamerica.com

Fun Zone Boat Company

You and your pup can embark on a scenic harbor cruise with the **Fun Zone Boat Company** in Newport Beach. The company features a fleet of four vessels that welcome man's best friend on narrated tours around the Newport Beach Harbor. Choose the 45-minute sea lion tour that ventures into the Pacific Ocean or opt for the smooth sailing celebrity homes tour, which stays in the harbor for the duration of the 45-minute cruise. If you can't decide, the company also offers a 90-minute trip that includes both attractions. Enjoy the captain's entertaining narration as you get a glimpse of Catalina Island. If you cruise in winter, you may spot some whales too. Tours depart several times daily from the Harbor Cruise boat docks adjacent to the **Balboa Island Ferry**. Rates start at $14 for adults and $7 for children. Add $5 for the 90-minute cruise. Dogs are always welcome aboard for free.

Fun Zone Boat Company
600 E Edgewater Avenue
Balboa Island, CA 92661
(949) 673-0240
www.funzoneboats.com

Where to Stay:

Balboa Bay Resort is Newport Beach's only full-service waterfront resort. Enjoy the bay view from your private balcony, lounge beside the massive outdoor swimming pool, rent a kayak or paddle boat, or schedule a massage at the award-winning spa. One dog up to 50 lbs is welcome for an additional fee of $100 per stay. Those traveling with larger dogs should opt for the **Pacific Edge Hotel** in Laguna Beach, where dogs of any size are welcome for no extra fee.

Balboa Bay Resort
1221 West Coast Highway
Newport Beach, CA 92663
(949) 645-5000
www.balboabayresort.com
Rates from $209/night

Calistoga Ranch

Discerning travelers in search of a few days of serenity should look no further than the **Calistoga Ranch**. Tucked away on 157 secluded acres in the northern stretch of Napa Valley, this Auberge Resort combines world-class service with luxurious private accommodations to create a rejuvenating experience for all visitors, including your pampered pooch. Upon arrival, Fido will be greeted by the attentive staff with an assortment of treats and gifts. After settling in to your room, take your furry friend on a hike along one of the property's scenic trails. The resort offers a number of activities to round out your trip to California's wine country. Vinophiles will appreciate tasting seminars and wine-blending classes. Fitness enthusiasts can find their inner Zen at a Pilates or yoga class in the open-air fitness center overlooking a vineyard. Guests of the resort also enjoy complimentary use of a Mercedes-Benz vehicle during their stay.

Calistoga Ranch
580 Lommel Road
Calistoga, CA 94515
(707) 254-2800
www.calistogaranch.com

Where to Stay:

Each of **Calistoga Ranch**'s 48 guest lodges offer ample indoor and outdoor living spaces, complete with a private outdoor shower, garden, fireplace, and original artwork. Resort amenities include a heated swimming pool, full-service spa and fitness facility, as well as 24-hour concierge and in-room dining services. Lakeside dining under the stars is a culinary experience not to be missed during your stay. Up to three dogs of any size are welcome for an additional fee of $125 per stay.

Calistoga Ranch
580 Lommel Road
Calistoga, CA 94515
(707) 254-2800
www.calistogaranch.com
Rates from $525/night

Where to Stay:

Located a short walk from down-town Pacific Grove and Asilomar Beach, **Pacific Gardens Inn** is a lovely bed and breakfast that welcomes dogs of any size for no additional fee. Each evening you will be treated to a wine and cheese reception. Every morning, the inn provides a continental breakfast with goodies prepared by a local bakery. After your breakfast, take Fido on a walk to explore the trails leading to both the beach and the woods right outside your door.

Pacific Gardens Inn
701 Asilomar Boulevard
Pacific Grove, CA 93950
(831) 646-9414
www.pacificgardensinn.com
Rates from $99/night

17-Mile Drive

Considered one of the most scenic drives in the country, **17-Mile Drive** is the perfect way to see the California coastline. Pay the $10 toll and start from the southern access point off Highway 68 near Pebble Beach, rolling down the windows so you and your pup can enjoy the ocean breeze. Along the road you will see Shepherd's Knoll, Huckleberry Hill, Spanish Bay, and China Rock. Seal Rock is a great spot to stop for a picnic and watch the seals frolicking in the sun. Continue on to see Fanshell Overlook, Crocker Grove, the famous Lone Cypress, and the Ghost Tree. After your drive, Fido can stretch his legs at **Asilomar State Beach**. Rivaling 17-Mile Drive's beauty, the 107-acre property gives you and your pooch the opportunity to enjoy coastal bluffs, sand dunes, forests, swamps, and wildlife. Dogs must be leashed and stay on boardwalks and trails at all times.

17-Mile Drive
Highway 1 & Highway 68
Carmel, CA 93923
(800) 654-9300
www.bringfido.com/attraction/49/

Fountain of Woof

Nicknamed the dog-friendly capital of the world, the town of Carmel caters to man's best friend like no other. In the heart of Carmel's shopping district, you will find **Carmel Plaza**, offering a wide range of outdoor dining options, as well as fabulous boutiques and studios that cater to dog lovers. Nestled in the courtyard of the plaza is the famous **Fountain of Woof**, a popular spot for dog and people-watching on a hot sunny day. Be sure Fido takes a sip from the fountain for good luck, and then head to **Forge in the Forest**, where you can enjoy delicious American cuisine and California wines on the pup-friendly patio. Carmel Plaza is also just a half-mile away from the pet-friendly **Carmel Beach**, where dogs can roam off-leash on the gorgeous white sand beaches. With so much to see and do, your pup will love his visit to canine-centric Carmel.

Fountain of Woof
Carmel Plaza
Ocean Avenue & Mission Street
Carmel, CA 93921
(831) 624-1385
www.carmelplaza.com

Where to Stay:

After an off-leash romp at Carmel Beach, make your way to the nearby **Cypress Inn**. Stop by the pet wash station in the hotel courtyard before retreating to your magnificently appointed guest room. For a cocktail with your canine, be sure to visit Terry's Lounge, where your dog's adventures are sure to become a topic of conversation. The hotel welcomes dogs of any size for an additional fee of $30 per night ($50 for two dogs). Pet blankets, treats, and bowls will be provided.

Cypress Inn
Lincoln Street & 7th Avenue
Carmel, CA 93921
(831) 624-3871
www.cypress-inn.com
Rates from $245/night

Where to Stay:

Located a short drive from downtown Carmel and adjacent to Garland Ranch, the **Carmel Valley Ranch** sits on 500 acres of rolling hills with sweeping views of the central coast landscape. Resort amenities include golf, tennis, yoga, hiking, and other daily activities designed to keep you active. Fido is welcome to explore the trails, dine with you on the restaurant's patio, and enjoy the evening marshmallow roast. Dogs of any size are permitted for an additional fee of $100 per pet, per stay. Pet beds, bowls, and treats are provided.

Carmel Valley Ranch
1 Old Ranch Road
Carmel, CA 93923
(831) 625-9500
www.carmelvalleyranch.com
Rates from $375/night

Garland Ranch Regional Park

One of the best ways to enjoy the allure of the Carmel Valley is a day of hiking with your furry friend in the 4,462-acre **Garland Ranch Regional Park**. Offering trails for nearly every level of hiking ability, from beginner to advanced, this park is the perfect place to appreciate the gorgeous views of the Carmel River, Garzas Creek, and the Ventana Wilderness. Some trails offer interpretive signs, explaining elements of the natural surroundings, while others wind through sites formerly inhabited by the Rumsien Indians and 19th century homesteading settlements. Trail maps can be found at the park's visitor center. Many of the hiking trails have a water fountain designed for both human and canine rehydration. When not on-leash, Fido must be within your eyesight and under strict voice control. Garland Ranch Regional Park is open daily from sunrise to sunset. There is no admission fee.

Garland Ranch Regional Park
700 W Carmel Valley Road
Carmel, CA 93923
(831) 372-3196
www.bringfido.com/attraction/205

Coronado Surfing Academy

Located across the bay from downtown San Diego, the town of Coronado is home to some of Southern California's finest beaches, as well as the Loews Surf Dog Competition held annually in June. Does your dog have what it takes to win the top prize? You can find out by signing up for a dog surfing lesson from the crew at **Coronado Surfing Academy**. One-hour private lessons are offered year-round for $80 and will give your pooch the chance to 'Hang 20' on the waves of the Pacific Ocean. After your lesson, head to Ocean Beach, home of the **Original Dog Beach**, for more leash-free fun in the sun. Once Fido is finished playing, get him cleaned up at the **Dog Beach Dog Wash** on Voltaire Street. Following your pup's bath, enjoy an evening in San Diego's Gaslamp Quarter by bringing your pooch to the 'wooftop' bar at **Hotel Indigo**.

Coronado Surfing Academy
116 B Avenue
Coronado, CA 92118
(619) 293-3883
www.coronadosurfing.com

Where to Stay:

After a day of riding the waves, you won't have to go far for the perfect beachside accommodations for you and your surf dog. The **Loews Coronado Bay Resort** is perfectly situated within 10 minutes of two dog-friendly beaches on Coronado Island. Be sure to let Fido sample one of the 'Surf & Turf' selections from the gourmet room service menu for dogs. He deserves it! Dogs of any size are welcome for an additional fee of $25 per night.

Loews Coronado Bay Resort
4000 Coronado Bay Road
Coronado, CA 92118
(619) 424-4000
www.tinyurl.com/ruff03
Rates from $189/night

Where to Stay:

Outdoor enthusiasts who like to 'ruff it' will feel right at home in the Tent Cabins at **Big Basin Redwoods State Park**. You can choose a basic cabin with thin mattresses on platforms, or upgrade to a 'Total Camping Package' with sleeping bags, pillows, cooking stove, lantern, cooler, pots and pans, wood, and ice for a nightly fee of $50. Well-behaved dogs of any size stay for free and are welcome at the state park's ranger-led evening campfire programs.

Big Basin Redwoods State Park
21600 Big Basin Way
Boulder Creek, CA 95006
(831) 338-4745
www.bigbasintentcabins.com
Rates from $79/night

Roaring Camp Railroads

Located just six miles from Santa Cruz, Roaring Camp is a re-creation of an 1880's logging town with a general store, Chuckwagon BBQ, and lots of old-time activities like gold panning, candle making, and blacksmithing. However, the star attraction here is **Roaring Camp Railroads**. You and your canine companion can climb aboard an authentic 19th century steam train for a 75-minute trip through the magnificent redwood forests. As you travel along the historic, winding narrow-gauge track to the summit of Bear Mountain, the conductor will entertain you with the history of the railroad and its locomotives, which were once used to haul giant redwood logs out of the forest. Tours are offered daily (except Christmas), and departure times vary by season. Fares are $26 for adults and $19 for children. Dogs are welcome to ride for no additional fee as long as there is room on the open-air train.

Roaring Camp Railroads
5401 Graham Hill Road
Felton, CA 95018
(831) 335-4484
www.roaringcamp.com

Mendocino Botanical Gardens

When planning a visit to Fort Bragg, allow time for a leisurely stroll through the gorgeous **Mendocino Coast Botanical Gardens** with your canine companion. Savor the breathtaking beauty of the formal gardens, coastal bluffs, pine forests, and fern-covered canyons. The mild coastal climate ensures that something is always in bloom. Rhododendrons, magnolias, heritage roses, heathers, lilies, and succulents are just some of the flora you will see as you wander along the trails with Fido. Your dog is welcome throughout the entire property—just keep your pup on a leash and clean up after him. The Mendocino Coast Botanical Gardens are open year-round, with the exception of Thanksgiving, Christmas, and the Saturday before Labor Day. From March through October, the gardens are open from 9:00 am to 5:00 pm. In winter, they close an hour earlier. Admission is $14 for adults, $5 for children, and free for dogs.

Mendocino Coast Botanical Gardens
18220 N Highway One
Fort Bragg, CA 95437
(707) 964-4352
www.gardenbythesea.org

Where to Stay:

Overlooking the Pacific Ocean in Mendocino, the **Little River Inn** features an assortment of pet-friendly guest rooms to fit every budget. The property offers on-site golf, dining, and spa services. With advance reservations, the hotel can even provide a private, dog-friendly dining table for breakfast or dinner in the parlor. The hotel features designated pet walking areas and offers treats, food bowls, and pet towels upon arrival. Up to two dogs are welcome for an additional fee of $25 per pet, per night.

Little River Inn
7901 N Highway One
Little River, CA 95456
(707) 937-5942
www.littleriverinn.com
Rates from $135/night

Where to Stay:

Showered with treats and toys at check-in, Fido will love his stay at **The Inn at Schoolhouse Creek** in Mendocino. For amazing views of the ocean, choose the Water Tower cottage, which features an enclosed courtyard for Fido and a private hot tub and rooftop deck for you. The property also offers a private beach, where your pup can romp off leash. Dogs of any size are welcome. The fee is $50 for one dog or $75 for two.

The Inn at Schoolhouse Creek
7051 N Highway One
Little River, CA 95456
(707) 937-5525
www.schoolhousecreek.com
Rates from $159/night

Skunk Train

Snaking through 40 miles of majestic redwood forests, the famous **Skunk Train** offers human and canine passengers excellent views of gorgeous Mendocino County. Originally built as a logging railroad in 1885, the train takes its current name from the description locals gave to the smell of gasoline-powered engines after the introduction of motorcars in 1925. Bring Fido on a half-day tour beginning in Fort Bragg or Willits, and journey along the Redwood Route to Northspur, where the train stops for an extended break. Stretch your pup's legs and enjoy the lunch offered from April through November before making the return trip. Photo opportunities and entertainment are provided. Snacks and beverages are available to purchase on the train. Fares start at $49 for adults and $24 for children. Your well-behaved, leashed dog is welcome to accompany you on the vintage locomotives for an additional fee of $10.

Skunk Train
100 W Laurel Street
Fort Bragg, CA 95437
(707) 964-6371
www.skunktrain.com

Russian River Adventures

Join **Russian River Adventures** on a SOAR inflatable canoe trip down the Russian River in Healdsburg. The inflatable canoes are perfect for dog owners with little paddling experience because they are virtually untippable—even with a rambunctious Great Dane aboard. The company's nine-mile, full-day float covers a stretch of river that's unobstructed by buildings or roads, so Fido can remain off-leash whenever and wherever you decide to pull ashore for a break from paddling. Cool off in one of the river's many swimming holes, show off on a rope swing, or enjoy a picnic lunch on the first sandbar that looks good to you. Tours are offered seven days a week in the summer and every weekend in the fall. The fees are $50 per adult, $25 per child, and $10 per dog (with a guarantee that he'll be happy and tired at the end of the trip).

Russian River Adventures
20 Healdsburg Avenue
Healdsburg, CA 95448
(707) 433-5599
www.russianriveradventures.com

Where to Stay:

After a day on the Russian River, you and your pup can relax at the **Healdsburg Inn on the Plaza** in downtown Healdsburg. Enjoy luxury accommodations, daily breakfast buffet, and complimentary wine and hors d'oeuvres each afternoon. Up to two dogs (40 lbs or less) are welcome for an additional fee of $65 per stay. If you have a larger dog, opt for the nearby **h2hotel**, where dogs up to 85 lbs are welcome for an extra fee of $99 per stay.

Healdsburg Inn on the Plaza
112 Matheson Street
Healdsburg, CA 95448
(707) 433-6991
www.healdsburginn.com
Rates from $279/night

Huntington Dog Beach

Located on a mile-long stretch of sand between Seapoint Avenue and 21st Street on the famous Pacific Coast Highway, the **Huntington Dog Beach** is a canine lover's paradise. Nicknamed 'Surf City USA' by the locals, this strand is home to several annual dog events, including the Surf City Surf Dog Weekend. The three-day event attracts four-legged competitors from around the world, seeking the title of canine surfing champion. Whether your pooch wants to ride a board or just romp leash-free on the sand, Huntington Beach is the place for some fun in the sun. After your day at the beach, take a short walk with Fido to the **Dirty Dog Wash**. For the do-it-yourself price of $15, the service will provide you with all of the equipment and supplies you need to get Fido freshened up for a night on the town. Full-service grooming is also available by appointment.

Huntington Dog Beach
100 Goldenwest Street
Huntington Beach, CA 92647
(714) 841-8644
www.dogbeach.org

Where to Stay:

After catching some waves, check into the **Shore-break Hotel**, a beachfront property with an upscale surf motif. Relax with Fido by the courtyard fire pits as you enjoy a complimentary glass of wine. Have dinner together at **Zimzala Restaurant**, which offers a gourmet dog menu. Book the 'Dog is Good' package and you'll get a $25 restaurant credit, along with a basket of pet toys at check-in. Up to two dogs of any size are welcome for no additional fee.

Shorebreak Hotel
500 E Pacific Coast Highway
Huntington Beach, CA 92648
(714) 861-4470
www.shorebreakhotel.com
Rates from $209/night

Where to Stay:

Dog-loving history buffs will enjoy spending a night aboard **The Queen Mary**. Permanently docked in Long Beach since 1967, this floating hotel offers visitors the chance to stay on a vessel that carried dignitaries, royalty, and celebrities around the world in the 1930s, 40s and 50s. Dogs were welcome on the Queen Mary then, and they're just as welcome today. The fee is $75 per stay for dogs up to 25 lbs. Larger dogs are allowed with management approval.

The Queen Mary
1126 Queens Highway
Long Beach, CA 90802
(800) 437-2934
www.queenmary.com
Rates from $97/night

The Queen Mary

Start off a full day of dog-friendly activities in Long Beach with a morning jog at **Rosie's Dog Beach**. Located on Ocean Boulevard between Roycroft and Argonne Avenues, the beach is open daily from 6:00 am to 8:00 pm. Access is free and metered parking is available. After your pooch has worked up an appetite, bring him to **Pussy & Pooch** for a full-service or do-it-yourself dog washing and grooming session, followed by a visit to the boutique's Pawbar for some gourmet dog grub. The store is located at 222 East Broadway, and prices vary depending upon services ordered. Finally, complete your Long Beach experience by visiting the historic **Queen Mary**. Small dogs are welcome to accompany you on overnight stays aboard this luxury ocean liner, which is now permanently docked in Long Beach. With boutique shops, tours, exhibits, and a spa, you will find plenty to do before retiring for the evening.

The Queen Mary
1126 Queens Highway
Long Beach, CA 90802
(800) 437-2934
www.queenmary.com

Lake Hollywood Park

Want to bring Fido to one of the best kept doggie secrets in Los Angeles? **Lake Hollywood Park** is where the locals bring their dogs for off-leash playtime and socialization under the famous Hollywood sign. Although the park is not fenced and you will see signs stating that dogs should be kept on a leash, you might consider taking the lead from the friendly locals. Those in the know say that only aggressive dogs causing a disturbance are cited for being unleashed. There is a great view of the Hollywood Sign from Lake Hollywood Park, but if you want to get an even closer look, head to Griffith Park afterwards. A 6.5-mile hike up the **Bronson Canyon Trail** will take you to the rear of the Hollywood Sign in less than three hours. Along the way, you'll also get a look at the 'bat cave' from the 1960's Batman TV show.

Lake Hollywood Park
3204 Canyon Lake Drive
Los Angeles, CA 90068
(323) 913-4688
www.bringfido.com/attraction/11147

Where to Stay:

Make new friends at the **Pod-Share Hollywood Lofts**, a trendy property in the heart of Hollywood. Each loft space has a modern feel with high ceilings and concrete floors. Units include a king-size bed, private bathroom, and kitchen. You and Fido can venture to the rooftop garden, which offers a grill, lounge chairs and heaters, as well as terrific views of the city. Up to two dogs of any size are welcome in select loft rooms for no additional fee.

PodShare Hollywood Lofts
1617 Cosmo Street
Los Angeles, CA 90028
(310) 800-6696
www.thehollywoodloft.com
Rates from $150/night

Where to Stay:

Fido will feel like an A-list movie star upon arrival at the fashionable **Loews Hollywood Hotel**. Located just steps from the Hollywood Walk of Fame, the property features a pool, fitness center, spa, and spacious guest rooms. Pet amenities include bowls, mats, bones, and bedding. Dog-walking services can be arranged by the concierge, and there's even a doggie room service menu for your pooch! Up to two dogs of any size are welcome for an additional fee of $25 per stay.

Loews Hollywood Hotel
1755 N Highland Avenue
Hollywood, CA 90028
(323) 856-1200
www.tinyurl.com/ruff04
Rates from $199/night

Runyon Canyon Park

If your idea of 'star gazing' involves a celebrity crush instead of a distant constellation, skip the Griffith Observatory and take a hike with your pooch at **Runyon Canyon Park** in Los Angeles. While celebrity sightings aren't guaranteed at this Hollywood hotspot with a 90-acre designated off-leash area, they are very common on the aptly named Star Trail. And even if Fido doesn't get to rub tails with Justin Timberlake's boxers or Gwen Stefani's Pomeranian on the three-mile loop, he will be treated to an amazing view of Los Angeles just half a mile into the hike at Inspiration Point. Runyon Canyon Park is open from sunrise to sunset. There is no admission fee, but parking can be a challenge. After your hike, visit the **Hollywood Walk of Fame** along Hollywood Boulevard. Bring your camera to snap a picture of your dog next to the stars of Lassie and Rin Tin Tin!

Runyon Canyon Park
2000 N Fuller Avenue
Los Angeles, CA 90046
(323) 666-5046
www.bringfido.com/attraction/50

Devils Postpile

Don't miss the chance to see a rare geologic wonder in Mammoth Lakes. **Devils Postpile National Monument** was formed a hundred thousand years ago when a volcanic eruption cooled into an impressive wall of columns. Today, the 60-foot-tall rock formation can be accessed via an easy half-mile hike. Dogs must be leashed at the monument but can remain under voice control on all other trails. Early birds may drive themselves to the Devils Postpile Ranger Station, but after 7:00 am, all visitors are required to take a shuttle bus from the **Adventure Center** at Mammoth Mountain. The shuttle costs $7 for adults and $4 for children. Dogs ride for free but must be muzzled during the short trip. After returning to the Adventure Center, take the **Scenic Gondola** to the summit of the mountain for lunch at the **Top of the Sierra Café**. Tickets are $24 for adults and free for dogs.

Devils Postpile National Monument
Ranger Station & Trailhead
1 Reds Circle
Mammoth Lakes, CA 93546
(760) 934-2289
www.nps.gov/depo

Where to Stay:

After a full day of hiking, the signature 'Heavenly Bed' at the **Westin Monache Resort** in Mammoth will be calling your name. Sink in for a while or unwind in the hot tub while Fido relaxes on the plush 'Heavenly Dog Bed' next to the fire. Westin's four-legged guests also receive a basket of treats, food and water bowls, and map of dog-friendly hiking trails at check-in. Up to two dogs of any size are welcome for no additional fee.

Westin Monache Resort
50 Hillside Drive
Mammoth Lakes, CA 93546
(760) 934-0400
www.westinmammoth.com
Rates from $179/night

Where to Stay:

When you arrive at the **Stanford Inn** following your Big River adventure, Fido will likely be greeted by the innkeeper's dogs, Murphy and Ellie. While you warm up by the fire in the main lodge, the three of them can feast on organic sweet potato biscuits made by the inn's chef. But don't be jealous—you'll also be treated to one of his delicious creations at breakfast the next morning. One dog of any size is welcome for $45 per stay; additional pets are $23.

Stanford Inn
44850 Comptche Ukiah Road
Mendocino, CA 95460
(707) 937-5615
www.stanfordinn.com
Rates from $195/night

Catch a Canoe & Bicycles Too

If you'd like to paddle with your dog, but haven't tried it before, you might want to start by renting a handcrafted, redwood outrigger canoe from **Catch a Canoe & Bicycles Too** in Mendocino. Outriggers are the perfect vehicle for novice paddlers because they're extremely stable and easy to paddle on the water—even with an excited dog on board. And when Fido sees all of the herons, ducks, harbor seals, and river otters on the Big River estuary, he is definitely going to be excited! Families with multiple dogs should request the aptly named 'Canine Cruiser' outrigger. It can safely accommodate up to four dogs and has a raised fabric platform that allows them to walk, sit, and lie down comfortably. Catch a Canoe is open daily from 9:00 am to 5:00 pm year-round. Fees are $28 per person for up to three hours or $40 for longer trips.

Catch a Canoe & Bicycles Too
1 S Big River Road
Mendocino, CA 95460
(707) 937-0273
www.catchacanoe.com

Monterey Bay Whale Watch

For a whale of a time with your pup, take a ride on *Sea Wolf II* with **Monterey Bay Whale Watch** in Monterey. Tours on this 70-passenger vessel depart twice daily for three to five hour trips. All tours are guided by a marine biologist, and, depending on the season, your dog is almost sure to spot killer whales, humpbacks, blue whales, or gray whales in the Monterey Bay National Marine Sanctuary. Tour prices start at $40 for adults and $27 for children, with no additional charge for your pooch. After your adventure on the bay, park yourself at one of the outdoor tables at **Abalonetti's Seafood Trattoria**. In addition to having the largest dog-friendly dining area on Fisherman's Wharf, they also feature a dog menu with $5 items like a grilled chicken breast or a hamburger patty. Both are served on a souvenir Frisbee that Fido can take home.

Monterey Bay Whale Watch
84 Fisherman's Wharf
Monterey, CA 93940
(831) 375-4658
www.montereybaywhalewatch.com

Where to Stay:

You and your four-legged friend will be treated like VIPs at the lavish **Portola Hotel & Spa**. Munch on fresh-baked cookies at check-in, sleep in elegant guest rooms, dine al fresco at one of the property's pet-friendly restaurants, or take a half-mile walk to **Cannery Row** on the Monterey Bay Coastal Recreation Trail. Dogs of any size are welcome for an additional fee of $50 per stay. A comfy dog bed, food and water bowls, and treats are provided at check-in.

Portola Hotel & Spa
2 Portola Plaza
Monterey, CA 93940
(800) 342-4295
www.portolahotel.com
Rates from $289/night

Knight Wine Tours

Touring California's wine country with your dog couldn't be easier with Napa-based **Knight Wine Tours**. The company offers fully customizable guided tours of the entire Napa Valley region and encourages you to bring your dog along for the ride. Stan Knight and his team will assist you with planning your visit by making recommendations specifically geared toward your interests. Stroll village shops, take in scenic vistas, and enjoy a picnic lunch on the manicured lawns of one of the region's finest vineyards. You may even meet some famous vineyard dogs roaming the pet-friendly estate wineries. Dog owners can relax on the trip, knowing that Stan will plan all the details and make sure that your four-legged friend gets plenty of exercise while you enjoy wine tastings. Prices vary depending on itinerary and season. Rates for a seven-hour tour start at $550 for up to five guests and a dog.

Knight Wine Tours
1436 2nd Street
Napa, CA 94558
(707) 738-4500
www.knightwinetours.com

Where to Stay:

Following a day of strolling through vineyards and sipping vino, retire to the luxurious accommodations offered by **Bardessono** in Yountville. Spacious suites featuring gas fireplaces, steam showers, personal massage tables, and private courtyards will ensure that you'll never want to leave. But, for Fido's sake, walk around the corner to **Bouchon Bakery** and treat him to a foie gras biscuit while you're there. Up to two dogs of any size are welcome for an additional fee of $150 per stay.

Bardessono
6526 Yount Street
Yountville, CA 94599
(707) 204-6000
www.bardessono.com
Rates from $450/night

Where to Stay:

Nestled at the base of the Squaw Valley ski area, the **PlumpJack Squaw Valley Inn** is conveniently located just steps away from the aerial tram and other attractions in Olympic Valley—the home of the 1960 Winter Olympics. This lodge-style property offers relaxing accommodations, picturesque Sierra Nevada views, and delectable dining (including a complimentary gourmet breakfast buffet). One dog of any size is welcome for an additional fee of $150 per stay. Add $50 for a second pet.

PlumpJack Squaw Valley Inn
1920 Squaw Valley Road
Olympic Valley, CA 96146
(530) 583-1576
www.tinyurl.com/ruff05
Rates from $175/night

Squaw Valley Aerial Tram

The North Lake Tahoe area offers plenty of warm-weather adventures for you and your pooch, including a hiking excursion at Squaw Valley. Start at the base of the mountain and hit the Shirley Lake Trail for a three-hour moderate-to-difficult trek up to high camp (elevation 8,200 feet). During your ascent, take a break at Shirley Lake, a popular dog-friendly swimming hole. Following your hike, enjoy a complimentary trip down the mountain via the **Squaw Valley Aerial Tram**. For those inclined to see the summit without the rigor of an uphill hike, Fido is welcome to join you on the roundtrip tram ride ($32 for adults, $10 for children, and free for dogs). If your dog prefers swimming to hiking, schedule time for a float down the nearby Truckee River in a rental raft from **Truckee River Rafting**. Rates start at $35 for adults and $23 for kids. Fido rides for free.

Squaw Valley Aerial Tram
1960 Squaw Valley Road
Olympic Valley, CA 96146
(800) 403-0206
www.bringfido.com/attraction/10404

Ace Hotel & Swim Club

Doggie nirvana awaits man's best friend at the **Ace Hotel & Swim Club** in Palm Springs. Relax in style at this desert oasis, where both you and your pooch will receive the VIP treatment. The fun starts poolside, where Fido is free to lounge on the deck while you soak up some rays or go for a swim. Grab a fruity drink for yourself and a bowl of ice water for your pup at the club's Amigo Room bar. When it's time to grab lunch, you won't have to go far. The on-site King's Highway restaurant offers pet-friendly patio tables that overlook the pool. Your furry friend can even join you for an outdoor hot stone massage at the resort's Feel Good Spa. In the evening, kick back and relax in one of the resort's comfy hammocks as you and your dog listen to nightly entertainment while gazing at the stars above.

Ace Hotel & Swim Club
701 E Palm Canyon Drive
Palm Springs, CA 92264
(760) 325-9900
www.acehotel.com/palmsprings

Where to Stay:

Continue your retreat by staying overnight at the **Ace Hotel & Swim Club**. The resort features a number of bohemian-inspired rooms with canvas-draped walls that give the accommodations a poolside cabana feel. Many rooms come with private enclosed patios—perfect for guests traveling with pets. Although you're in the desert, the hotel even provides a small grassy fenced-in area to walk your pup. Dogs of any size are welcome for an additional fee of $25 per pet, per night.

Ace Hotel & Swim Club
701 E Palm Canyon Drive
Palm Springs, CA 92264
(760) 325-9900
www.acehotel.com
Rates from $119/night

Where to Stay:

Luv San Diego Surf is a boutique vacation rental company specializing in pet-friendly rentals. All of their homes are located in the heart of Mission Beach and come fully stocked with everything a dog could need for a weekend at the beach. Most even have fenced patios with doggie doors! Dogs of any size are welcome for no additional fee. Be sure to visit the company's pet-friendly restaurant, **The Patio on Lamont Street**, for half-price dog-themed cocktails during brunch on the weekends.

Luv San Diego Surf
4439 Lamont Street
San Diego, CA 92109
(858) 230-6682
www.luv-surf.com
Rates from $165/night

Aqua Adventures

Spend a day on Mission Bay with your dog by renting a kayak or stand-up paddleboard from **Aqua Adventures Kayak Center** in San Diego. With a large variety of kayaks, canoes, and paddleboards to choose from, you'll find exactly what you need for an unforgettable day on the water. Beginners will appreciate the advice offered by the company's experienced staff. The outfitter will help you plan your route and make sure that the equipment is ready when you and your pooch get to the water. Gorgeous views of the Coronado Bay Bridge and San Diego skyline await you. If your pup is a novice at paddlesports, Aqua Adventures offers free clinics designed to introduce him to these activities to ensure success and enjoyment for both of you. Hone your skills with one of their regular doggie paddles out to **Fiesta Island Park** for off-leash play time. Rental rates start at $17.

Aqua Adventures Kayak Center
1548 Quivira Way
San Diego, CA 92109
(619) 523-9577
www.aqua-adventures.com

Presidio of San Francisco

Dog owners visiting San Francisco will get some great views of the Golden Gate Bridge as they walk their furry friends along **Baker Beach**. Located in the **Presidio**, a decommissioned military base which is now part of **Golden Gate National Recreation Area**, Baker Beach is a one-mile stretch of coastline that is popular with locals and tourists alike. The entire beach is leash-optional, making it a great choice for active dogs. But, be forewarned, the northernmost section is also clothing-optional (and frequented by nude sunbathers). For more off-leash fun in the Presidio, bring your pup to nearby **Crissy Field** for a stroll along the promenade. Dogs are welcome to join you off-leash as you enjoy a picnic, play Frisbee, or fish at Torpedo Wharf. Baker Beach and Crissy Field are free to the general public and can become quite crowded, especially on weekends, but ample parking is available.

Presidio of San Francisco
103 Montgomery Street
San Francisco, CA 94129
(415) 561-4323
www.nos.gov/prsf

Where to Stay:

Military and history aficionados, along with anyone else looking for a unique hotel experience in San Francisco, should look no further than the **Inn at the Presidio**. Beautifully restored in 2011, the Georgian-Revival-style building known as Pershing Hall housed bachelor officers when the Presidio was a US Army post in the early 1900s. Today, the hotel welcomes the general public, as well as their four-legged friends. Dogs of any size are permitted for an additional fee of $40 per stay.

Inn at the Presidio
42 Moraga Avenue
San Francisco, CA 94129
(415) 800-7356
www.innatthepresidio.com
Rates from $215/night

Where to Stay:

Perched on a bluff overlooking the Pacific Ocean, the **Seacrest OceanFront Hotel** in Pismo Beach offers pet-friendly patio rooms that have direct access to the lawn and dog-friendly beach below. Fido will also enjoy a comfy bed, treats, and bowls. One dog (up to 50 lbs) is welcome for no additional fee. Add $20 for a second pup. Guests traveling with larger pets can stay at the adjacent **Pismo Lighthouse Suites**, where dogs of any size are welcome for $25 per pet, per night.

Seacrest OceanFront Hotel
2241 Price Street
Pismo Beach, CA 93449
(805) 773-4608
www.seacrestpismo.com
Rates from $129/night

City to the Sea Trail

Start your morning with an on-leash stroll along Pismo Beach with your pooch, and then hop in your car for a 10-minute drive north to tackle the **City to the Sea Trail** in San Luis Obispo. Before starting the 2.5-mile (each way) trek, make a pit stop at the **Avila Valley Barn** to grab some fresh fruit, baked goods, and other snacks for a delicious picnic lunch. Next, make your way to the trailhead, located less than half a mile from the Avila Valley Barn on Ontario Road. Known locally as the Bob Jones Trail, this easy-to-moderate paved course meanders through the beautiful Avila Valley and ends at the Avila Beach promenade. For some off-leash fun with your pup, extend your walk by another half-mile along a bike path that leads to **Fisherman's Beach**. Once there, your dog is welcome to enjoy a leash-free romp in the sand and the bay.

City to the Sea Trail
7001 Ontario Road
San Luis Obispo, CA 93405
(805) 781-5930
www.bringfido.com/attraction/11145

Arroyo Burro Beach

If you're in the mood for a day at the beach with your pup, head to **Arroyo Burro Beach** in Santa Barbara. Known to the locals as Hendry's Beach, this strip of sand has a great dog-friendly area where Fido can run, play, and swim. Just be sure to keep your pooch on a leash until you reach the designated doggie area. Parking and beach access are free, but bring a little coin for the on-site, self-service dog washes that make cleanup easy after your dog's fun in the sun. If you're in the mood for a less sandy adventure, head to the **Douglas Family Preserve** overlooking Arroyo Burro Beach. This 70-acre undeveloped park area boasts gorgeous views of the ocean below and welcomes visitors and their off-leash dogs for no fee. On-street parking is also free, but there are no public facilities. Both sites are open daily from dawn to dusk.

Arroyo Burro Beach
2981 Cliff Drive
Santa Barbara, CA 93109
(805) 687-3714
www.bringfido.com/attraction/574

Where to Stay:

For a weekend getaway to Santa Barbara that won't break the bank, check out the charming **Beach House Inn**. Located only three blocks from the beach, restaurants, and shopping along Cabrillo Boulevard, the property offers comfortable accommodations at affordable prices. Many rooms feature fully furnished kitchens and gas fireplaces. Bring Fido for an additional fee of just $10 per pet, per night. At the end of the street, you'll find a park that is perfect for walking your furry friend.

Beach House Inn
320 W Yanonali Street
Santa Barbara, CA 93101
(805) 966-1126
www.thebeachhouseinn.com
Rates from $118/night

DeeTours of Santa Barbara

Enjoy some fun in the California sun with your four-legged friend in an open-air Jeep limousine tour. **DeeTours of Santa Barbara** features two popular driving tours, including the Scenic Santa Barbara and Montecito City Tour, which takes you on a fast-paced journey around some of the most famous landmarks and residences in the 'American Riviera'. The Wine Country Adventure Tour offers a more relaxing pace, as you and your group are treated to a scenic drive to the Santa Ynez Valley for a day complete with wine tastings, shopping in Solvang, and a picnic lunch. City tour prices are $25 for adults and $10 for children. Wine country tour prices (which include all tasting fees and lunch) are $135 per person for a five to six hour tour. Well-behaved dogs of any size are welcome on all tours for no additional fee. Fully customized trips are also available.

DeeTours of Santa Barbara
1 Garden Street
Santa Barbara, CA 93101
(805) 448-8425
www.deetoursofsb.com

Where to Stay:

After seeing the highlights of Santa Barbara with DeeTours, you'll get an amazing view of the Pacific Ocean when you arrive at **El Encanto by Orient-Express**. Unwind in one of the resort's private bungalows, which feature luxurious king-size beds, rainforest showers, and private patios. Fido will love exploring the botanical gardens that canvas the seven-acre property. Dogs of any size are welcome for an additional fee of $35 per stay, and a special gift is provided at check-in.

El Encanto by Orient-Express
800 Alvarado Place
Santa Barbara, CA 93103
(805) 845-5800
www.elencanto.com
Rates from $375/night

Where to Stay:

Wake up to views of the Golden Gate Bridge from your guest room at **Cavallo Point** on the San Francisco Bay. Located within the **Golden Gate National Recreational Area**, the property offers plenty of acreage for you and your pup to explore. The resort caters to pet owners with its 'Eco Luxe Pups' program, featuring locally-made treats, luxury pet bedding, and designer dishes. Up to two dogs of any size are welcome in select ground floor rooms for an additional fee of $75 per stay.

Cavallo Point
601 Murray Circle
Sausalito, CA 94965
(415) 339-4700
www.cavallopoint.com
Rates from $360/night

Bluerush Boardsports

Bring Fido to Sausalito to spend a day on the water, learning the sport of stand-up paddleboarding. Every other Thursday evening, the crew at **Bluerush Boardsports** takes dog owners and their adventurous pooches on a 90-minute guided 'Dog Paddle' around the Sausalito houseboat community. The short excursions are perfect for experienced and novice boarders alike. Local residents enjoy watching the pups paddling by and will often come out to greet you and your canine companion. The trip ends at **Fish,** a restaurant where you and your dog can enjoy a delicious meal on the waterfront with your new friends. Although there is no extra cost to participate in the Dog Paddle, SUP rentals are $30, and doggie life jackets are available for purchase. If you want to test your skills before signing up for the guided paddle, Bluerush Boardsports also offers private lessons.

Bluerush Boardsports
400 Harbor Drive
Sausalito, CA 94965
(415) 339-9112
www.bluerushboardsports.com

Tahoe Sport Fishing

Spend the day fishing with your canine companion aboard a charter from **Tahoe Sport Fishing** in South Lake Tahoe. Listen to stories from the captain as you cast your hook in search of mackinaw, brown trout, rainbow trout, and kokanee salmon. Don't have your gear? No worries, as the outfit provides bait, tackle, poles, and doggie life jackets, along with a continental breakfast, coffee, and soda. They'll even clean and bag your catch at the end of the trip. Rates start at $90 per person, and Fido goes for free. When making your reservation, just mention that he'll be coming along for the ride. After returning to shore, take your catch to the **Blue Angel Café** or **MacDuff's Public House**, where you and your pup can watch your fresh catch become dinner. If you go to MacDuff's, your pooch should be prepared to share with Bob, the resident Rottweiler!

Tahoe Sport Fishing
900 Ski Run Boulevard
South Lake Tahoe, CA 96150
(530) 541-5448
www.tahoesportfishing.com

Where to Stay:

Dog lovers will find warm and inviting accommodations at the **Fireside Lodge** in South Lake Tahoe. Upon arrival, you'll be greeted as if you were staying at a friend's home. The gracious innkeepers welcome travelers with an afternoon wine and cheese reception and property tour. Families with children will particularly enjoy the nightly marshmallow roasts and retro game room. Complimentary kayak, bike, and snowshoe rentals are also provided. Well-behaved dogs of any size are welcome for an additional fee of $25 to $35 per night.

Fireside Lodge
515 Emerald Bay Road
South Lake Tahoe, CA 96150
(530) 544-5515
www.tahoefiresidelodge.com
Rates from $119/night

Where to Stay:

Located seven miles from Garden of the Gods in Colorado Springs, **The Broadmoor** defines modern elegance. Spectacular views of Cheyenne Mountain, Cheyenne Lake, and three on-site golf courses are available in most suites and cottages. Amenities include a full-service spa, tennis, three swimming pools, and numerous restaurants. Fido can sample canine cuisine from the gourmet pet menu. Bedding and bowls are provided. Up to two dogs of any size are welcome for an additional fee of $50 per pet, per night.

The Broadmoor
1 Lake Avenue
Colorado Springs, CO 80906
(719) 577-5775
www.broadmoor.com
Rates from $220/night

Garden of the Gods

Garden of the Gods in Colorado Springs is known for its incredible red rock formations, beautiful hiking trails, and breathtaking views of Pikes Peak. Start your visit by taking a free 30-minute guided walk to give you an overview of this National Natural Landmark. After working up an appetite, enjoy a meal at the Café at the Garden, where your dog is welcome to join you on the patio, or pack a lunch and enjoy the views from one of the picnic areas. With over 15 miles of trails, the park offers plenty of hiking opportunities for you. Dogs must remain leashed throughout most of the park, but there is one designated off-leash area where your pup can roam free. The park is open daily from 8:00 am to 8:00 pm, Memorial Day through Labor Day, and 9:00 am to 5:00 pm throughout the rest of the year. There is no admission charge.

Garden of the Gods
1805 N 30th Street
Colorado Springs, CO 80904
(719) 634-6666
www.gardenofgods.com

Sundance Trail Guest Ranch

Bring Fido to Red Feather Lakes for an unforgettable experience at the **Sundance Trail Guest Ranch**. This northern Colorado dude ranch offers a variety of ranch activities, including rifle-shooting, archery, roping lessons, rock climbing, hiking, fishing and horseshoe tournaments. Explore the trails by horseback as Fido comes along for the ride. The ranch caters to a limited number of visitors each week, so all activities can be tailored for beginners or those experienced in the many activities offered during your stay. Nightly offerings such as square dancing, cowboy poetry, and evening campfires are designed for the whole family to enjoy. Relax after a full day of fun with a soak in the hot tub, a massage, or a good book by the warm fire. Listen to cowboy stories on the expansive front porch in the company of your new friends. Well-socialized dogs can enjoy all of the ranch activities with their humans.

Sundance Trail Guest Ranch
17931 Red Feather Lakes Road
Red Feather Lakes, CO 80545
(970) 224-1222
www.sundancetrail.com

Where to Stay:

Settle in for the night in a cozy lodge room or spacious cabin at the **Sundance Trail Guest Ranch**. Rooms feature comfortable beds, private baths, outdoor entrances, refrigerators, and daily housekeeping. Cookies, lemonade, and coffee are available any time, and three hearty western meals are served daily. The dinner bell is rung before all meals and activities, so you can enjoy your vacation without a watch. Dogs of any size are welcome at the ranch for no additional fee.

Sundance Trail Guest Ranch
17931 Red Feather Lakes Road
Red Feather Lakes, CO 80545
(970) 224-1222
www.sundancetrail.com
Rates from $109/night

Skijor-n-More

Skijoring is a winter sport where a cross-country skier is pulled by a dog, several dogs, or even a horse! In the snow-covered Colorado Rockies, it's a great way to exercise and bond with your pooch while enjoying the jaw-dropping scenery all around you. Dogs of all breeds can participate in skijoring, and most animals over 30 lbs are capable of pulling an average-sized skier. All they need is an innate desire to run down a trail and pull! If you'd like to give it a try, Louisa Morrissey of **Skijor-n-More** offers private lessons and workshops at **Devil's Thumb Ranch** (and many other locations throughout central Colorado). You and Fido will start with an indoor session on training tips and dog care before heading out on the snow for a hands-on lesson on basic commands and techniques. Two-hour workshops cost $55 and include your ski rental, trail pass, and all skijoring equipment.

Skijor-n-More
PO Box 1875
Silverthorne, CO 80498
(970) 406-0158
www.skijornmore.com

Where to Stay:

Located just outside of Winter Park, **Devil's Thumb Ranch** has been welcoming city folk (and their dogs) to the property since 1938. Today, the luxury resort boasts two gourmet restaurants, a full-service spa, and some of the best Nordic trails in North America. Up to two dogs of any size are welcome in cabins for an additional fee of $50 per pet, per night. Each four-legged guest receives a dog bed, homemade treat, and leash to use while exploring the 6,000-acre property.

Devil's Thumb Ranch
3530 County Highway 83
Tabernash, CO 80478
(970) 726-5632
www.devilsthumbranch.com
Rates from $174/night

Where to Stay:

With slope-side cabins and ski-in/out access less than 100 yards away, you couldn't ask for a more convenient location for your Colorado vacation than the **Mountain Lodge at Telluride**. The pet-friendly Telluride Gondola is only a few blocks away too, so once you park your car at the lodge, you won't need it again until you leave. Just relax and enjoy the view! Dogs of any size are welcome for an additional fee of $50 per night (maximum $150 per stay).

Mountain Lodge at Telluride
457 Mountain Village Boulevard
Telluride, CO 81435
(970) 369-5000
www.tinyurl.com/ruff06
Rates from $139/night

Telluride Gondola

Telluride is best known for its world-class alpine skiing, but with hundreds of pet-friendly trails originating in or near town, it is also heaven-on-earth for hounds that like to hike once the snow melts. Your adventure starts with a 13-minute trip on the **Telluride Gondola**. Free to ride, this popular attraction connects Telluride with Mountain Village via a scenic tram traversing the San Juan Mountains. Located halfway between the two towns, the Station San Sophia stop is your gateway to mountaintop hiking and biking with your canine companion. The gondola operates daily from 7:00 am to midnight, and pet-friendly cabins are marked with stickers in the window. After a day on the trails, give tired paws a break by hopping aboard the town's free shuttle—the Galloping Goose. Hop off at **Mountain Tails** to buy a souvenir for your pooch, or warm up with an Irish coffee at **The Steaming Bean**.

Telluride Gondola
W San Juan Avenue & S Oak Street
Telluride, CO 81435
(970) 728-3041
www.bringfido.com/attraction/10277

Vail Nature Center

While Vail is famous for winter sports, it's also a popular summertime destination. Enjoy the warm Colorado weather on a visit to the **Vail Nature Center** with your pup. Visit on a Monday or Wednesday for a one-hour 'Wildflower Walk' through the woods and meadows. The cost is $5 for adults and free for dogs. On Sundays during the summer, you and your pup can join a free walking tour that departs from the **Vail Farmers Market & Art Show**. You'll see beautiful birds and flower gardens as you journey along the forested banks of Gore Creek. The nature center is open daily from Memorial Day through Labor Day, and special canine-centric hikes are scheduled throughout the season. After your walk, head to nearby Edwards for a brewery tour and tasting at **Crazy Mountain Brewing Company**. Well-behaved, leashed dogs are welcome to join you in the tasting room, where you can sample a delicious craft brew.

Vail Nature Center
601 Vail Valley Drive
Vail, CO 81657
(970) 479-2291
www.vailrec.com/nature.cfm

Where to Stay:

Enjoy your summer visit to the Colorado Rockies with a stay at the **Ritz-Carlton Bachelor Gulch**. Situated in Avon at the gateway to Vail-area attractions, this resort offers luxurious guestrooms with awe-inspiring mountain views. Your pooch can enjoy doggie room service, as well as an in-room canine massage. A dog bed, treats, toys, and bowls are also provided. Dogs of any size are welcome for a fee of $125 for stays up to three nights. Add $25 for each additional night.

Ritz-Carlton Bachelor Gulch
130 Daybreak Ridge
Avon, CO 81620
(970) 748-6200
www.tinyurl.com/ruff07
Rates from $269/night

Mystic Seaport

Delve into American maritime history with a trip to **Mystic Seaport**. Fido is welcome to join in the fun as you explore the grounds of the nation's leading maritime museum. Stroll through the shipyard before visiting the re-creation of a 19th-century seafaring village with more than 30 historic trade shops and businesses. Historians, storytellers, and musicians in period dress bring an air of authenticity to the experience. Walk with your pup through Mystic Seaport's nine gardens to learn more about New England flora and fauna in a beautiful outdoor setting. If maritime history inspires you to venture off shore, end a trip to the seaport aboard a rowboat with your pup. Rentals cost just $10 for a 30-minute ride. Mystic Seaport is open daily from 10:00 am to 4:00 pm (with extended seasonal hours). Admission is $24 for adults and $15 for children. Dogs are welcome for no additional fee.

Mystic Seaport
75 Greenmanville Avenue
Mystic, CT 06355
(860) 572-5302
www.mysticseaport.org

Where to Stay:

For a lovely seaside getaway, plan a stay at **Saybrook Point Inn & Spa** in Old Saybrook. Dogs up to 50 lbs are welcome for a fee of $50 (plus $25 for each additional night). Your pup will be welcomed with an assortment of pet amenities, including a plush dog bed, gourmet treats, and a souvenir bandana. Guests with larger dogs should opt for the **Harbour Inne & Cottage** in Mystic, where dogs of any size stay for free.

Saybrook Point Inn & Spa
2 Bridge Street
Old Saybrook, CT 06475
(860) 395-2000
www.saybrook.com
Rates from $259/night

Where to Stay:

Homestead at Rehoboth is an adults-only bed & breakfast with two acres of grounds and a large fenced yard that is perfect for Fido. If you visit during the off-season (when dogs are allowed on Rehoboth Beach), you'll find their doggie shower and towels convenient for cleaning up after a trip to the beach. Pets under 80 lbs are welcome for an additional fee of $25 per pet. Larger dogs and children over 12 may be allowed with prior approval.

Homestead at Rehoboth
35060 Warrington Road
Rehoboth Beach, DE 19971
(302) 226-7625
www.homesteadrehoboth.com
Rates from $110/night

Delaware Family Fishing

Exercise Fido's sea legs with a charter boat rental from **Delaware Family Fishing** in Lewes. Captain Brian welcomes you and your pooch to climb aboard the *Lil Angler II*, a 38-foot vessel that can accommodate up to 16 passengers. Cruise the Delaware Bay and Atlantic Ocean in waters ideal for catching sea bass, shark, tuna, marlin, and swordfish. The company offers full-day and half-day charters, bottom and wreck fishing trips, and scenic bird-watching and sightseeing cruises. Rates start at $375 for a three-hour Family Shark Fishing Adventure (for up to 10 people) and go up to $1100 for a 12-hour Sea Bass and Wreck Fishing Trip (for up to six people). Prices include all rods, reels, bait, tackle, ice, and a cooler. If you want to bring your lucky pole, they will be happy to rig it for you too. Dogs are welcome on all trips for no additional fee.

Delaware Family Fishing
Anglers Marina
400 Anglers Road
Lewes, DE 19958
(302) 430-3414
www.delawarefamilyfishing.com

DC by Foot

One of the easiest and least expensive ways to see our nation's capital is by taking one of the tours offered by **DC by Foot**. Fortunately for Fido, the company allows well-behaved dogs to join in the fun. Try out their All-in-One or National Mall Tour for a comprehensive visit to the memorials and monuments around our National Mall. Other special interest tours feature visits to sites including Capitol Hill and Arlington Cemetery. Tours are offered daily, but reservations are required in advance to guarantee a spot for you and your pooch. DC by Foot doesn't charge a set price for most tours. Instead, they ask you to pay at the end based on what the tour was worth to you. If you and your pup would rather ride than walk, you can enjoy one of the many tour options offered by **Discover DC Pedicab Tours**. Rates vary based upon itinerary, and dogs ride for free.

DC by Foot
Constitution Ave NW & 15th St NW
Washington, DC 20560
(202) 370-1830
www.freetoursbyfoot/dc

Where to Stay:

The Jefferson hotel is the perfect spot for your canine companion to rest his weary paws after a long walking tour of Washington DC. Located just a few blocks from the White House, the hotel features elegant rooms, delectable dining, and an impressive private collection of antique furnishings, period artwork, and historical documents. Dogs up to 100 lbs are welcome for no additional fee. Pet amenities include bedding, food dishes, and a tasty treat provided at check-in.

The Jefferson
1200 16th Street NW
Washington, DC 20036
(202) 448-2300
www.jeffersondc.com
Rates from $324/night

Where to Stay:

Located four blocks from downtown Apalachicola, the **Water Street Hotel and Marina** features 30 spacious guest suites, each with Hemingway-style furnishings, a fully-equipped kitchen, and private balcony overlooking the Apalachicola River. Enjoy the complimentary continental breakfast and evening wine reception. Fishing and boating activities are right outside your door, courtesy of the full-service marina. You can also lounge by the pool and soak in the Florida sun. Dogs of any size are welcome for an additional fee of $25 per pet, per night.

Water Street Hotel and Marina
329 Water Street
Apalachicola, FL 32320
(850) 653-3700
www.waterstreethotel.com
Rates from $179/night

Captain Gill's River Cruises

You and your canine companion will love spending a day on the lower Apalachicola River with **Captain Gill's River Cruises**. Enjoy a private two, three, or four-hour tour aboard the *Lily*, a 28-foot Adventure Craft that features an air-conditioned cabin with private bathroom. Captain Gill will entertain you with stories and history of the biologically diverse Apalachicola River System. A two-hour tour will provide you with an overview of the area and glimpses of the flora and fauna that inhabit the region. Longer tours will allow more time to explore the scenic tributaries flowing into the river. Cruises can be tailored to your specific interests, and fishing charters are available. Departing from the Water Street Dock, tours are offered seven days a week. Rates start at $250 for a two-hour trip. Bring your own refreshments. Man's best friend is welcome to join the fun for no additional fee.

Captain Gill's River Cruises
501 Bay City Road
Apalachicola, FL 32320
(850) 370-0075
www.captgill.com

Florida Manatee Adventures

Bring Fido on a trip to see Florida's gentle giants with Captain Greg of **Florida Manatee Adventures**. Crystal River is one of the premier manatee-spotting destinations in the world, and the year-round warm waters also make it an ideal location to swim with the manatees in their natural habitat. With more than 25 years of experience as a captain, fisherman and scuba diver, Captain Greg has a wealth of knowledge about the Crystal River area. Climb aboard the boat with your pup and enjoy a three-hour tour, complete with narration, gear, snacks and beverages. Tours prices start at $50 for adults and kids age 10 and older. Younger children and dogs are welcome aboard for free. Call ahead for reservations, as space on each tour is limited. Dolphin-watching tours are also available, and the family-owned company is happy to offer customized tours to make your experience unique. Hours vary by season.

Florida Manatee Adventures
2880 N Seabreeze Point
Crystal River, FL 34429
(352) 476-7556
www.floridamanateeadventures.com

Where to Stay:

Following your swim with the manatees, check into the **Plantation on Crystal River** for a relaxing weekend retreat. Situated on 232 picturesque acres, the resort offers 27 holes of golf and a full-service spa. Allow plenty of time to leisurely explore the grounds with your furry friend. A wide range of accommodations from garden view rooms to golf villas are offered, and dogs up to 50 lbs are welcome for an additional fee of $25 per pet, per night.

Plantation on Crystal River
9301 W Fort Island Trail
Crystal River, FL 34429
(352) 795-4211
www.tinyurl.com/ruff08
Rates from $107/night

Where to Stay:

If you and Fido don't want to 'ruff it' on a deserted island overnight, you'll find comfortable accommodations at the **Beachside Inn** in Destin. This cozy motel will inspire you to unplug and relax by its two-tiered swimming pool and hot tub. The inn is conveniently located across the street from Crystal Beach and just a few blocks from **Henderson Beach State Park**, where Fido is free to explore the trails. The hotel welcomes dogs of any size for an additional fee of $25 per stay.

Beachside Inn
2931 Scenic Highway 98
Destin, FL 32541
(888) 232-2498
www.destinbeachsideinn.com
Rates from $89/night

Crab Island Cruises

Journey to Crab Island in the Santa Rosa Sound and bring Fido along for the fun! With a tour from **Crab Island Cruises** in Destin, you and your pup can enjoy a half-day or full-day chartered boat trip without the hassle of renting your own equipment. Half-day fares start at $250, and full-day cruises start at $350. If you go in the spring, try the 'Cruise-n-Camp' tour for an overnight visit to an uninhabited island. While you explore the island, your tour guide will set up your tent (including bedding) and prepare a delicious BBQ dinner for you to enjoy as you watch the sun set. After dinner, roast marshmallows over the fire before retiring for the night. In the morning, you'll enjoy breakfast before heading back to the mainland. If you'd rather visit Crab Island on your own, pontoon boat rentals are available from **Dockside Watersports** in Destin.

Crab Island Cruises
US 98 at Destin Bridge
Destin, FL 32541
(850) 685-7027
www.crabislandcruises.com

Key West Aquarium

You and your pooch can get up close and personal with marine life without ever getting in the water at the **Key West Aquarium**. Located on bustling Mallory Square, the aquarium welcomes well-behaved pets of any size, provided they remain leashed at all times. Start your visit with one of the guided tours and feedings, which take place several times throughout the day. The 30-40 minute guided walks will teach you about the history of Key West and the native marine life that inhabits the waters surrounding the island. Visitors can feed stingrays and touch a shark's tail as they browse the touch tanks filled with conch, sea stars, and crabs. Tour a living mangrove ecosystem, as well as alligator and jellyfish exhibits. The aquarium is open daily from 10:00 am to 6:00 pm. Admission is $15 for adults and $9 for children. Dogs are allowed for no additional fee.

Key West Aquarium
1 Whitehead Street
Key West, FL 33040
(305) 296-2051
www.keywestaquarium.com

Where to Stay:

Located half a mile from the aquarium, **Ambrosia Key West** is a tropical compound featuring rooms with private entrances that open onto the property's lush garden and pool. Up to two dogs of any size are welcome for an additional fee of $35 per pet, per stay. For a more lively Key West experience, the **Speakeasy Inn and Rum Bar**, located on bustling Duval Street, has its very own dog-friendly bar and welcomes pets for a fee of $50 per stay.

Ambrosia Key West
622 Fleming Street
Key West, FL 33040
(305) 296-9838
www.ambrosiakeywest.com
Rates from $189/night

Lazy Dog Kayak

Bring Fido on a two-hour guided tour with **Lazy Dog Kayak** in Key West. Paddle through the mangrove creeks and shallow waters of Key West on a kayak or stand-up paddleboard, while spotting marine life such as jellyfish, conch, sea cucumbers, stingrays, and maybe even a shark or manatee. If you've never paddled with your dog before and would prefer to learn at your own pace, Lazy Dog also offers kayak and paddleboard rentals. Their staff will give you tips on how to introduce your dog to the sport, help you select the proper board, and provide a map with suggestions on the top spots to explore with your pup. Half-day rentals are $25, and guided tours start at $40. Dogs ride for no additional fee. After your adventure, bring Fido next door to **Hurricane Hole Bar & Grill** for a 'fresh off the boat' meal on their waterfront deck.

Lazy Dog Kayak
Hurricane Hole Marina
5114 Overseas Highway
Key West, FL 33040
(305) 295-9898
www.lazydog.com

Where to Stay:

Banana Bay Resort & Marina is an adults-only oceanfront resort in Key West, located just two miles from famous Duval Street. The grounds feature an abundance of tropical foliage with a large 'topless optional' pool, relaxing whirlpool, and dog-friendly sunning beach. A complimentary continental breakfast is served at the Tiki Bar each morning, and the oversized guest rooms with private balconies are bargain-priced by Key West standards. Up to two dogs of any size are welcome for no additional fee.

Banana Bay Resort & Marina
2319 N Roosevelt Boulevard
Key West, FL 33040
(305) 296-6925
www.bananabayresortkeywest.com
Rates from $149/night

Where to Stay:

After your airboat experience, hit the road with Fido for a half-hour drive to **Chalet Suzanne**. Tucked away on a 100-acre estate in Lake Wales, this historic inn has been welcoming people and their pets since the Great Depression. The lakefront property features 26 guest rooms, five RV sites, a soup cannery, citrus groves, and a ceramic studio. Don't miss dining at the hotel's award-winning restaurant. Dogs of any size are welcome for an additional fee of $50 per stay.

Chalet Suzanne
3800 Chalet Suzanne Drive
Lake Wales, FL 33859
(863)-676-6011
www.chaletsuzanne.com
Rates from $169/night

Airboat Nature Tours

Whether you request a mild or wild ride from Captain John, you pup is sure to enjoy the wind in his fur while cruising along the Kissimmee River with **Airboat Nature Tours** in Lake Wales. Travel through Central Florida's swampland to observe turtles, exotic birds, and other native wetland species in their natural environment. Keep your eyes peeled for alligators too! You will likely see several on the two-hour tour. Tours operate daily from 7:00 am to 4:00 pm. Rates are $50 for adults and $25 for children age 8 and under. Dogs ride for free. Call ahead for reservations because seating is very limited. After the airboat ride, take a trip to nearby **Lake Kissimmee State Park** to let your leashed pup stretch his legs on more than 13 miles of hiking trails. The park is open every day from 7:00 am to sundown. Admission is $5 per vehicle.

Airboat Nature Tours
14400 Reese Drive
Lake Wales, FL 33898
(863) 696-0313
www.airboatnaturetours.com

Art Deco Tours

Take a walking tour with **Art Deco Tours** and enjoy learning about the history of South Beach while observing the exterior architecture and interior décor of some of Miami Beach's most famous Art Deco buildings. Christine & Company will enlighten and entertain on this two-hour pet-friendly tour. Because some of the buildings on the tour don't allow dogs, the tour company brings along a pet sitter to keep the pups entertained as you get to experience the full tour. Pet-friendly tour reservations must be made two weeks in advance. The tour costs $30 for adults. Add an additional fee of $30 for up to two pets (to offset the cost of the sitter). Art Deco Tours provides water, bowls, and cleanup bags. After your tour, head to **Lincoln Road Mall** where you and your pup can people-watch as you dine al fresco at one of the many pet-friendly restaurants.

Art Deco Tours
Collins Avenue & 10th Street
Miami Beach, FL 33139
(305) 218-9952
www.artdecotours.com

Where to Stay:

After learning about South Beach's architectural history, stay at the **Surfcomber Hotel** to relax and enjoy beachfront views with your dog. In addition to on-site dining and spa options, this Kimpton resort offers a variety of daily activities and an evening wine reception. Dogs of any size are welcome for no extra fee, and the property provides pet beds, food and water bowls, and pet waste bags. The hotel concierge is also happy to make arrangements for pet sitting or grooming services.

Surfcomber Hotel
1717 Collins Avenue
Miami Beach, FL 33139
(305) 532-7715
www.surfcomber.com
Rates from $203/night

Where to Stay:

Kick back and relax or get ready for an adventure with your dog at the **Naples Bay Resort**. Guests can book the 'Boatel Sea & Suite' package to enjoy a private boat cruise to Keewaydin Island along with their posh beachfront suite. Land lubbers might prefer the 'U Naugti Dog' package which provides a signature pet bed, treats, and pet amenity kit instead of the boat ride. Dogs up to 40 lbs are welcome to stay at the resort for no additional fee.

Naples Bay Resort
1500 5th Avenue S
Naples, FL 34102
(239) 530-1199
www.naplesbayresort.com
Rates from $144/night

Keewaydin Island

Escape civilization with your pooch on a day trip to **Keewaydin Island** in southwest Florida. Located along the coast between Naples and Marco Island, this eight-mile long barrier island boasts sugar sand beaches and some of the finest shelling in the Sunshine State. The area is accessible only by boat, but if you don't have one of your own, you can rent a powerboat from the marina at **Naples Bay Resort**. Rates vary depending upon the season, but full-day weekday rentals are often available for $149. All boats come with a sun top, cooler, GPS, and map of the local waters. Because Keewaydin Island is a conservation area, dogs must remain leashed during your time on the beach. If your sea dog wants some off-leash fun, return to the mainland and head north to the **Lee County Dog Beach**, located on the south end of Lovers Key in Fort Myers Beach.

Keewaydin Island
Boat Rentals at Naples Bay Resort
1500 5th Avenue S
Naples, FL 34102
(239) 530-5134
www.nbrboatrental.com

Palm Beach Lake Trail

Gaze at gorgeous, waterfront Palm Beach mansions as you stroll down the **Palm Beach Lake Trail** with your pup. Stretching along the Intracoastal Waterway, this five-mile paved biking and walking trail was constructed by Henry Flagler in 1894 as a promenade for elite guests staying at his Royal Poinciana Hotel. Start at the Flagler Museum for free parking and access to the public trail. If you prefer to bike with your pooch, rentals are available for $15 at the **Palm Beach Bicycle Trail Shop**. After enjoying the island, hit the water with a kayak or stand-up paddleboard rental from the **Jupiter Outdoor Center**. Rentals start at $25 per hour. Guided tours of the Loxahatchee River are also available from $40 per person. For some off-leash beach fun, head to the **Jupiter Dog Beach**, located between beach markers 25 and 59. Free parking is available along the public beach.

Palm Beach Lake Trail
Flagler Museum Parking
1 Whitehall Way
Palm Beach, FL 33480
(800) 554-7256
www.bringfido.com/attraction/11022

Where to Stay:

The Chesterfield Palm Beach offers elegant accommodations with twice-daily maid service, unique homemade turndown treats, and fresh flowers in every suite. Located a short walk from the world famous Worth Avenue shopping district, the hotel will spoil your pet with a welcome basket of toys and treats upon arrival. The staff will also make arrangements for grooming, pet sitting, and dog walking services upon request. Dogs of any size are welcome for an additional fee of $90 per pet, per stay.

The Chesterfield Palm Beach
363 Cocoanut Row
Palm Beach, FL 33480
(561) 659-5800
www.chesterfieldpb.com
Rates from $158/night

Where to Stay:

Just a short stroll from Algiers Beach, you'll find **Signal Inn Beach & Racquetball Club**, a collection of 19 fully-furnished condos that welcome man's best friend. On-site amenities include a solar-heated pool and spa, butterfly garden, barbeque grills, and a shell cleaning station. Dogs stay for an additional fee of $45 to $95, depending on the length of stay. For shorter visits, check out nearby **Tropical Winds Beachfront Motel & Cottages**, where dogs are welcome for $15 per night.

Signal Inn
1811 Olde Middle Gulf Drive
Sanibel, FL 33957
(239) 472-4690
www.signalinn.com
Rates from $217/night

Tarpon Bay Explorers

If your dog likes to walk where the wild things are, bring him to the **J.N. Ding Darling National Wildlife Refuge** in Sanibel. Besides being home to over 300 species of animals, the refuge is also part of the largest undeveloped mangrove system in the country. Follow the four-mile Wildlife Drive through the refuge in your car, hike one of six nature trails, or rent a pontoon boat, kayak, canoe, or stand-up paddleboard from **Tarpon Bay Explorers** for an intrepid journey through the mangrove forest. Admission is $5 per vehicle, and boat rentals start at $25. Afterwards, do the famous 'Sanibel Stoop' at **Gulfside Beach**, which is literally covered with shells and sand dollars at low tide. Simply bend down to pluck the perfect shell from the sand and repeat. Now you're doing the Sanibel Stoop! After you've worked up an appetite, head to **The Island Cow** for 'udderly' delicious seafood and frozen concoctions.

Tarpon Bay Explorers
900 Tarpon Bay Road
Sanibel, FL 33957
(239) 472-8900
www.tarponbayexplorers.com

Fountain of Youth

You and your pooch can walk in the footsteps of explorer Juan Ponce de León in search of the legendary Fountain of Youth in sunny St. Augustine. Start your day by visiting the **Fountain of Youth Archaeological Park**, where you and your pup can enjoy exhibits on the Native Americans and Spanish explorers who once inhabited the grounds. After learning about the historic settlements, make your way to the 600-foot long observation platform over the marsh. Be sure to pack a picnic lunch, which you can enjoy at one of the many picnic tables throughout the park. Before you leave, stop by the Spring House for a cool drink from the Fountain of Youth. Fido can have a sip too! Admission is $12 for adults and $8 for children. Dogs are welcome for no additional fee. The park is open daily from 9:00 am to 5:00 pm.

Fountain of Youth Archaeological Park
11 Magnolia Avenue
St. Augustine, FL 32084
(904) 829-3168
www.fountainofyouthflorida.com

Where to Stay:

Once you and your four-legged friend have walked in the footsteps of explorers past at the Fountain of Youth, take a five-minute drive to the **Saint Augustine Beach House** for a relaxing overnight stay. The innkeepers welcome dogs with open arms and yummy treats. The pet fee is only $15 per stay, regardless of the number of dogs, and pet beds are available upon request. After a comfy night's sleep, take a morning stroll on the dog-friendly beach right outside your door.

Saint Augustine Beach House
10 Vilano Road
St. Augustine, FL 32084
(904) 217-3765
www.sabhonline.com
Rates from $159/night

Where to Stay:

Located just one block from the Eco Tours dock in the heart of the historic district, the **Bayfront Marin House** is a great place to rest and relax on your St. Augustine vacation. Each guest room has a private entrance, convenient for early morning and late night walks with your pup. The property also offers complimentary parking, daily hot breakfast, and evening happy hours. Dogs of any size are welcome in most rooms for an additional fee of $25 per night.

Bayfront Marin House
142 Avenida Menendez
St. Augustine, FL 32084
(904) 824-4301
www.bayfrontmarinhouse.com
Rates from $139/night

St. Augustine Eco Tours

Cruise around St. Augustine with your dog on a guided boat tour from **St. Augustine Eco Tours**. Experience the popular Dolphin & Nature Eco Tour, which takes you on a 90-minute journey around the rivers and creeks surrounding the historic city. Your boat captain will serve as your guide, educating you on marine ecology, as you keep an eye out for turtles, dolphins and various bird species that call Florida home. If you are lucky, you may even spot a manatee or two! Up to six guests and their furry friends can enjoy a private tour for $175. The company also offers two-hour sailing adventures aboard a 27-foot catamaran, which can also accommodate six passengers. Learn to sail with instruction provided by your guide, or simply sit back and enjoy the ride along the rivers of the estuary. Prices start at $250. Dogs ride for no extra fee on either tour.

St. Augustine Eco Tours
111 Avenida Menendez
St. Augustine, FL 32084
(904) 377-7245
www.staugustineecotours.com

Barnsley Gardens

One of the few surviving antebellum gardens in the southern United States, **Barnsley Gardens** offers its visitors and their pups over 3,000 acres to explore just an hour's drive from Atlanta. Located in Adairsville, the 160-year old estate grounds were once home to a grand Italianate mansion, the ruins of which form the centerpiece of this attraction. A team of master gardeners maintains the property, where Fido can stop and smell the heirloom roses in spring, see a spectacular display of daylilies in summer, and pose for a picture-perfect Christmas card during the holidays (when the halls of the villa are decked with boughs of holly). After touring the gardens, you can hike 12 miles of trails or share a meal at the Beer Garden. Self-guided tours are complimentary for resort guests, but day visitors are also welcome. Tickets are $10 for adults, $5 for children under 12, and free for dogs.

Barnsley Gardens
597 Barnsley Gardens Road
Adairsville, GA 30103
(770) 773-7480
www.barnsleyresort.com

Where to Stay:

Extend your visit to Adairsville with an overnight stay at **Barnsley Resort**. Choose between the property's pet-friendly Garden or Meadow suites, or opt for a one-bedroom Arbor Cottage, which offers a private entrance and front porch. The resort's 'Fairy Godmother' will ensure that your pup has an enjoyable stay by delivering an assortment of treats, food and water dishes, and a pet bed to your room. Dogs of any size are welcome for an additional fee of $75 per stay.

Barnsley Resort
597 Barnsley Gardens Road
Adairsville, GA 30103
(770) 773-7480
www.barnsleyresort.com
Rates from $225/night

Seventy-Four Ranch

Give your pup an authentic dude ranch experience at **Seventy-Four Ranch** in Jasper. A working cattle ranch and cozy bed and breakfast nestled in the foothills of the Blue Ridge Mountains, Seventy-Four Ranch provides an escape from daily life just an hour from Atlanta and Chattanooga. Their popular guided trail rides offer a taste of the cowboy life as you ride across thousands of acres of fields and creeks. This isn't your typical nose-to-tail trail ride. Your guide will set a course based on your experience and then let you ride to your heart's content. Fido can come along to enjoy a full-day or half-day trail ride, too. During your stay on the ranch, you can also learn to rope like a cowboy or fish for your dinner in Parker Pond. They've got the poles, bait, and plenty of fish. Just bring your best fishing dog!

Seventy-Four Ranch
9205 Highway 53 W
Jasper, GA 30143
(706) 692-0123
www.seventyfourranch.com

Where to Stay:

All of the rooms at the **Seventy-Four Ranch** allow pets, but, for a true rustic ranch experience, skip the main house in favor of the property's Saddle House. Originally designed as a cowboy bunkhouse, this room offers four full-size double bunk beds (which can sleep up to eight). The room shares a bathroom with the Porch Cabin, and both rooms may be reserved together for a family-friendly accommodation. Dogs of any size are welcome to stay in guest rooms for no additional fee.

Seventy-Four Ranch
9205 Highway 53 W
Jasper, GA 30143
(706) 692-0123
www.seventyfourranch.com
Rates from $85/night

Where to Stay:

After you see Rock City, bring Fido to the historic **Chattanooga Choo Choo Hotel**, where you can sleep aboard an authentic train car. The Victorian train car rooms feature a queen-size bed. Some rooms also have a trundle bed to accommodate more than two guests. Dogs are welcome for an additional fee of $35 per stay. The property offers a fenced dog exercise area, as well as a formal garden that your pooch is welcome to visit while on a leash.

Chattanooga Choo Choo Hotel
1400 Market Street
Chattanooga, TN 37402
(800) 872-2529
www.choochoo.com
Rates from $98/night

Rock City Gardens

Located atop Lookout Mountain on the Tennessee-Georgia border, **Rock City Gardens** provides a unique adventure for you and your pup. A stroll along The Enchanted Trail will take you through the manicured 14-acre property. Pose for some photos at the 100-foot waterfall or the 1,000-ton balanced rock. Conquer Fido's fear of heights by crossing the Swing-A-Long Bridge, or stay on solid ground by choosing the sturdy Stone Bridge. Perched 1,700 feet above sea level, Lover's Leap offers panoramic views of seven states, as well as breathtaking vistas of the scenic Chattanooga Valley below. Amid the rock formations, you'll find expansive botanical gardens, displaying over 400 varieties of native flowers, shrubs, and trees year-round. Well-behaved leashed dogs are welcome throughout the gardens. Rock City hours vary by season. Admission is $20 for adults, $12 for children ages 3 to 12, and free for dogs. Free parking is also available.

Rock City Gardens
1400 Patten Road
Lookout Mountain, GA 30750
(706) 820-2531
www.seerockcity.com

Bonaventure Cemetery

In a city well-known for its elaborate burial grounds, Savannah's **Bonaventure Cemetery** is certainly the most famous. Spanning over 100 acres and filled with live oaks towering over ornate tombs, this graveyard is open daily from 8:00 am to 5:00 pm. Visit on your own for free, but be sure to leave by 5:00 pm sharp—according to local legend, a pack of ghost dogs roam the grounds at night and will chase away any visitors still there after dark. If your pup's not afraid, check out **Ghost City Tours**, which offers nightly walking tours of Savannah. A 90-minute tour costs $20 for adults and $10 for kids. For another frightfully fun experience, enjoy a trip with **Hearse Ghost Tours**. Your mode of transportation is an authentic hearse once used to transport the dearly departed. Prices are $15 for adults and $10 for children. Dogs are free on both tours.

Bonaventure Cemetery
330 Bonaventure Road
Savannah, GA 31401
(912) 651-6843
www.bonaventurehistorical.org

Where to Stay:

If you haven't had your fill of frights after a cemetery tour, be sure to stay at the **Olde Harbour Inn** in downtown Savannah, which boasts its own resident ghost. The all-suite property has large rooms with separate sitting areas overlooking the Savannah River. Be sure to check the freezer in your efficiency kitchen each night too. The housekeeping staff leaves ice cream bars during turn-down service! Dogs of any size are welcome for an additional fee of $40 per stay.

Olde Harbour Inn
508 E Factors Walk
Savannah, GA 31401
(912) 234-4100
www.oldeharbourinn.com
Rates from $142/night

Where to Stay:

Top off your tour of Savannah with an overnight stay in one of the city's historic mansions. The **Foley House Inn** will welcome you with tea and cookies in the afternoon or wine and cheese in the evening. And the innkeepers extend the same Southern hospitality to their four-legged guests! Multiple dog-friendly parks are nearby, including Chippewa Square, where Forrest Gump ate his box of chocolates. Dogs of any size are welcome for an additional fee of $50 per pet, per stay.

Foley House Inn
14 W Hull Street
Savannah, GA 31401
(912) 232-6622
www.foleyinn.com
Rates from $179/night

Oliver Bentleys

Savannah is home to many pet-friendly tour companies, but only one features a guide with four legs. Retailer **Oliver Bentleys** invites you to 'embark on a tour of tales' with their Historic Dog Walk Tour. Led by Ollie B. himself—a Cavalier King Charles Spaniel—the tours are tailored specifically for dogs and their humans. Groups depart from their bakery on Tuesdays through Saturdays at 4:30 pm. Tickets are $20 for adults and $10 for children over nine. If you want to soak up even more Savannah history, climb aboard an **Oglethorpe Tours** trolley for a driving tour of the city. You can hop on/off as many times as you'd like 'til 5:30 pm for $20. Film buffs can catch a glimpse of some of their favorite movie backdrops with **Savannah Movie Tours**. Their 90-minute tour costs $26 and visits more than 60 film locations. Dogs are free on all three excursions!

Oliver Bentleys
13 W York Street
Savannah, GA 31401
(912) 201-1688
www.oliverbentleys.com/tour

Tybee Jet Ski & Watersports

Take your dog on an unforgettable ocean adventure with a Jet Ski rental from **Tybee Jet Ski & Watersports** (rates from $95/hour). Your pup is welcome to ride on your personal watercraft as you speed across the waves, enjoying the ocean breezes and the thrill of being out on the open water. For a more leisurely experience, rent a kayak and paddle through Tybee's waters with your canine companion. Be sure to bring your Jet Ski or kayak over to Little Tybee for some beach-time fun with Fido. If you want someone else to escort you around the island, book a 90-minute cruise with **Captain Mike's Dolphin Tours**. You and your leashed pooch will enjoy spotting bottlenose dolphins frolicking in their natural habitat, while also seeing some of Tybee Island's most famous sights. Rates are $15 for adults and $8 for kids under 13. Dogs ride for free.

Tybee Jet Ski & Watersports
1 Old Tybee Road
Tybee Island, GA 31328
(912) 786-8062
www.tybeejetski.com

Where to Stay:

After catching some waves, head to **The Crab Shack**, an eclectic pet-friendly restaurant serving up tasty seafood and cold concoctions. Then spend the night in one of 17 dog-friendly coastal cottages available from **Mermaid Cottages** in Tybee Island. Fido will love the 'Paws & Paddles' cottage thanks to its fenced-in backyard and partial view of the salt marsh. Dog treats are also provided. Up to two dogs of any size are welcome for an additional fee of $100 per stay.

Mermaid Cottages
1517 Chatham Avenue
Tybee Island, GA 31328
(912) 313-0784
www.mermaidcottages.com
Rates from $160/night

Where to Stay:

After Fido learns to 'Hang 20' on the water, kick back and relax at the **Aqua Waikiki Wave**, a trendy boutique hotel with affordable accommodations. Conveniently located one block from where you'll be taking your surfing lessons, the Wave is just minutes away from Honolulu's shopping, dining, and nightlife district. Pets receive treats, beds, and a toy to take home. Up to two dogs under 40 lbs are welcome for an additional fee of $35 per pet, per night.

Aqua Waikiki Wave
2299 Kuhio Avenue
Honolulu, HI 96815
(808) 922-1262
www.aquawaikikiwave.com
Rates from $96/night

Gone Surfing Hawaii

If you're planning a getaway to Honolulu and want to bring Fido along for the trip, reward him with a day on the water with **Gone Surfing Hawaii**. Don't worry if you've never surfed before. The crew at Gone Surfing Hawaii offers beginner lessons for you and your dog and will equip you with all the necessary gear. During your private lesson, they'll provide an on-land demonstration of surfing basics before you get wet. After entering the water, you'll receive instruction on reading the waves and properly using the board. The two-hour lessons take place on Waikiki Beach and cost $135 per person. If surfing is not for you, the company also offers stand-up paddleboard lessons. You and your four-legged friend can enjoy a two-hour private lesson for $155, which includes all equipment. Gone Surfing Hawaii even has a videographer on staff to capture your adventure for posterity.

Gone Surfing Hawaii
330 Saratoga Road
Honolulu, HI 98615
(808) 429-6404
www.gonesurfinghawaii.com

Brooks Sea Plane

Experience an aerial tour of beautiful Coeur d'Alene on a flightseeing adventure with **Brooks Sea Plane**. Your canine companion is welcome to join you on a 20-minute flight that circles Lake Coeur d'Alene and offers panoramic views of the lake and scenic terrain below. Your tour will depart from the City Dock at Independence Point in downtown Coeur d'Alene via a Cessna 206 or a de Havilland Beaver. Flights are offered daily, and rates are $60 per adult and $30 per child ($120 minimum per flight). A longer 40-minute tour is also available. If you and your pooch want to keep your feet firmly planted on the ground, you can still enjoy the lake by visiting **Tubbs Hill** for an afternoon hike. The park encompasses over 120 acres of trails, beaches, overlooks, and caves bordering Lake Coeur d'Alene. There is no admission fee to enjoy this magnificent public area.

Brooks Sea Plane
Independence Point City Dock
Coeur d'Alene, ID 83814
(208) 664-2842
www.brooks-seaplane.com

Where to Stay:

After his flightseeing adventure with Brooks Sea Plane, Fido can watch other 'pawsengers' land on the lake from the wall-to-wall windows in your room at the **Coeur d'Alene Resort**. Located in a 17-story tower at the lake's edge and nicknamed the 'Playground of the Pacific Northwest,' the resort features a large marina with a mile-long floating walkway, lakeside pool, full-service spa, and a dozen dining options. Dogs of any size are welcome for an additional fee of $75 per stay.

The Coeur d'Alene Resort
115 S 2nd Street
Coeur d'Alene, ID 83814
(208) 765-4000
www.cdaresort.com
Rates from $129/night

Dog Bark Park Inn

Located near the border of Washington and Oregon, you'll find Idaho's most famous dog-friendly landmark in the sleepy town of Cottonwood. Nicknamed 'Sweet Willy' by the locals, the world's largest beagle stretches to a height of 30 feet. But this is no ordinary dog—it's actually a bed and breakfast! The **Dog Bark Park Inn** was created by a husband and wife team of chainsaw artists in 1997. The unusual structure has garnered worldwide attention as a slice of roadside Americana ever since, and travelers come from around the globe to spend a night 'in the dog house.' Even if you're not able to stay overnight, you can still browse the gift shop and watch Dennis and Frances carve wooden statues of more than 60 dog breeds in their studio. Passers-by can even take a potty break in the giant fire hydrant! Visitors are welcome daily from 11:00 am to 4:00 pm.

Dog Bark Park Inn
2421 Business Highway 95
Cottonwood, ID 83522
(208) 983-1236
www.dogbarkparkinn.com

Where to Stay:

No trip to the **Dog Bark Park Inn** is complete without an overnight stay. Inside the belly of the beast, you'll find a queen bedroom and full-size bathroom. Additional loft space (accessible by ladder) contains twin futons and a variety of books and games. A self-serve breakfast of homemade treats is included with your stay. Plan to get there early on your day of arrival, as check-in is from 3:30 pm to 5:30 pm. Well-behaved dogs are welcome for an additional $15 each.

Dog Bark Park Inn
2421 Business Highway 95
Cottonwood, ID 83522
(208) 983-1236
www.dogbarkparkinn.com
Rates from $98/night

Where to Stay:

Located just one mile from the Navy Pier, the **Hotel Palomar** will make your Chicago visit one to remember. Floor-to-ceiling windows in your luxurious guest room provide fantastic views of the Chicago skyline. Treat yourself to an in-room spa service or visit to the health club, while the concierge makes grooming arrangements for your canine companion. Dogs of any size are welcome to stay for no additional fee. Treats, bowls, and bedding are provided for Fido during your stay.

Hotel Palomar
505 N State Street
Chicago, IL 60654
(312) 755-9703
www.tinyurl.com/ruff09
Rates from $179/night

Seadog Cruises

See the Windy City with your pooch on a **Seadog Cruises** speedboat tour. Departing from Chicago's famous Navy Pier, the company offers four pet-friendly cruise options. If you're short on time, opt for the half-hour Lakefront Speedboat Tour, which hits the highlights on a fast-paced cruise on Lake Michigan. With more time to spare, choose the 75-minute River and Lake Architecture Tour, which extends your trip through the Chicago River Locks. Cruises operate from April through October. Humans traveling with their pooch receive 10% off regular ticket prices, which start at $24 for adults and $17 for kids 12 and under. Dogs ride for free! If you'll be in town from July through September, check out **Mercury's** famous Canine Cruise. Taking place on Sunday mornings in late summer, the Canine Cruise highlights many of Chicago's pet-friendly restaurants, attractions, and parks. Rates are $29 for adults, $11 for kids, and $8 for Fido.

Seadog Cruises
600 E Grand Avenue
Chicago, IL 60611
(877) 902-6216
www.seadogcruises.com

Shawnee National Forest

With more than 270,000 acres across 10 counties in Southern Illinois, the **Shawnee National Forest** is a hiking enthusiast's dream. Dozens of trails in the area invite you and your canine companion to explore hundreds of miles of scenic landscape and amazing rock formations. Amateurs should feel comfortable starting out at the **Rim Rock National Recreation Area** near Elizabethtown. Fido will enjoy the short one-mile hike around the forested bluffs, with interpretive signs guiding the way. More experienced hikers will be eager to backpack a nearby portion of the River to River Trail, which extends approximately 150 miles from Battery Rock on the Ohio River to Devil's Backbone Park on the Mississippi River. Finally, you won't want to miss the **Garden of the Gods Recreation Area**, with its unique rock formations and miles of interconnected trails. Leashed dogs are welcome on all trails throughout the Shawnee National Forest.

Shawnee National Forest
Illinois 34
Harrisburg, IL 62946
(618) 253-7114
www.fs.usda.gov/shawnee

Where to Stay:

Located in the Shawnee Hills of Southern Illinois, **Rim Rock's Dogwood Cabins** are great for hiking enthusiasts who want to 'ruff it' for a few days with their dogs. This collection of five well-appointed cabins sits on 77 acres of forestland adjacent to the Rim Rock National Recreation Trail and only seven miles from the Garden of the Gods. Countless other trails are located in the surrounding area. Up to two dogs of any size are welcome to stay in the cabins for no additional fee.

Rim Rock's Dogwood Cabins
3900 Pounds Hollow Blacktop
Elizabethtown, IL 62931
(618) 264-6036
www.tinyurl.com/ruff10
Rates from $100/night

Where to Stay:

A clean modern atmosphere will greet you at the **I Hotel & Conference Center** in Champaign. Guest rooms feature local artwork and a shelf of books to peruse at your leisure. Squeeze in a workout at the fitness center, schedule a deep tissue massage at the spa, and grab a bite to eat on one of the pet-friendly patio tables at the adjacent **Houlihan's Restaurant**. One dog up to 50 lbs is welcome for an additional fee of $100 per stay.

I Hotel & Conference Center
1900 S 1st Street
Champaign, IL 61820
(217) 819-5000
www.stayatthei.com
Rates from $119/night

Allerton Park & Retreat Center

Borne out of Robert Allerton's love of nature and artistic expression, **Allerton Park & Retreat Center** exists today as a 1,500-acre oasis of forests, hiking trails, gardens, statuary, sculptures, grassy fields, rivers, and ponds. You and Fido will find plenty to love about this park as you hike the 14 miles of trails, visit the 30-acre demonstration prairie, and enjoy more than 100 outdoor sculptures and ornamental pieces found throughout the property. Twelve park gardens, including the Peony Garden, Chinese Maze Garden, Fu Dog Garden, Parterre Garden, and the Sunken Garden are waiting for you and your pup to explore them. Bring a picnic and make a day of your visit. Leashed dogs are welcome to join their humans throughout the park (other than the park building). Allerton Park is open daily from 8:00 am to sunset with the exception of Thanksgiving, Christmas, and New Year's Day. There is no admission fee.

Allerton Park & Retreat Center
515 Old Timber Road
Monticello, IL 61856
(217) 333-3287
www.allerton.illinois.edu

French Lick Scenic Railway

The **French Lick Scenic Railway** has been a popular stop for train enthusiasts for many years. You and Fido can enjoy a 20-mile roundtrip ride from French Lick to Cuzco aboard a historic passenger train. The locomotives pass through portions of the Hoosier National Forest and take passengers through the 2,200-foot-long Burton Tunnel. You will hear about the history of the French Lick area as you pass the structural remains of a bygone era. Trains travel to Cuzco, where you can disembark, stretch your pup's legs and purchase a snack from the shop adjacent to the train tracks. After the stop, the train reverses direction and heads back to French Lick. Fares are $18 for adults and $9 for children. Well-behaved dogs are welcome aboard the train during scenic tours for no additional fee! After the roundtrip, head to **French Lick Resort** for a historical tour of their famous domed atrium.

French Lick Scenic Railway
1 Monon Drive
French Lick, IN 47432
(812) 936-2405
www.frenchlickscenicrailway.org

Where to Stay:

Fido can exchange his conductor hat for poker chips at the **French Lick Resort**, a Victorian-style hotel and casino that dates back to 1845. Whether you prefer golfing, spa treatments, gaming or concerts, this French Lick establishment has something for everyone. Dogs up to 40 lbs are welcome for an additional fee of $50 per stay. Guests with larger dogs can stay in a pet-friendly cottage at the nearby **Artist's Inn & Cottages** for an additional fee of $25 per night.

French Lick Resort
8670 W State Road 56
French Lick, IN 47432
(812) 936-9300
www.frenchlick.com
Rates from $159/night

100 Acres Art and Nature Park

Art lovers will want to bring Fido to the **100 Acres Art and Nature Park** in Indianapolis. Adjacent to the Indianapolis Museum of Art, 100 Acres is one of the largest contemporary sculpture parks in the world and features a number of unique exhibits designed for human (and canine) interaction. Be sure to check out The Pulliam Family Landscape Journeys exhibit and take a canoe ride to the fully-inhabitable living structure on the water known as Indy Island. There is no admission fee, so you are free to stroll through on a morning walk with your pup and return for an afternoon picnic by the 35-acre lake. To round out your Indianapolis art tour, head over to the **Indianapolis Art Center Artspark**, where you and your pup will find even more outdoor exhibits. Both parks are open daily from sunrise to sunset, and dogs should remain leashed at all times.

100 Acres Art and Nature Park
4000 N Michigan Road
Indianapolis, IN 46208
(317) 923-1331
www.imamuseum.org/visit/100acres

Where to Stay:

Doubling as a museum of sorts, **The Alexander** is an eclectic alternative to chain hotels. Boasting its own impressive art collection, this contemporary hotel features stylish guest rooms and an array of comforting amenities. Dogs up to 40 lbs are welcome for an additional fee of $100 per stay. If your pooch is on the larger side, plan on staying at the **Residence Inn on the Canal**, which welcomes dogs of all sizes for an extra fee of $100 per stay.

The Alexander
333 S Delaware Street
Indianapolis, IN 46204
(317) 624-8200
www.thealexander.com
Rates from $170/night

Where to Stay:

In keeping with the pioneer theme of Living History Farms, the **Stoney Creek Inn** in Johnston features Western-style suites with stone fireplaces and lodge-themed décor. Families will love the bunk bed suites that comfortably sleep six. Enjoy a free hot breakfast, splash away at the Wilderness Park Pool, and grab a slice of pizza at Bearly's Bar, all without ever leaving the grounds. Up to two dogs under 50 lbs are welcome for an additional fee of $25 per pet, per night.

Stoney Creek Inn
5291 Stoney Creek Court
Johnston, IA 50131
(515) 334-9000
www.stoneycreekinn.com
Rates from $84/night

Living History Farms

Take your pup on a stroll through the past at **Living History Farms** in Urbandale. Visit exhibits designed to engage and educate you on life in the Midwest during the 1700s, 1800s, and 1900s. Each site is authentically farmed according to the time period and features interpreters dressed in period garb. The 1700 Iowa Farm boasts gardens, bark lodges, and demonstrations in tanning, cooking, and making pottery. At the 1850 Pioneer Farm, you might see men cultivating the fields while the women work on domestic projects inside the period cabin. See how farming changed with the arrival of machinery at the 1900 Horse-Powered Farm, or take in the sights and sounds of a bustling frontier community at the 1875 Town of Walnut Hill. Dogs must be leashed at all times and remain outside of the buildings. Hours vary by season. Admission is $13 for adults, $8 for children, and free for dogs.

Living History Farms
11121 Hickman Road
Urbandale, IA 50322
(515) 278-5286
www.lhf.org

Greyhound Hall of Fame

Hop in the car for a road trip to Abilene with your faithful canine companion to celebrate the noble greyhound at the **Greyhound Hall of Fame**. Two loving, retired racers, Gary and Jade, will greet you at the door, welcoming you to this fascinating experience. Enjoy learning about the history of the breed, from ancient to modern times, at what is considered to be the 'Greyhound Capital of the World.' Get to know the Hall of Fame inductees at various displays throughout the building. You'll see some of the finest representations of the breed in the museum exhibits. Keep Fido leashed when inside unless you receive permission from the staff to browse with your pup off-leash. The Greyhound Hall of Fame is open daily from 9:00 am to 5:00 pm. Admission is free, but gift shop purchases and donations to help the museum remain open are greatly appreciated.

Greyhound Hall of Fame
407 S Buckeye Avenue
Abilene, KS 67410
(785) 263-3000
www.greyhoundhalloffame.com

Where to Stay:

You won't have to venture far from the Greyhound Hall of Fame to find comfortable accommodations for you and your pooch. The **Holiday Inn Express Abilene** is directly across the street and in close proximity to other historical attractions in the area. Relax in clean, spacious rooms, swim in the heated indoor pool, and unwind in the on-site sauna. Enjoy complimentary breakfast every morning. Dogs of any size are welcome for an additional fee of $20 per pet, per night.

Holiday Inn Express Abilene
110 E Lafayette Avenue
Abilene, KS 67410
(785) 263-4049
www.tinyurl.com/ruff11
Rates from $99/night

Where to Stay:

Cap off a day of boating, fishing, and hiking by putting your feet up in a 'Floating Cabin' at the **Green River Marina**. Soak up the tranquil lake scenery from your balcony or deck in either a one or two-story boathouse. All cabins come fully furnished with kitchens and outdoor gas grills so that you can cook your fresh catch. A minimum stay of three nights is required. Dogs are welcome for an additional fee of $25 per pet, per night.

Green River Marina
2892 Lone Valley Road
Campbellsville, KY 42718
(270) 465-2512
www.greenrivermarina.com
Rates from $100/night

Green River Lake

Considered one of the best kept secrets in Kentucky, **Green River Lake** in Campbellsville is a perfect spot for a day in nature with your furry friend. Start off at the marina and rent a boat for a day of relaxation on the water with your pup. Drop a line over the side of the boat and fish for bass, crappie, bluegill, and catfish. If you want to stay on land, you and Fido can tackle the 28 miles of hiking trails in the **Green River Lake State Park**. With hikes ranging from easy to difficult, you can choose to embark on a leisurely stroll through the woods or challenge yourself to conquer the most strenuous trail. Keep your eye out for deer, resident and migratory birds, rabbits, and other wildlife. Dogs must be on a leash throughout Green River Lake State Park. There is no admission fee.

Green River Marina
2892 Lone Valley Road
Campbellsville, KY 42718
(270) 465-2512
www.greenrivermarina.com

Dinosaur World

Give Fido a chance to get up close and personal with dinosaurs of all sizes at **Dinosaur World** in Cave City. Life-size replicas made from steel, concrete, and fiberglass line the paths of this educational outdoor attraction. You and your pup can stroll through natural settings on the lookout for more than 100 prehistoric animals on the Dinosaur Walk. Explanatory signs are found at each display. Dinosaurs are not the only giants, though. Head over to Mammoth Gardens to see the woolly creatures that once roamed the earth. The Movie Cave gives you an opportunity to watch an interpretive film before or after your walk. Unearth the life-size bones of a dinosaur in the Boneyard or go hunting for fossils in the Fossil Dig. Well-behaved, leashed pets are welcome throughout the park and gift shop. Hours vary by season. Admission is $13 for adults and $10 for children. Dogs are free!

Dinosaur World
711 Mammoth Cave Road
Cave City, KY 42127
(270) 773-4345
www.dinosaurworld.com

Where to Stay:

Step out of the Jurassic period and into frontier times at **Jellystone Park of Mammoth Cave**. Located a half-mile from Dinosaur World, Jellystone Park allows pets in its log cabins. With room for up to eight people, these modernized cabins come equipped with a full kitchen, satellite TV, Wi-Fi, covered porch, and a fire ring with charcoal grill. Don't forget to bring your own linens. Two dogs of any size are welcome for an additional fee of $10 per pet, per night.

Jellystone Park
1002 Mammoth Cave Road
Cave City, KY 42127
(270) 773-3840
www.tinyurl.com/ruff13
Rates from $75/night

SECRETARIAT

Where to Stay:

Following a day at the Kentucky Horse Park, take a short drive to Versailles for a stay at the **Rose Hill Inn**. Built in 1823 and fully restored, this Kentucky mansion now serves as a bed and breakfast, welcoming visitors from around the country with southern hospitality. Fido will be greeted by Roxie, the resident English bulldog, who loves to frolic in the fenced yard. Dogs are welcome in four of the seven guest rooms for an additional fee of $20 per stay.

Rose Hill Inn
233 Rose Hill Avenue
Versailles, KY 40383
(859) 873-5957
www.rosehillinn.com
Rates from $159/night

Kentucky Horse Park

Aficionados of all things equestrian are certain to enjoy a visit to the **Kentucky Horse Park** in Lexington. Bring Fido to the barns, rings, courses, arenas, and memorials on the park's 1,032 acres. Browse the exhibits at the two museums and visit the guest horses staying at the park in the summer. Stroll through the Memorial Walk of Champions before visiting the famous Man o' War statue. Tour the barns or enjoy one of several events that take place on the grounds each year. Dogs of any size are welcome at nearly all outdoor areas. Small dogs that can be carried are welcome in the gift shop. If you want to visit the museums, someone in your party will need to stay outside with your pup. Park hours are 9:00 am to 5:00 pm, and prices range from $10-16 for adults and $5-8 for children, depending on the season. Dogs are free.

Kentucky Horse Park
4089 Iron Works Parkway
Lexington, KY 40511
(800) 678-8813
www.kyhorsepark.com

Mega Cavern

Bring Fido on an underground adventure inside Louisville's **Mega Cavern**. Founded in 1930, this man-made cavern is one of the largest in the country. Nearly 100 acres in size, Mega Cavern is part of a 15-mile network of corridors located beneath the city of Louisville. Climb aboard the tram with your pup and enjoy a tour that includes cave formations, a replica of the Cuban Missile Crisis Fallout Bunker, early mining sites, and a worm recycling room. Strategic lighting and expert narration enhance your cavern experience. The temperature underground stays at 58 degrees Fahrenheit throughout the year, providing you with a refuge from the summer heat or the chill of winter. The hour-long tram tour departs promptly on the hour, so make sure to arrive early to pick up tickets. Hours vary by season. Admission is $14 for adults and $8 for children. Dogs ride for free.

Mega Cavern
1841 Taylor Avenue
Louisville, KY 40213
(877) 614-6342
www.louisvillemegacavern.com

Where to Stay:

When you're finished exploring Louisville's underground past, climb into the city's cultured present at the **21c Museum Hotel**, a unique convergence of art and hospitality. Rest in luxurious modern rooms, enjoy a soothing spa treatment, dine at Proof on Main, and browse the diverse collection of contemporary artwork, sculpture, and photography spanning the entire property. You can't miss the ubiquitous red penguins and mirrored convertible. Dogs up to 50 lbs are welcome for an additional fee of $100 per stay.

21c Museum Hotel
700 W Main Street
Louisville, KY 40202
(502) 217-6300
www.21cmuseumhotels.com
Rates from $179/night

Where to Stay:

After trekking through the scenic Louisiana wilderness, you and Fido will welcome the charming appeal of the **Bois de Chenes Bed & Breakfast** in Lafayette. Pet-friendly accommodations are available in the property's Carriage House, where up to two dogs of any size are welcome for no additional fee. While enjoying your stay in Lafayette, be sure to visit the **Blue Dog Café**. Displaying the art of George Rodrigue, the restaurant features an eclectic menu and a pet-friendly patio.

Bois de Chenes Bed & Breakfast
338 N Sterling Street
Lafayette, LA 70501
(337) 233-7816
www.boisdechenes.com

Atchafalaya Experience

Enjoy America's largest river swamp with your pup on the **Atchafalaya Experience** in Breaux Bridge. Louisiana's Atchafalaya River is a perfect place to spot beavers, deer, alligators, crocodiles, and over 30 bird species. Tour the swamp with experienced naturalists, whose love of the area and expertise make each trip memorable. Tours begin daily at the Atchafalaya Welcome Center, but you should call ahead for reservations. Prices are $50 for adults and $25 for children. Well-behaved, leashed pets are welcome for no additional fee. For another nearby adventure with Fido, travel to **Avery Island** for a visit to the Tabasco Country Store and the 170-acre Jungle Gardens. Dogs are welcome on the grounds of both attractions but should remain leashed at all times. Visitors pay a $1 toll per vehicle to enter Avery Island. Admission to Jungle Gardens is $8 for adults and $5 for children. Dogs are welcome for free.

Atchafalaya Experience
Atchafalaya Welcome Center
1908 Atchafalaya River Highway
Breaux Bridge, LA 70517
(337) 277-4726
www.theatchafalayaexperience.com

Bloody Mary's Tours

If you're a fan of spooks and specters, enjoy a nighttime tour of New Orleans with **Bloody Mary's Tours**. On the Moonlight Graveyard Tour, you'll wander through at least two cemeteries with Fido and get a peek at many more from behind the gates. History and haunts will come to life as your guide entertains you with ghost stories and historical facts about the famous graveyards. Tours depart from the Beachcorner Bar at 5:00 pm on Fridays and Saturdays. Tickets cost $30 per person, and reservations are required. Well-behaved dogs are welcome for no additional fee. For a less-spooky look at New Orleans, climb aboard the pet-friendly **Algiers Ferry** and enjoy incredible views of the city as you head to Algiers Point. Experience the charming neighborhood before completing your round-trip back to the Crescent City. The trip to Algiers Point is free, and the return costs $1 per car.

Bloody Mary's Tours
4905 Canal Street
New Orleans, LA 70119
(504) 523-7684
www.bloodymarystours.com

Where to Stay:

Conveniently located a block away from the Algiers Ferry dock, the **Windsor Court Hotel** is a veritable French Quarter oasis that will make you and Fido feel like royalty during your stay in New Orleans. Marvel at the impressive European architecture, take in spectacular city skyline views from the gorgeous rooftop swimming pool, schedule a relaxing spa treatment, grab a drink at the Polo Lounge, and peruse the museum quality art collection. Dogs of any size are welcome for no additional fee.

Windsor Court Hotel
300 Gravier Street
New Orleans, LA 70130
(504)523-6000
www.windsorcourthotel.com
Rates from $225/night

Acadia National Park

Spend a glorious day with your pup surrounded by the beauty of **Acadia National Park** on a tour with **Carriages of Acadia**. You and Fido will enjoy traveling down Acadia's historic roads in a horse-drawn carriage on one of four guided excursions. Tours start at $20. If you would rather explore on your own, take the free, pet-friendly **Island Explorer** shuttle into Acadia and wander the trails, hike the granite peaks, and savor the natural beauty of the flora and fauna. Visit the **Jordan Pond House** for famous popovers, lobster stew, or a refreshing glass of hand-squeezed lemonade on the lawn. See Acadia's wonders from the water with a scenic nature cruise aboard the **Sea Princess**. Narrated by an Acadia Park Ranger, the pet-friendly cruise will take you through Mount Desert Island's Great Harbor and the Somes Sound fjord. Rates start at $23 for adults and $7 for children. Dogs ride for free.

Acadia National Park
20 McFarland Hill Drive
Bar Harbor, ME 04609
(207) 288-3338
www.nps.gov/acad

Where to Stay:

Constructed in 1900, the **Canterbury Cottage Bed & Breakfast** is a cozy alternative to traditional lodgings in Bar Harbor. The home is within walking distance of downtown shops and the harbor, as well as a short drive from the hiking trails in Acadia National Park. While you're there, Fido can also make friends with the owner's two dogs, Ellie May and Clinton. Dogs of any size are welcome in the Cottage Room for an additional fee of $20 per night.

Canterbury Cottage Bed & Breakfast
12 Roberts Avenue
Bar Harbor, ME 04069
(207) 288-2112
www.canterburycottage.com
Rates from $99/night

Where to Stay:

When you and Fido are finished on the links, take a leisurely 30-minute drive to the **Lakeside Motel & Cabins**. Situated on the quiet shores of Cobbosseecontee Lake in East Winthrop, the property offers standard motel rooms, efficiency suites, and one or two bedroom cabins. Fishing enthusiasts will be in heaven, casting away on one of the Northeast's best bass lakes. Dogs of any size are welcome with prior notice for an additional fee of $10 per night or $50 per week.

Lakeside Motel & Cabins
77 Turtle Run Road
East Winthrop, ME 04343
(207) 395-6741
www.lakesidelodging.com
Rates from $98/night

Belgrade Lakes Golf Club

Grab your clubs and hit the links with Fido in tow at the **Belgrade Lakes Golf Club**. This award-winning golf course was designed by architect Clive Clark and features 18 holes on a stunning 240-acre landscape. The Maine hills and rustic woodlands surrounding the meticulously manicured greens provide an unrivaled ambience for you and your four-legged friend to enjoy a relaxing day of golf. Upon arrival, you'll be shuttled to the top of the hill to meet the club's Director of Outside Happiness before teeing off on a challenging course in an unforgettable setting. After finishing your round, hit the back deck of the clubhouse, where your canine companion is free to join you for a tasty meal from the club's restaurant. The golf course is open May through October. Green fees range from $75 to $135 and include cart rental. Well-behaved dogs are always welcome.

Belgrade Lakes Golf Club
46 Clubhouse Drive
Belgrade Lakes, ME 04918
(207) 495-4653
www.belgradelakesgolf.com

Cap'n Fish's Boat Trips

Bring your pup on one of Boothbay Harbor's most unique attractions by embarking on a Puffin Nature Cruise with **Cap'n Fish's Boat Trips**. Grab your binoculars before leaving the harbor on this 2.5-hour tour around Eastern Egg Rock. Along the way, admire Maine's charming coastline as the onboard marine biologists and naturalists answer questions and introduce you to the wildlife you're likely to encounter on your voyage. Watch for seals, herons, gulls, and perhaps a whale or two before beginning the search for puffins. Cruising around Eastern Egg Rock—the southernmost nesting island in all of North America for the Atlantic Puffin—you're sure to enjoy the sights and sounds of this busy colony. The Puffin Nature Cruise is offered from June through late August; other tours are available through October. Rates are $29 for adults, $15 for children, and $10 for dogs. Call for reservations and departure times.

Cap'n Fish's Boat Trips
1 Wharf Street
Boothbay Harbor, ME 04538
(207) 633-3244
www.boothbayboattrips.com

Where to Stay:

Following your cruise with Cap'n Fish, check in at **Spruce Point Inn Resort & Spa**—a seaside retreat offering sensational views of Boothbay Harbor. Choose from several pet-friendly room types, each decorated with authentic New England furnishings. Fido will get plenty of exercise on the many wooded walking trails located around the resort, which sits on 57 acres of shoreline. You can also sail Maine's only wooden lobster boat from the resort's dock. Dogs of any size are welcome for no additional fee.

Spruce Point Inn Resort & Spa
88 Grandview Avenue
Boothbay Harbor, ME 04538
(207) 633-4152
www.sprucepointinn.com
Rates from $195/night

Where to Stay:

Located a short drive from Portland, **Inn by the Sea** is a true doggie delight on Crescent Beach. The hotel offers an 'Inncredible Pets' package, which includes a two-night stay in a one-bedroom suite, personalized L.L.Bean dog bed, 30-minute in-room pet massage, nightly dining from the gourmet pet menu, and evening turndown service (complete with a locally made seasonal dog treat). The property's human perks are great too, and dogs of any size stay for no additional fee.

Inn by the Sea
40 Bowery Beach Road
Cape Elizabeth, ME 04107
(207) 799-3134
www.innbythesea.com
Rates from $249/night

Casco Bay Lines

Explore the islands of Casco Bay with Fido aboard one of the daily cruises offered by **Casco Bay Lines** in Portland. Start your morning with a beautiful 'Sunrise on the Bay' cruise, a two-hour tour that starts at the peak of dawn, giving you opportunities for great early morning photographs. If island hopping is more your style, check out the 'Mailboat Run' instead. As the name implies, the Mailboat navigates the many small islands of Casco Bay, delivering mail and freight, and hauling passengers and their furry friends. Round-trip cruises take approximately three hours and depart twice daily. Ticket prices are $16 for adults, $8 for children, and $4 for dogs. Dogs must remain leashed at all times. After you've worked up an appetite helping to deliver mail, stop by the **Portland Lobster Company** to enjoy a classic Maine lobster roll. The restaurant welcomes your pooch with ample outdoor seating.

Casco Bay Lines
56 Commercial Street
Portland, ME 04112
(207) 774-7871
www.cascobaylines.com

Captain Jack Lobster Tours

Make your way to Rockland for a once-in-a-lifetime adventure aboard a working lobster boat. On the 90-minute adventure with **Captain Jack Lobster Tours**, you'll get a glimpse at the life of lobster man, Steve Hale, as he seeks out the day's fresh catch. Fido will be nose-to-nose with lobster, crabs, starfish, and sea urchins when Steve hauls in the traps. You may also see harbor seals and whales as you're whisked through Rockland Harbor and West Penobscot Bay. Those wishing to add more flavor to their adventure can purchase lobster fresh off the boat at market price or rent their own lobster trap for $250 a season (plus shipping). With the latter purchase, you are guaranteed at least 25 pounds of fresh Maine lobster delivered to your home throughout the year. Tours are limited to six people and cost $30 for adults and $18 for kids. Well-behaved dogs are free.

Captain Jack Lobster Tours
Middle Pier
1 Park Drive
Rockland, ME 04841
(207) 542-6852
www.captainjacklobstertours.com

Where to Stay:

Only 15 minutes from Rockland, the **Lord Camden Inn** offers upscale amenities befitting its regal name. Enjoy harbor and river views from your cozy room, or take Fido on a hike at nearby **Camden Hills State Park**. Dogs are given the royal treatment with the inn's 'Pampered Pooch' program, which includes a plush fleece-lined bed, gourmet biscuits, and food and water bowls. Up to two dogs of any size are welcome for an additional fee of $25 per pet, per night.

Lord Camden Inn
24 Main Street
Camden, ME 04843
(207) 236-4325
www.lordcamdeninn.com
Rates from $99/night

Where to Stay:

After a day on the water, you and your furry friend can take it easy at the deluxe **Loews Annapolis Hotel**. In addition to offering first-rate rooms and amenities, the hotel welcomes visiting pups with dog tags, bowls, beds, and treats. Pet sitting and walking services can be arranged by the concierge, and the 'Loews Loves Pets' room service menu is sure to satisfy your canine's cravings. Up to two dogs of any size are welcome for an additional fee of $25 per stay.

Loews Annapolis Hotel
126 West Street
Annapolis, MD 21401
(410) 263-7777
www.tinyurl.com/ruff14
Rates from $139/night

Watermark Cruises

You and your canine compatriot can cruise the Chesapeake Bay in style with **Watermark Cruises** in Annapolis. Whether you have just an hour or want to enjoy an entire day on the water, the company has got you covered. Enjoy a quick 40-minute trip around the bay as you learn about Annapolis history, or set off on a 90-minute excursion highlighting the scenic Severn River. If you want to see Maryland's historic lighthouses, choose the three-hour Bay Lighthouse Cruise. Or spend an entire day on the water with a tour to St. Michaels, where you'll disembark to explore the charming streets as you shop, sightsee, and dine. If your dog needs to shake off his sea legs, head to **Quiet Waters Park** after your cruise for off-leash playtime in the dog park or along the hiking trails. Cruise prices start at $14 for adults and $6 for children. Well-behaved dogs ride for free.

Watermark Cruises
1 Dock Street
Annapolis, MD 21401
(410) 268-7601
www.watermarkcruises.com

Ayers Creek Adventures

Experience the natural beauty of Maryland's coastal waterways with **Ayers Creek Adventures** in Berlin. Located just a stone's throw from Ocean City, the family-owned business can introduce you to the quiet side of this bustling beach town with a kayak, canoe, or stand-up paddleboard rental. As you paddle Ayers Creek with your canine companion, he's likely to see bald eagles, herons, egrets, and osprey nesting in the salt marsh. If you'd prefer to paddle Sinepuxent Bay, boats can also be delivered to **Castaways Campground** by request. Either way, you'll get a brief lesson, water trail map, and guide to the local wildlife before you set off. Ayers Creek Adventures is open daily from 8:00 am to 5:00 pm between May and October. Hourly rates start at $15 for kayaks, $20 for canoes, and $25 for stand-up paddleboards. Half-day, full-day, and weekend rates are also available. Dogs paddle for free!

Ayers Creek Adventures
8628 Grey Fox Lane
Berlin, MD 21811
(888) 602-6288
www.ayerscreekadventures.com

Where to Stay:

Sheltered on the shores of Sinepuxent Bay, **Castaways Campground** offers pet-friendly cottage and RV rentals. The property also features dog-friendly perks including a bark park, bark beach, and dog wash station. One large dog or two small dogs are welcome for an additional fee of $8 per night. Add $8 per night for each additional pet. Fido is also welcome to join you for a drink at Jackspot Waterfront Tiki Bar, which features live entertainment during the summer.

Castaways Campground
12550 Eagles Nest Road
Berlin, MD 21811
(410) 213-0097
www.castawaysrvoc.com
Rates from $39/night

Where to Stay:

From the acres of outdoor fun to the daily homemade dog biscuits given to all visiting pooches, **Savage River Lodge** is a doggie paradise. Fido can even savor canine casserole and mutt meatballs from the 'Bone Appetit' menu. After a full day, cozy up in one of the private, two-story cabins appointed with everything you and your pooch need to enjoy a comfortable night. Dogs of any size are welcome for an additional fee of $30 per pet, per night.

Savage River Lodge
1600 Mount Aetna Road
Frostburg, MD 21532
(301) 689-3200
www.savageriverlodge.com
Rates from $190/night

Savage River Lodge

Spend some quality time with your furry friend on an outdoor adventure at **Savage River Lodge** in Frostburg. Located within the 700-acre **Savage River State Forest**, the lodge provides a peaceful oasis from the distractions of daily life. In the spring, try your hand at fly fishing for trout in the cold mountain streams. Summer is the perfect time to take man's best friend for a hike along the 13 miles of maintained trails looping through the property and surrounding state forest. Relax amid the changing scenery during the brilliant fall foliage season. Enjoy a winter escape on the cross-country ski trails, or take a snowshoe expedition with Fido by your side. If you are visiting in the spring, summer or fall, don't miss the weekly 'Yappy Hour' held each Saturday afternoon in the meadow. Dogs are welcome anywhere on the property except inside the lodge and on the porches.

Savage River Lodge
1600 Mount Aetna Road
Frostburg, MD 21532
(301) 689-3200
www.savageriverlodge.com

Appalachian Trail

Take a fantastic day hike with your pup along a 10-mile stretch of the Appalachian Trail from Crampton's Gap in Maryland to Harpers Ferry in West Virginia. Start your adventure by staying overnight at **The Treehouse Camp**, located just a quarter of a mile from the trailhead in **Gathland State Park**. Spend some time learning about the Civil War Battle of South Mountain and admire the War Correspondent's Arch before heading south toward Harpers Ferry. The mild elevation change along this portion of the Appalachian Trail makes the trek appropriate for both skilled and novice hikers. Stop for a picnic lunch before crossing the banks of the Potomac River into West Virginia. Don't worry about the hike back once you've reached Harpers Ferry. **River & Trail Outfitters** will shuttle you to your accommodations for a small charge. Dogs must remain leashed on the trail and during the shuttle ride.

Gathland State Park
900 Arnoldstown Road
Jefferson, MD 21718
(301) 791-4767
www.bringfido.com/attraction/11151

Where to Stay:

Located just a stone's throw from the Appalachian Trail, **The Treehouse Camp** in Rohrersville features 18 elevated tree cottages and tree houses that welcome Fido. Cottages are insulated for year-round use and come furnished with tables, mattresses, and wood stoves. Tree houses are rustic, screened-in structures without stoves or mattresses. Campground amenities include fire pits, charcoal grills, picnic areas, and private bathrooms. Remember to bring your own bedding and a lantern. Dogs are welcome for no additional fee.

The Treehouse Camp
20716 Townsend Road
Rohrersville, MD 21779
(301) 432-5585
www.thetreehousecamp.com
Rates from $43/night

The Freedom Trail

Fido can walk in the footsteps of America's founding fathers by following the **Freedom Trail** through downtown Boston. All you need to enjoy this free attraction is your dog's leash and a good pair of walking shoes. The 2.5-mile red brick trail will lead you right to 16 of Boston's most historic sites, so you don't even need a map! Starting at the **Boston Common**, America's oldest public park, you'll pass by Faneuil Hall, Paul Revere's House, and the site of the Boston Massacre before ending at the USS Constitution in Charlestown. Once there, you can hitch a ride back to Faneuil Hall on the **City Water Taxi** for a $1 fare. Or, better yet, ask them to drop you off at **Joe's American Bar & Grill** for a lobster roll! Both the City Water Taxi and Boston's subway system, **The T**, allow dogs for no additional fee.

The Freedom Trail
139 Tremont Street
Boston, MA 02111
(617) 357-8300
www.thefreedomtrail.org

Where to Stay:

After conquering the Freedom Trail, Fido can rest his weary paws at **XV Beacon Hotel**. Centrally located in Beacon Hill, less than two blocks from the Boston Common, the property offers a boutique hotel feel with full-service amenities. After a restful night's sleep, bring your pooch to the nearby **Public Garden** to enjoy a 'morning constitutional' through America's first public botanical garden. The hotel welcomes dogs of any size for no additional fee. Treats are provided at check-in, and dog-walking services are available.

XV Beacon Hotel
15 Beacon Street
Boston, MA 02108
(617) 670-1500
www.xvbeacon.com
Rates from $385/night

Where to Stay:

Indulge in a relaxing Berkshires retreat at the charming **Birchwood Inn**, where guest rooms are named after former owners of the nearly 250-year old mansion. Each morning, wake up to a scrumptious breakfast, including homemade breads, muffins, and soufflés. Afternoon tea on the porch is a treat not to be missed. Fido will be welcomed with homemade biscuits, a comfy dog bed, towels, and a water bowl. Up to two dogs are permitted for a fee of $25 per pet, per night.

Birchwood Inn
7 Hubbard Street
Lenox, MA 01240
(413) 637-2600
www.birchwood-inn.com
Rates from $200/night

Birchwood Inn

Foodies will feel right at home at the cozy **Birchwood Inn** in Lenox. The elegant property offers a variety of themed packages to food lovers seeking out unique experiences during their Berkshires getaway. Your four-legged companion will thank you for choosing the 'Dog Day Afternoon' experience, where you will learn how to bake made-from-scratch, nutritious dog cookies for your furry friend. While you are whipping up the homemade treats in the Birchwood Inn kitchen, your pooch will be introduced to Quinn, the resident golden retriever, who is sure to teach him the proper way to sample the gourmet delicacies. After your biscuit-making class, let Fido work off some of the calories by taking him on a walk on one of several nearby hiking trails. The Dog Day Afternoon package is available by pre-arrangement from November through April. The fee is $50 for one person or $75 for a pair.

Birchwood Inn
7 Hubbard Street
Lenox, MA 01240
(413) 637-2600
www.birchwood-inn.com/foodies

deCordova Sculpture Park

Bring Fido along as you observe contemporary art at the **deCordova Sculpture Park** in Lincoln. This 30-acre park is the largest of its kind in New England and is home to over 60 large-scale, modern and contemporary sculptures. Most of the exhibits are on loan to the museum and are constantly changing, making each visit to the park unique. Your pup is welcome to wander the trails with you as you marvel at the beautiful lawns, gardens, fields, and forests. Take a guided tour of the park, or set your own pace and pause for a picnic on the grounds. Dogs must remain leashed at all times while in the park, which is open daily from 10:00 am to 5:00 pm. Admission is $14 for adults, except on the first Wednesday of each month when everyone is admitted for free. Children under 12 and pets always enjoy complimentary admission.

deCordova Sculpture Park
51 Sandy Pond Road
Lincoln, MA 01773
(781) 259-8355
www.decordova.org

Where to Stay:

Following your art walk, spend some time admiring the hip, modern décor of your accommodations at the **Aloft Lexington**. Grab drinks at the Re:Mix Lounge, splash around in the indoor saltwater pool, and listen to live music at the XYZ Bar. Aloft pays special attention to its canine clientele with its 'ARF Program' and provides dog beds, bowls, toys, and woof-alicious treats upon arrival. Dogs up to 40 lbs (larger with management approval) are welcome for no additional fee.

Aloft Lexington
727 Marrett Road
Lexington, MA 02421
(781) 761-1700
www.aloftlexington.com
Rates from $99/night

The Cottages
& Lofts
RECEPTION

Nantucket Island

Bring Fido by air or sea to beautiful Nantucket Island. Start your adventure with a flight from Hyannis on **Nantucket Airways**. One dog of any size can sit in the aisle beside you for a modest $10 fee. If your pup would rather float than fly, dogs ride free on the **Steamship Authority**'s high-speed ferry. Once your feet are on the ground, catch '**The Wave**' (the island's pet-friendly public bus service). Take the Madaket Route to **Sanford Farm** for the stimulating six-mile Ocean Walk, or visit the island's unofficial dog park at **Tupancy Links**. Hop on the route to Surfside Beach and walk a mile east to **Nobadeer Beach**, where Fido can run off-leash year-round. Enjoy a tasty clam roll and lavender lemonade popsicle from the **Blue Bellies** food truck, which operates beachside from 11:00 am to 3:00 pm daily. Before your day is over, grab a cold beer at **Cisco Brewers**.

Nantucket Airlines
Barnstable Municipal Airport
660 Barnstable Road
Hyannis, MA 02601
(508) 228-6234
www.nantucketairlines.com

Where to Stay:

For a quintessential Nantucket experience, spend the night in a 'Woof Cottage' at **The Cottages & Lofts at the Boat Basin**—a waterfront property located right on the dock at Straight Wharf. Fido will find a comfy pet bed, food and water bowls, and a basket of beach toys in your cottage. Doggie turndown service is provided nightly. Dogs of any size are welcome for an additional fee of $60 per stay ($75 for stays of four nights or more).

The Cottages & Lofts at the Boat Basin
24 Old South Wharf
Nantucket, MA 02554
(508) 325-1499
www.thecottagesnantucket.com
Rates from $175/night

Where to Stay:

Located just one block from Provincetown Harbor, the **Provincetown Hotel at Gabriel's** is made up of four historic buildings that surround a lovely courtyard (which serves as the gathering spot for a made-to-order breakfast each morning). With beautiful gardens, decks, private sitting areas, and a fire pit, it's easy to forget you are just steps away from bustling Commercial Street. Dogs of any size are welcome for an additional fee of $25 per night, per pet.

Provincetown Hotel at Gabriel's
102 Bradford Street
Provincetown, MA 02657
(508) 487-3232
www.provincetownhotel.com
Rates from $125/night

Dog Gone Sailing Charters

Strap a doggie life vest on your pup and go sailing with **Dog Gone Sailing Charters** in Provincetown. After climbing aboard The Moondance II with Captain Ro and her trusty sea dog Mini Mate, you'll sail to Long Point—the site of the original Provincetown settlement. Choose a two-hour sunrise or sunset tour, or relax on a half-day or full-day sailing adventure. Rates start at $35 for shrimp sails to Toro. Sunrise and sunset cruises are $40 per person. Half-day charters begin at $325 and can accommodate six passengers. If your salty dog is up for more water fun, take a whale watching cruise with **Dolphin Fleet of Provincetown**. An interpretive guide accompanies each three to four-hour cruise to narrate the natural history of Cape Cod and to help identify marine life spotted on the trip. Prices are $44 for adults and $29 for children. Dogs float for free.

Dog Gone Sailing Charters
8 Macmillan Wharf
Provincetown, MA 02657
(508) 566-0410
www.doggonesailingcharters.com

Argo Canoe Livery

Float down the Huron River with Fido in beautiful Ann Arbor. Start your day at the **Argo Canoe Livery**, where you can rent a canoe or kayak for your leisurely trip down the water. Bring your pup on a river trip to Gallup Park or enjoy a four-hour paddle from Delhi to Argo Park. Although you're in the heart of the city, you'll enjoy a peaceful day on the river as you spot turtles, cranes, ducks, and swans. Hours vary per itinerary, and rates start at $18 for a one-person kayak (including van transportation and life jackets). After your river adventure, head to the **Nichols Arboretum** at the University of Michigan. Open daily from sunrise to sunset, the arboretum offers complimentary admission, and visitors are free to bring their dogs. Stroll along the trails and paths, exploring the Main Valley, Magnolia Glen, Gateway Garden, and art exhibits.

Argo Canoe Livery
1055 Longshore Drive
Ann Arbor, MI 48105
(734) 794-6241
www.a2gov.org/canoe

Where to Stay:

After your day of fun at the Argo Canoe Livery and Nichols Arboretum, call it a night at the **TownePlace Suites Ann Arbor**. This centrally located property features comfortable bedding, separate living areas, and fully-equipped kitchens in each guest suite. Other amenities include an indoor pool and hot tub, fitness center, complimentary breakfast, free Wi-Fi, business center, and an outdoor picnic area with gas grills. Dogs of any size are welcome for an additional fee of $100 per stay.

TownePlace Suites Ann Arbor
1301 Briarwood Circle Drive
Ann Arbor, MI 48108
(734) 327-5900
www.tinyurl.com/ruff15
Rates from $119/night

Where to Stay:

Nicknamed 'Michigan's Little Bavaria' for its German heritage and architectural style, the town of Frankenmuth is home to many Bavarian-themed shops and attractions. Extend your visit with Fido by staying at the **Drury Inn & Suites Frankenmuth**. Located on Main Street, within easy walking distance of the downtown shops and restaurants, the hotel offers comfortable rooms, an indoor pool, and a free hot breakfast buffet and nightly happy hour. Up to two dogs are welcome for no additional fee.

Drury Inn & Suites Frankenmuth
260 S Main Street
Frankenmuth, MI 48734
(989) 652-2800
www.tinyurl.com/ruff16
Rates from $110/night

Bavarian Belle Riverboat

Docking near River Place Shopping Center, the **Bavarian Belle Riverboat** is a popular attraction for visitors to Frankenmuth. Board the Belle with your pup to enjoy the views of town from the Cass River and learn more about the history of the region. The authentic, stern-driven paddlewheel riverboat has an open-air canopied upper deck and a fully-enclosed lower deck. Well-behaved, leashed pets are always welcome aboard for free. The company also sponsors a 'Canine Cruise' during the Dog Bowl Festival, held annually the last weekend in May. The Bavarian Belle sails from early May to mid-October, seven days a week. Tour departure times vary. Tickets are $10 for adults and $4 for children 10 and under. After enjoying the river, head to nearby **Grandpa Tiny's Farm** to show Fido what a working farm looks like. The farm is open from 10:00 am to 5:00 pm, April to October.

Bavarian Belle Riverboat
925 S Main Street
Frankenmuth, MI 48734
(866) 808-2628
www.bavarianbelle.com

Gilmore Car Museum

If you love cars almost as much as you love your dogs, bring them along for a day at the **Gilmore Car Museum**. Over 300 cars and motorcycles are featured at the museum, including an 1899 Locomobile, a 1929 Duesenberg, and a Chrysler Turbine. As you stroll around the historic campus with your pup, you'll pass by the carriage house, Disney movie set, depot, train tower, and a 1930s gas station. Other on-site attractions include the Midwest Miniatures Museum and the Pierce-Arrow Museum. Time your visit right and you'll be able to enjoy one of the many events held on the property. Leashed dogs are welcome throughout the grounds. Small dogs are allowed in the buildings if they can be carried or confined to a stroller. Gilmore Car Museum is open daily from 9:00 am to 5:00 pm, April through November. Admission is $12 for adults, $9 for children, and free for dogs.

Gilmore Car Museum
6865 W Hickory Road
Hickory Corners, MI 49060
(269) 671-5089
www.gilmorecarmuseum.org

Where to Stay:

After touring the Gilmore Car Museum, take a 30-minute drive to **Kara's Kottages** in downtown Kalamazoo. Each of the three units in this urban bed and breakfast has a cozy living room, private bathroom, one or two separate bedrooms, and a well-stocked kitchen (so you can make breakfast in the morning). There's also a shared yard with a fenced patio, gas grill, and fire pit. Up to two dogs under 50 lbs are welcome for an additional fee of $15 per night.

Kara's Kottages
837 W Main Street
Kalamazoo, MI 49006
(269) 491-0765
www.karaskottages.com
Rates from $150/night

Where to Stay:

Enjoy four seasons of fun at the **Beachfront Hotel** on Houghton Lake. Gaze at serene lake views from your balcony or patio, take a dip in the indoor pool, or relax in the hot tub. If you are visiting in summer, enjoy the sandy beach, convenient boat dock, and outdoor grilling area. Up to two dogs under 25 lbs are welcome for an additional fee of $25 per pet, per night. Larger pets may be allowed with prior management approval.

Beachfront Hotel
4990 W Houghton Lake Drive
Houghton Lake, MI 48629
(855) 235-9709
www.beachfronthl.com
Rates from $75/night

Houghton Lake Ice Fishing

If you'd like to give ice fishing a try, bring Fido to the **Beachfront Hotel** in Houghton Lake. The hotel is located on Michigan's largest inland lake and offers an ice fishing package from January through March. Your party will be picked up early in the morning and transported to a private shanty on the ice, complete with pre-drilled fishing holes and a propane heater to keep you and your pooch warm. Get ready to catch the 'big one' as you fish for walleye, pike, bass, and bluegill. The fishing excursion costs $199 for up to four people. The rate includes a one-night stay in a Lakeview Room with continental breakfast and a shanty rental from 7:00 am to 7:00 pm. For more wintertime fun, take a 20-minute drive to **South Higgins Lake State Park** in Roscommon, where your leashed pup can enjoy 11 miles of cross-country ski trails.

Beachfront Hotel
4990 W Houghton Lake Drive
Houghton Lake, MI 48629
(855) 235-9709
www.beachfronthl.com

Mackinac Island

Mackinac Island is filled with fun activities you can enjoy with your pup, and nearly all of the historic sites and buildings allow leashed pets. Your adventure begins with a 15-minute ride to the island aboard **Shepler's Ferry**. Round-trip fares start at $25 for adults, and dogs ride for free. Motorized vehicles are not allowed on Mackinac Island, so upon arrival, you'll have to get around on two (or four) legs. With a circumference of only eight miles, it is possible to walk around the entire island. However, if you'd prefer not to 'hoof it,' you can pay a horse to do it for you! **Mackinac Island Carriage Tours** offers fully narrated two-hour tours of the island with stops at Arch Rock, **Fort Mackinac**, and several other points of interest. Tickets are $25 for adults and $10 for children. Lap dogs are free, and larger dogs ride for the price of a child's ticket.

Mackinac Island Carriage Tours
7278 Main Street
Mackinac Island, MI 49757
(906) 847-3325
www.mict.com

Where to Stay:

After a day of exploring Mackinac Island, you and your dog can stay overnight at **Mission Point Resort**. Situated on 15 acres, the resort offers a plethora of amenities including a swimming pool, putting course, bocce ball lawn, arcade, and movie theater. You can even rent a bicycle and Burley trailer from the Activities Center to ride around the island with your pooch in tow! Dogs of any size are welcome for an additional fee of $50 per stay.

Mission Point Resort
6633 Main Street
Mackinac Island, MI 49757
(906) 847-3312
www.missionpoint.com
Rates from $99/night

Where to Stay:

Hop off the trail in Montague for a stay at **The Weathervane Inn**, a waterfront property on beautiful White Lake. Guest rooms feature hot tubs, fireplaces, and private balconies overlooking the lake. Enjoy a complimentary breakfast before taking your pup for a walk on the adjacent Hart-Montague Trail. Kayak, stand-up paddleboard, and bike rentals are available on-site through **White Lake Excursions**. Up to two dogs under 60 lbs are welcome for an additional fee of $10 per pet, per night.

The Weathervane Inn
4527 Dowling Street
Montague, MI 49437
(231) 893-8931
www.theweathervaneinn.net
Rates from $79/night

Silver Lake Buggy Rentals

Take your pooch on a wild dune buggy ride with a rental from **Silver Lake Buggy Rentals** in Mears. Pick up a two-seat or four-seat cart for an off-road adventure between the shores of Lake Michigan and Silver Lake. Your dog is welcome to ride along as you speed across the sand. You'll need eye protection when navigating the dunes, so don't forget to pack Fido's goggles! Bring a change of clothes too—you'll probably get wet. The recreation area is open from April through October, and buggy rentals are available from May through September. Rental rates start at $163 for a 90-minute rental. After your ride is over, bring your pup on a walk or bike ride through the nearby **Hart-Montague Trail State Park**, a scenic 22-mile paved path that was formerly a railroad line. Stop to enjoy lunch on one of the picnic tables found along the trail.

Silver Lake Buggy Rentals
8288 W Hazel Road
Mears, MI 49436
(231) 873-8833
www.silverlakebuggys.com

Toonerville Trolley

Climb aboard the **Toonerville Trolley** in Soo Junction to set off on an adventure with Fido through the thick forests of Michigan's Upper Peninsula. Operating since 1927, the train gives you the chance to see deer, bears, moose, wolves, and birds from the comfort of your seat. Let Fido sit on your lap, and he'll help you spot them! At the end of the line, you'll get your first peek of the Tahquamenon River and board the *Hiawatha Riverboat* for a 21-mile cruise to its rapids. Well-behaved, leashed dogs can ride on the top deck of the boat. After reaching the rapids, disembark for a half-mile hike to Tahquamenon Falls with your pooch. Tours depart at 10:30 am on Mondays, Wednesdays, and Saturdays from mid-June through September. The journey takes approximately six hours to complete and costs $45 for adults. Dogs and children under four ride for free.

Toonerville Trolley
7195 Soo Junction Road
Soo Junction, MI 49000
(888) 778-7246
www.trainandboattours.com

Where to Stay:

Extend your outdoor adventure in Michigan's Upper Peninsula with an overnight stay at **Northland Outfitters** in Germfask. Located adjacent to the **Seney National Wildlife Refuge** (where leashed pets are welcome on all trails), their heated and furnished cabins are available from May through mid-October. Dogs of any size are welcome for an additional fee of $5 per night. You and your pooch can also sign up for Northland Outfitters' overnight canoe and fishing trips down the Fox and Manistique Rivers.

Northland Outfitters
8174 Highway M-77
Germfask, MI 49836
(906) 586-9801
www.northoutfitters.com
Rates from $50/night

Sky Dan Air Tours

Even the most well-traveled pups will find a unique experience awaiting them at **Sky Dan Air Tours** in Grand Marais. Dubbed 'Minnesota's Only Aerial Moose Adventure,' the scenic airplane tour company will take you and your pooch on a 60-minute moose scouting flight. Soar over Devil's Kettle, Eagle Mountain, Devil Track Canyon, and the Gunflint Trail as you observe wild moose grazing in the pastures below. Fly high above the Cascade Mountains for breathtaking views of Lake Superior and Superior National Forest as your pilot navigates the plane and points out native wildlife on the ground. Scenic flights start at $50 per person (two person minimum per flight). A moose flight for two adults and a dog costs $300. There is no specified weight limit, but size restrictions may apply to ensure aircraft safety. Tours depart from Cook County Airport, which is located eight miles south of downtown Grand Marais.

Sky Dan Air Tours
80 Skyport Lane
Grand Marais, MN 55604
(218) 370-0645
www.skydanairtours.com

Where to Stay:

Your pooch will love exploring Minnesota's Northwoods during your stay at **Gunflint Lodge** in Grand Marais. Cabins feature wood-burning fireplaces, plush bedding, and kitchenettes. Hiking, biking, fishing, and canoeing are just a few of the property's recreational offerings. Dogs of any size are welcome for an additional fee of $20 per pet, per night. Visit during one of the popular 'Dog Lover's Weekends' when pet fees are waived and the lodge offers classes and seminars geared toward man's best friend.

Gunflint Lodge
143 S Gunflint Lake Road
Grand Marais, MN 55604
(218) 388-2296
www.gunflint.com
Rates from $79/night

Where to Stay:

If you and your four-legged friend are feeling lucky, your best bet is to head to the **Hard Rock Hotel & Casino Biloxi** for the night. While you're in the casino, Fido can enjoy the gulf front view from your glamorous suite. Resort amenities include a full-service spa, fitness center, pool with swim-up bar, live entertainment, and multiple on-site dining options. Dogs up to 25 lbs are welcome for an additional fee of $75. Add $50 for a larger pet.

Hard Rock Hotel & Casino Biloxi
777 Beach Boulevard
Biloxi, MS 39530
(228) 374-7625
www.hardrockbiloxi.com
Rates from $129/night

Biloxi Shrimping Trip

Bring your canine companion to the Mississippi Gulf Coast for an educational outing with **Biloxi Shrimping Trip**. Climb aboard the *Sailfish* for a 70-minute journey into the unexpectedly fascinating world of shrimping. The crew will tell you everything you ever wanted to know about shrimp, from the life cycle of the crustaceans to the best ways to catch, cook, and eat them. Watch the crew demonstrate the proper techniques for catching the tasty shellfish as they drop the net and drag the bottom of the Mississippi Sound. After learning some history of the industry, the day's catch will be hauled in, and the captain will help you identify the various sea creatures that found their way into the net. Rates start at $15 for adults and $10 for children. Dogs float for free. After your tour, stop by **Shaggy's Beach Bar & Grill** to enjoy some tasty barbeque shrimp at a beachfront table.

Biloxi Shrimping Trip
693 Beach Boulevard
Biloxi, MS 39530
(228) 392-8645
www.biloxishrimpingtrip.com

AKC Museum of the Dog

Celebrate all things canine with a trip to the AKC Museum of the Dog in Ballwin. You and Fido will find more than 700 original works of art celebrating man's best friend. After your pup is greeted with treats and water, browse the 14,000 square foot museum and enjoy drawings, watercolors, prints, bronzes, porcelain figurines, and sculptures. The museum is open daily (except Mondays), and admission is $5 for adults and free for your furry friend. After your visit, head to Purina Farms in nearby Gray Summit to see Purina's Pro Plan Performance Team in action. Several shows take place daily, and well-behaved dogs are always welcome to watch the competitors perform feats of skill and agility. There is no admission fee. At the end of the day, enjoy dinner at The Boathouse in Forest Park, where Fido is welcome to join you on the outdoor patio and for an after-dinner paddleboat ride.

AKC Museum of the Dog
1721 S Mason Road
Ballwin, MO 63011
(314) 821-3647
www.museumofthedog.org

Where to Stay:

Bring Fido on a trip to England without leaving St. Louis by staying at The Cheshire. Each room in this European-style boutique hotel is named after a popular English author. The property features a number of themed suites, a courtyard pool, and the popular Fox & Hounds Tavern. Your pup gets the royal treatment, which includes dog biscuits, food bowls, bed, and a Purina coupon. Dogs up to 70 lbs are welcome for an additional fee of $25 per pet, per stay.

The Cheshire
6300 Clayton Road
St. Louis, MO 63117
(314) 647-7300
www.cheshirestl.com
Rates from $126/night

Where to Stay:

Only two miles from the heart of Branson, a relaxing stay awaits you at **Lilley's Landing Resort & Marina** on Lake Taneycomo. Fish from the covered dock, lounge on the poolside sundeck, play a game of horseshoes, or gather with friends and family at the outdoor pavilion overlooking the lake. Fido is free to sniff the grounds as long as he remains leashed. Dogs of any size are welcome for an additional fee of $10 per pet, per night.

Lilley's Landing Resort & Marina
367 River Lane
Branson, MO 65616
(417) 334-6380
www.lilleyslanding.com
Rates from $64/night

National Tiger Sanctuary

Introduce Fido to the big cats at the **National Tiger Sanctuary** in Saddlebrooke. This 501c-3 non-profit facility is home to 18 exotic animals, including a black leopard, mountain lion, African lion, and many tigers. What sets the sanctuary apart is the stress-free environment in which the animals live, along with the love and care given to all the animals for their entire lives. The 75-minute 'Awareness Tour' includes a brief classroom presentation and the chance to see tigers from three feet away. The 'Feeding Tour' highlights the different personalities of each cat and lets tour-goers tag along for the feeding. Well-behaved, leashed pets are welcome on all tours. The National Tiger Sanctuary is only open to visitors during scheduled tours. The tours take place Wednesday through Sunday at 10:00 am, 1:00 pm, and 3:00 pm. Prices start at $20 for adults and $10 for kids. Dogs visit for free.

National Tiger Sanctuary
518 State Highway BB
Saddlebrooke, MO 65630
(417) 587-3633
www.nationaltigersanctuary.org

Fantastic Caverns

Discovered by a farmer's dog in 1862, **Fantastic Caverns** was first explored by a dozen local women who answered a Springfield newspaper ad seeking explorers. During Prohibition, the massive cave was used by bootleggers as a speakeasy and casino. And in the 1950's, it was transformed into an underground auditorium by country greats like Buck Owens. Today, your dog can 'mark his territory' on America's only Jeep-drawn cave tour. During the one-hour tour, you'll hear more fascinating tales about this Springfield landmark and see stunning stalactites and stalagmites at every turn. With a natural temperature of 60 degrees year-round, Fantastic Caverns is a perfect spot to visit with Spot in any season. The caverns are open daily from 8:00 am until dusk. Since no walking is required, the tour is appropriate for guests of all ages. Admission is $23 for adults and $15 for kids. Dogs and children under six are free.

Fantastic Caverns
4872 N Farm Road 125
Springfield, MO 65803
(417) 833-2010
www.fantasticcaverns.com

Where to Stay:

After a day of spelunking with your canine companion, spend a night at Springfield's **Drury Inn & Suites**. Nestled in the foothills of the Ozark Mountains, the property features oversized guestrooms, a fitness center, and an indoor/outdoor pool. The hotel also offers a slew of complimentary extras. High-speed internet, a daily hot breakfast, and a nightly cocktail hour with a rotating menu are all included in your room rate. Dogs of any size are also welcome for no additional fee.

Drury Inn & Suites Springfield
2715 N Glenstone Avenue
Springfield, MO 65803
(417) 863-8400
www.tinyurl.com/ruff17
Rates from $95/night

Where to Stay:

After your float down the Yellowstone River, spend a night of relaxation at **Chico Hot Springs Resort** in Pray. Although your pooch can't join you for a dip in the hotel's famous spring-fed pools, the grounds and garden offer plenty of outdoor space to explore. The property also features an on-site spa, lively saloon, and highly acclaimed dining room. Dogs of any size are welcome in standard rooms and cabins for an additional fee of $20 per pet, per stay.

Chico Hot Springs Resort
1 Old Chico Road
Pray, MT 59065
(406) 333-4933
www.chicohotsprings.com
Rates from $55/night

Paradise Adventure Company

Enjoy a delightful and relaxing float down the Yellowstone River with **Paradise Adventure Company** in Pray. Led by a certified river guide, the two-hour tours depart daily from **Chico Hot Springs Resort**. Your guide will narrate the tour as you leisurely meander down the river. No paddling is required, so the excursion is perfect for all ages and abilities. You likely won't even get wet, so feel free to bring your camera and take photos of the scenic views you'll encounter along the journey. You may also want to pack some binoculars for better wildlife viewing, as well as some beverages to enjoy on the river. Prices start at $41 for adults and $31 for kids. Dogs are welcome on float trips, but a private boat fee may be required if other guests object to dogs. The company also offers tours from its Gardiner location.

Paradise Adventure Company
1 Old Chico Road
Pray, MT 59065
(406) 333-7183
www.paradiserafting.com

Lava Creek Adventures

For a $25 entry fee, your dog can scratch Old Faithful off his bucket list in **Yellowstone National Park**. While dogs aren't allowed on any hiking trails beyond the geyser, they can accompany you on a 'photo safari' with **Lava Creek Adventures**. For $299, their knowledgeable guide will take you to all of the best spots to see moose, elk, bears, and buffalo from the comfort of your car window. The company also rents stand-up paddleboards and kayaks to guests of **Yellowstone Under Canvas**, a luxury campground just six miles from the national park. You can put in right beside your tipi or safari tent and paddle downstream on the Madison River. Once you reach Heben Lake, the company will shuttle you back to Yellowstone Under Canvas in time for the evening marshmallow roast. Rates start at $39 for four-hour kayak rentals and $35 for a one-way shuttle.

Lava Creek Adventures
433 Targhee Pass Highway
West Yellowstone, MT 59758
(406) 646-5145
www.lavacreekadventures.com

Where to Stay:

Located on a beautiful ranch just outside the national park, **Yellowstone Under Canvas** brings a new meaning to the phrase 'ruffing it.' Budget-minded travelers can choose a canvas tipi tent, which sleeps up to four and comes furnished with cots, sleeping bags, pillows, and towels. For a true 'glamping' experience, upgrade to a deluxe safari tent with a king-size bed, wood-burning stove, and private tipi bathroom (with hot running water). Dogs are welcome for an additional fee of $25 per pet, per stay.

Yellowstone Under Canvas
3111 Targhee Highway
West Yellowstone, MT 59758
(406) 219-0441
www.mtundercanvas.com
Rates from $95/night

Where to Stay:

Following your airboat adventure, drive into Omaha for a stay at the **Element by Westin** in Midtown Crossing. This LEED-certified hotel boasts apartment-style rooms, complete with fully furnished kitchens. The area around the hotel offers ample green space, shops, and outdoor dining establishments, but Fido will likely lead you right to **Three Dog Bakery** on Davenport Street. The hotel welcomes dogs up to 40 lbs for no additional fee. Larger dogs may be permitted with prior management approval.

Element by Westin
3253 Dodge Street
Omaha, NE 68131
(402) 614-8080
www.tinyurl.com/ruff18
Rates from $149/night

Bryson's Airboat Tours

If Fido loves riding in your car with his head out the window, he is sure to enjoy an adventure with **Bryson's Airboat Tours** in Fremont, about 40 minutes outside of Omaha. Bryson's 21-foot Panther airboat comfortably seats 11 passengers and, thanks to its theater-style seating, provides a great view of the water to everyone. During your journey on the Platte River, you and your pup might encounter several species of wildlife, including bald eagles, deer, turkeys, river otters and beavers. This 700-horsepower boat can reach speeds of 60 mph, so it's a good idea to bring eyewear and a jacket. Ear protection is provided by Bryson's. Prices start at $150 for two passengers; children under 13 can ride for an additional fee of $20 per child. Dogs are welcome for no additional fee. Tours take place from mid-April to mid-October and can be scheduled from 10:00 am to dusk.

Bryson's Airboat Tours
839 County Road 19
Fremont, NE 68025
(402) 968-8534
www.brysonsairboattours.com

Little Outlaw Canoe

If you and your pup love being out on the water and are ready to try something new, it's time to schedule a 'Tanking Trip' with **Little Outlaw Canoe** in Valentine. One of the most unusual ways to spend a day on the water, tanking gives you the opportunity to enjoy a leisurely river float with a group of friends. Climb into a big plastic tank equipped with seating and a picnic table in the center and get ready to relax. Bring your lunch and plenty of drinks to sip as you travel down the scenic Niobrara River from Berry Bridge to Brewer Bridge, passing Smith Falls along the way. The total float time is approximately four hours, and the trip costs $35 per adult. There is a four person minimum and a six person maximum for tank rentals. Dogs can join the humans for no additional fee.

Little Outlaw Canoe
1005 E Highway 20
Valentine, NE 69201
(402) 376-1822
www.outlawcanoe.com

Where to Stay:

You and your furry friend won't have to go far to find a place to stay in Valentine after your scenic float down the Niobrara River. **Trade Winds Motel**, located right next door to Little Outlaw Canoe, features clean and spacious guest rooms with microwaves, refrigerators, and complimentary wireless internet. A free hot country breakfast is served up daily, along with a side of southern hospitality. Dogs are welcome for an additional fee of $10 per pet, per night.

Trade Winds Motel
1009 E Highway 20
Valentine, NE 69201
(402) 376-1600
www.tradewindslodge.com
Rates from $59/night

Where to Stay:

Moroccan-inspired décor and stunning views of the lake will greet you upon arrival at the **Westin Lake Las Vegas Resort**. Your pooch can relax on the 'Heavenly Dog Bed' in your guest room, stroll through the resort's botanical cactus garden, or enjoy a canine massage at Spa Moulay. During the 50-minute treatment, you'll learn a few techniques that'll make Fido want to roll over at home too! One dog of any size is welcome for an additional fee of $35 per stay.

Westin Lake Las Vegas Resort
101 Montelago Boulevard
Henderson, NV 89011
(702) 567-6000
www.westinlakelasvegas.com
Rates from $119/night

Gondola Adventures

Located just 25 miles from the Las Vegas Strip, the resort community of Lake Las Vegas in Henderson is a true oasis in the desert. In fact, when you first spot the sun-drenched Mediterranean village on a stunning 320-acre lake, you may have to pinch yourself to make sure you're still in Nevada. For a front-row view of the water, share a filet mignon with Fido at **Bernard's Bistro by the Lake**. Afterwards, you can book a 60-minute 'Champagne Cruise' with **Gondola Adventures** for a truly memorable aperitif. You and a guest will enjoy gourmet chocolates and a bottle of champagne, complete with a singing gondolier for $135. Dogs ride for free, and additional humans are $25 each. If you've always wanted to take the plunge into the world of 'SUPing,' swing by **Paddle to the Core** during the week. The company offers $30 'Dog Paddle' lessons every Wednesday throughout the summer.

Gondola Adventures
41 Costa Di Lago
Henderson, NV 89011
(949) 646-2067
www.gondola.com

Mount Charleston

If you're looking to escape the desert heat, head to **Mount Charleston** for some cool outdoor adventures with your pooch. Located less than an hour's drive from downtown Las Vegas, Mount Charleston offers the chance to explore over 50 miles of hiking trails in a climate with temperatures averaging 20 degrees lower than Sin City. That means from November through April, there is snow on the mountain! The Bristlecone Trail is particularly great for snowshoeing, but the most popular wintertime activities are sledding, snowman building, and good old-fashioned snowball fights. In fact, 'snow play' is so popular here, that there's even a designated location for it at the **Foxtail Picnic Area** in Lee Canyon. For $12 per vehicle, you'll have access to plenty of parking, a heated restroom, and lots of open space to play in the snow with Fido. The gates are open from 10:00 am to 4:00 pm, seven days a week.

Mount Charleston
Foxtail Picnic Area
Lee Canyon Rd & Forest Road 106
Las Vegas, NV 89124
(702) 872-5486
www.gomtcharleston.com

Where to Stay:

After a long day of hiking, your pooch will be happy to come home to a cozy cabin at the **Mount Charleston Lodge**. Relax in a jetted tub, warm up by the fire, or unwind on a private balcony overlooking the mountain. The Lodge serves breakfast, lunch, and dinner. Picnic baskets are available for day hikes around Mount Charleston too. One dog of any size is welcome for an additional fee of $30 per night. Add $20 per night for a second dog.

Mount Charleston Lodge
5375 Kyle Canyon Road
Las Vegas, NV 89124
(702) 872-5408
www.mtcharlestonlodge.com
Rates from $145/night

Wedding Bells Chapel

Ring bearer, flower dog, or best pooch? Say 'I do' as Fido stands witness at the **Wedding Bells Chapel** in Las Vegas. Located within the **Alexis Park Resort**, the chapel offers standard ceremonies, vow renewals, and even dog weddings. Packages for canine nuptials and human vow exchanges start at $167. After the ceremony, load the 'wedding pawty' into a stretch limo to cruise Sin City in style on a Las Vegas Strip Tour with **Omni Limousine**. Fido can sniff out all the excitement of Las Vegas as you ride down the strip in a limo driven by a friendly chauffeur. Make a stop at the famous 'Welcome to Las Vegas' sign for a not-to-be-missed photo opportunity with your pup or head out to **Red Rock Canyon** and let your canine companion stretch his legs on the trails. Dogs of any size are welcome. Rates start at $55 per hour for up to six passengers.

Wedding Bells Chapel
375 E Harmon Avenue
Las Vegas, NV 89169
(702) 731-2355
www.weddingbellschapel.com

Where to Stay:

You and Fido will feel like Roman emperors upon entering the opulent **Caesars Palace**. Prepare to experience first-class rooms and suites in this venerable Las Vegas property. Visiting pups receive treats at check-in and can dine from a special pet room service menu. Up to two dogs under 50 lbs are welcome to stay in select 'PetStay' rooms. For those traveling with larger dogs, the **Alexis Park Resort** offers all-suite accommodations that welcome dogs for an additional fee of $50 per stay.

Caesars Palace
3570 S Las Vegas Boulevard
Las Vegas, NV 89109
(702) 731-7110
www.caesarspalace.com
Rates from $109/night

Where to Stay:

If you and your four-legged out-law didn't strike gold on your first day in Virginia City, try again after a good night's sleep at the **Silver Queen Hotel**. Built in 1876, the hotel offers 28 guest rooms, each with a private bath. For those interested in ghosts of Virginia City past, be sure to meet up for the weekend ghost tours that depart from the hotel's western saloon. Dogs of any size stay at the property for no additional fee.

Silver Queen Hotel
28 North C Street
Virginia City, NV 89440
(775) 847-0440
www.silverqueenhotel.net
Rates from $45/night

TNT Stagelines

Take a step back in time with your pup during a visit to the historic mining town of Virginia City. Old West saloons, historic churches, and restored public buildings from the mid-1800s greet visitors captivated by the town's rich history. For a truly authentic Old West experience, look no further than **TNT Stagelines** for the opportunity to ride in a 19th-century stagecoach. Powered by a team of four horses, you'll race through town at speeds reaching up to 25 miles per hour. Tickets for the 10-minute ride are $12 per person, and dogs are welcome for no additional fee. After your stagecoach ride, head over to bustling C Street to pan for gold or take a 35-minute ride on the **Virginia & Truckee Railroad**. Dogs are welcome in both the open-air and enclosed railcars. Just keep your pup on a leash while you enjoy your Virginia City experience.

TNT Stagelines
F Street
Virginia City, NV 89440
(775) 721-1496
www.tntstagelines.com

Mt. Washington Auto Road

If you and your pooch are experienced hikers looking for a challenge, hike up New England's tallest peak, Mount Washington, and then take the pet-friendly shuttle back down. If your pup isn't up for the difficult ascent, you can still enjoy stunning views by driving the eight-mile **Mt. Washington Auto Road** to the top of the mountain. Your $26 toll includes a bumper sticker and audio guide detailing the famous road's history, legends, and geography. You can also enjoy breathtaking views of New Hampshire's White Mountains as you drive the famous **Kancamagus Highway** through the **White Mountain National Forest**. The Kanc, as it's known by the locals, is most popular during the fall foliage season, but this scenic byway is frequented year-round for its beautiful natural setting. Leash Fido up and spend some time outside the car, hiking on one of the many trails found along the highway.

Mt. Washington Auto Road
1 Mount Washington Auto Road
Gorham, NH 03581
(603) 466-3988
www.mtwashingtonautoroad.com

Where to Stay:

After a day of hiking in the White Mountains, treat Fido to a much-needed break at the aptly named **Lazy Dog Inn**. Located in Chocorua, the property offers plenty of pet-friendly amenities that make it popular with dog lovers near and far. Your pup can burn some energy in the fenced play area or chill out in the doggie lodge, which also features a dog wash station. Dogs of any size are welcome in all guest rooms for no additional fee.

Lazy Dog Inn
201 White Mountain Highway
Chocorua, NH 03817
(603) 323-8350
www.lazydoginn.com
Rates from $120/night

Where to Stay:

If you didn't get your fill of ski-joring at Muddy Paw Sled Dog Kennel, you can ski right out the back door of the **Bartlett Inn** on a connector trail to Bear Notch Ski Touring Center. After a full day of outdoor adventures, sleep in a cozy cottage with a fireplace and enjoy a hearty country breakfast the next morning. Up to two dogs of any size are welcome for an additional fee of $15 per pet, per stay.

Bartlett Inn
1477 Main Street
Bartlett, NH 03812
(603) 374-2353
www.bartlettinn.com
Rates from $99/night

Muddy Paw Sled Dog Kennel

Cross-country skiing with your dog (a.k.a. ski-joring), is a winter adventure not to be missed at **Muddy Paw Sled Dog Kennel** in Bartlett. The experienced staff at Muddy Paw will help you and your pup learn to work together as a team as you hit the snow. All you need to bring is a pair of cross-country skis and your pooch. Muddy Paw will outfit you with all of the other necessary equipment. Lessons vary in price, depending on the length of your sessions. After one or two lessons, you can practice your newly acquired skills at nearby **Bear Notch Ski Touring Center**. Enjoy skiing, skijor-ing, and snowshoeing through fields, forests, and mountains. Whether you're looking for a challenge or an easy day on the snow, you'll find a trail suited to you and your pup's abilities. Day passes are $17 for adults. Dogs and kids under 17 are free.

Muddy Paw Sled Dog Kennel
32 Valley Road
Jefferson, NH 03583
(603) 545-4533
www.dogslednh.com

Cape May Whale Watcher

Four-legged 'pawsengers' are invited to come aboard the 110-foot *Cape May Whale Watcher* for an unforgettable Jersey Shore experience. Departing from the Miss Chris Marina in Cape May, the company offers three tours daily from May through October. The morning and evening tours both circle the island in two hours, providing a unique view of Cape May's picturesque Victorian homes and lighthouse. The afternoon cruise is all about whales! On this three-hour 'Cetacean Spectacular' tour, Captain Jeff Stewart takes you deep into the Delaware Bay Estuary and guarantees you'll see whales, dolphins, or porpoises (or your next trip is free). Rates start at $30 for adults. Dogs and children under seven are free. After your cruise, Fido can walk off his sea legs with a stroll through the 150-acre vineyard at **Cape May Winery**. Admission is free, and you can sample six wines for $6 in the dog-friendly tasting room.

Cape May Whale Watcher
1218 Wilson Drive
Cape May, NJ 08204
(609) 884-5445
www.capemaywhalewatcher.com

Where to Stay:

Built in 1850, the **Highland House** is an ultra dog-friendly B&B in Cape May. The innkeepers are dog lovers, and all of the rooms are decorated with dog-themed knickknacks. The result is charmingly homey, so it may feel like you're sleeping over at grandma's house. Spend an afternoon lounging on the front porch, walk four blocks to the beach, or let Fido play with the other canine guests in the fenced yard. Dogs of any size are welcome for no additional fee.

Highland House
131 N Broadway
Cape May, NJ 08204
(609) 898-1198
www.tinyurl.com/ruff19
Rates from $140/night

Where to Stay:

After a fun-filled day of sightseeing, you might think you know everything about Albuquerque. But do you know where Conrad Hilton and Zsa Zsa Gabor spent their honeymoon? **Hotel Andaluz!** The property opened in 1939 and was the fourth hotel Hilton ever built. A recent redesign blends Moroccan and Southwest décor almost as well as the bartender mixes jalapeño margaritas at the dog-friendly rooftop bar. Up to three dogs of any size are welcome for a fee of $50 per pet, per night.

Hotel Andaluz
125 2nd Street NW
Albuquerque, NM 87102
(505) 242-9090
www.hotelandaluz.com
Rates from $149/night

ABQ Trolley Company

'The best first thing to do in Albuquerque' is the motto for the **ABQ Trolley Company**. Climb aboard the trolley with your pup for a comprehensive overview of the city's rich history and a unique perspective on all that Albuquerque has to offer. Operating daily tours of the Duke City from April 1 through October 31, owners Jesse Heron and Mike Silva personally guide visitors on each tour. If it's your first time in Albuquerque, choose the 'Best of ABQ' city tour. You and Fido will enjoy an 85-minute ride beginning in historic Old Town that highlights Route 66, Museum Row, and the Barelas Neighborhood, among other attractions. Tour prices start at $25 per person. Your canine companion must be leashed aboard the open-air trolley and is welcome for no additional fee. During the trip, your pooch might meet the ABQ Trolley mascot—a greyhound pit bull mix named Bill Murray.

ABQ Trolley Company
303 Romero Street NW
Albuquerque, NM 87104
(505) 240-8000
www.abqtrolley.com

Red River Offroad

How many people can say their dog has ridden a cat? Not many. But you can claim those bragging rights with a snowcat tour from **Red River Offroad** in the Taos Mountains! These incredibly resilient vehicles are able to climb the slipperiest of slopes, taking you into the snow-covered back country of Red River. On the two-hour tour, you'll see breathtakingly beautiful scenery and feel the adrenaline rush through your body as the cat climbs and crawls over varied mountain terrain. As an added bonus, the driver will cut a trail to the best sledding hill in Red River. Hop out for a while and enjoy some old-fashioned winter fun with the entire family! The snowcat seats up to six passengers, plus Fido. When the snow melts, their off-road Jeep tours are equally thrilling. Rates start at $49 for adults and $32 for kids. Dogs ride for no additional charge.

Red River Offroad
500A E Maine Street
Red River, NM 87558
(575) 754-6335
www.redriveroffroad.com

Where to Stay:

After your snowcat tour, warm up beside a cozy Kiva fireplace at **Casa Gallina** in Taos. Each of the property's five private casitas is decorated in authentic Southwestern style and equipped with a full kitchen (where you'll find a homemade snack and bottle of wine upon arrival). In the morning, step into the garden and collect some fresh eggs from the resident hens for breakfast. One 'chicken-friendly' dog of any size is welcome for an additional fee of $50 per stay.

Casa Gallina
613 Callejon
Taos, NM 87571
(575) 758-2306
www.casagallina.net
Rates from $185/night

Santa Fe Walkabouts

You and your canine companion can explore the mountains and canyons around Santa Fe on a guided tour with **Santa Fe Walkabouts**. With several half-day and full-day hiking tours to choose from, hikers of various skill levels are sure to find an excursion of interest. Take a four-mile hike though a magical grove of Aspen trees in the Sangre de Cristo Mountains. Or start at the rim of White Rock Canyon and descend 800 feet to the Rio Grande River. For the easiest hiking option, choose the sunset Pinz and Hike Tour, which will take you on an off-road adventure in a Pinzgauer all-terrain vehicle, followed by a short walk along easy hiking trails. Tour prices start at $80 per person. Lunch is available for an extra $10. Well-behaved dogs are welcome on all tours. The tour company mascot, Murjo, may even join you and your pup on the adventure.

Santa Fe Walkabouts
PO Box 1942
Santa Fe, NM 87504
(505) 216-9161
www.santafewalkabouts.com

Where to Stay:

For a relaxing retreat with Fido, visit the **Inn of the Five Graces** in Santa Fe. This distinguished property boasts amazing architectural details, including adobe exteriors and ornately decorated suites filled with intricate mosaics and tapestries from around the world. After breakfast in the private courtyard, browse the art galleries on Canyon Road or snap a photo of your pooch on the giant dog swing at **Railyard Park**. Dogs up to 50 lbs are welcome for a fee of $75 per pet, per night.

The Inn of the Five Graces
150 E De Vargas Street
Santa Fe, NM 87501
(505) 992-0957
www.fivegraces.com
Rates from $500/night

Where to Stay:

Located a block from the boutiques and galleries of East Hampton, the **Mill House Inn** is a lovely bed and breakfast with incredible service and creature comforts like down-stuffed dog beds, nightly turndown treats, and a fenced yard. The inn is known for serving the best breakfast in the Hamptons, and the chef will even prepare a fresh breakfast for Fido upon request. Dogs of any size are welcome in the cottages for a fee of $60 per pet, per night.

Mill House Inn
31 N Main Street
East Hampton, NY 11937
(631) 324-9766
www.millhouseinn.com
Rates from $225/night

The Hamptons

The Hamptons are known for being a summer playground of the rich and famous, but they are a great place to visit with Fido year-round. In the off-season, dogs are allowed off-leash on East Hampton's **Main Beach** at any time. During summer, they're only allowed on the beach before 9:00 am or after 6:00 pm, so it's better to head to **Cedar Point County Park** for an outdoor adventure with your pooch. The 5.6-mile hike to the lighthouse provides incredible views of Gardiner's Bay and a mile-long stretch of rocky shoreline where your pooch can swim in the ocean. Afterward, clean up at **The Classy Canine** in Southampton, where Fido can enjoy a bubble bath, hot towel wrap, and blueberry facial. Just be sure to make it back to East Hampton in time for Yappy Hour at **The Maidstone**, held nightly (except Saturday) from 5:00 pm to 6:30 pm.

East Hampton Main Beach
101 Ocean Avenue
East Hampton, NY 11937
(631) 324-0074
www.bringfido.com/attraction/11157

Gold Coast Mansions

Enjoy a day of history and adventure as you tour three of Long Island's Gold Coast Mansions. Bring Fido to Theodore Roosevelt's beloved **Sagamore Hill**, where animals of all sorts have been welcomed for more than a century. Although only humans are permitted to enter the historic Roosevelt home, you and your pup can explore the 83 acres of forests, meadows, and salt marshes on trails and boardwalks. Your canine companion can also explore the grounds of **Coindre Hall**, which was built for a pharmaceutical magnate in 1912. Spend time trekking the 33 acres of forested property and enjoying the beautiful views of Huntington Harbor. Finally, take advantage of the six trails in the **Sands Point Preserve at Falaise**. You can have a picnic on the manicured grounds before hiking through forests, meadows, gardens, and beach areas. Dogs must remain on a leash at all three of these historic properties.

Sagamore Hill
20 Sagamore Hill Road
Oyster Bay, NY 11771
(516) 922-4788
www.nps.gov/sahi

Where to Stay:

Guarded by magnificent formal gardens and infused with rich Long Island history, the French-style chateau known as **Oheka Castle** is an amazing estate hotel that conjures images from the classic novel *The Great Gatsby*. Dogs are not permitted on the historic mansion tours, but Fido can sleep like a king in the guest-rooms and suites of this storied mansion (and filming location for numerous movies and TV series). Dogs of any size are welcome for an additional fee of $200 per pet, per night.

Oheka Castle
135 W Gate Drive
Huntington, NY 11743
(631) 659-1400
www.oheka.com
Rates from $395/night

Where to Stay:

A true dog-friendly getaway awaits you and your pooch at **La Tourelle Resort & Spa** in Ithaca. The resort sits on 70 acres with two hiking trails for Fido to explore. Book a traditional room or splurge on the 'Where the Wild Things Stay' cottage. A short walk from the main resort, the cottage offers Fido a fenced yard with room to roam. Amenities include a dog washing station and fully stocked canine cabinet. And, best of all, dogs stay for free!

La Tourelle Resort & Spa
1150 Danby Road
Ithaca, NY 14850
(607) 273-2734
www.latourelle.com
Rates from $139/night

Robert H. Treman State Park

Enjoy the wild beauty of the Finger Lakes region of New York at the **Robert H. Treman State Park**. With over nine miles of pet-friendly hiking trails, your pup will have plenty of room to explore this state treasure just outside of Ithaca. The popular Enfield Glen Gorge Trail will bring you past 12 waterfalls, including the 115-foot Lucifer Falls, while providing stunning views of the wooded gorge. Continue your outdoor adventure by visiting nearby **Buttermilk Falls State Park**, which offers several more rim and gorge hiking trails. To extend the adventure, you and your pooch can camp overnight in either park. Dogs are welcome in tent sites and cabins, which are rustic with no bedding, cookware, or heat. Both parks are open year-round, but some trails may be inaccessible during the winter. Admission to each park is $7 per vehicle. Dogs must remain leashed at all times.

Robert H. Treman State Park
105 Enfield Falls Road
Ithaca, NY 14850
(607) 273-3440
www.nysparks.com/parks/135

Glen Highland Farm

Give your pup an unforgettable vacation during a 'Canine Country Getaway' at **Glen Highland Farm** in upstate New York. More than two dozen rescued border collies call Glen Highland Farm home, and by the end of his trip, your dog might wish he did too. Dogs are always welcome to play off-leash on the property's 175 acres of meadows, trails, ponds, creeks, and forests. Get your feet wet on one of the many dog beaches, or spend the day fishing with your four-legged friend at the two-acre pond stocked with trout and bass. After working with your pup on the agility course, fire up the grill and cook something tasty for dinner. Watch the sunset over the meadow at the end of an amazing day. Rates vary depending on the date of your stay, and the season runs from mid-June to mid-October. A week-long 'Canine Country Camp' is also held annually in September.

Glen Highland Farm
217 Pegg Road
Morris, NY 13808
(607) 263-5416
www.highlandvue.com

Where to Stay:

Glen Highland Farm offers a variety of lodging options during your canine-centric getaway. For those who prefer to 'ruff it,' there are three creekside tents furnished with a futon and two camping chairs. Well-equipped cottages and cabins with electricity are also available for those who love nature but prefer to sleep indoors. For the ultimate in privacy and comfort while at the farm, enjoy an air-conditioned RV, complete with separate living and sleeping areas, bathroom, kitchen, TV, and DVD player.

Glen Highland Farm
217 Pegg Road
Morris, NY 13808
(607) 263-5416
www.highlandvue.com
Rates from $100/night

Z-Travel and Leisure Tours

Whether you're visiting New York City for the first time or are a lifelong resident of the Big Apple, you can always learn more about the city that never sleeps on one of the many tours offered by **Z-Travel and Leisure**. Bring Fido along as historians, Art and Susan Zuckerman, guide you through Greenwich Village, Soho, Times Square, or another vibrant neighborhood. Or take a themed tour such as Women of New York, New York After Dark, or one of four ethnic food adventures. Each tour can be adapted for people traveling with dogs, but Fido will definitely enjoy the Central Park Dog Tour the most. He can drink from one of 15 dog fountains, wander through the 2.5-acre Strawberry Fields, and pose for a photo with the Balto statue. Afterwards, stop by the Shake Shack to get Fido a Pup Treat, Pooch-ini, or Bag-o-Bones. Tours are customized, so prices vary.

Z-Travel and Leisure Tours
81 Van Etten Boulevard
New Rochelle, NY 10804
(914) 633-6658
www.ztravelandleisure.com

Where to Stay:

The Surrey is located on New York's Upper East Side, just a stone's throw from Central Park and the **William Secord Gallery** (which specializes in fine 19th century dog paintings). After resting his weary paws on a monogrammed dog bed, your pooch can select a treat from the hotel's curated biscuit menu or visit **Sprinkles** for a doggie cupcake. The concierge can also arrange dog walking or grooming services. Pets of any size are welcome for an additional fee of $100 per stay.

The Surrey
20 E 76th Street
New York, NY 10021
(212) 288-3700
www.thesurrey.com
Rates from $575/night

Where to Stay:

Clean, comfortable accommodations await you and your pooch at the **Adirondack Motel** in the Village of Saranac Lake. Serene, lakefront views, on-site boat rentals, and close proximity to popular hiking trails and fishing holes make the Adirondack Motel a true hidden gem. Fido is free to swim in the lake or run off-leash on the property with the hotel's resident English springer spaniels, Jack and Daisy. Dogs are welcome for an additional fee of $15 per pet, per night.

Adirondack Motel
248 Lake Flower Avenue
Saranac Lake, NY 12983
(518) 891-2116
www.adirondackmotel.com
Rates from $79/night

St. Regis Canoe Outfitters

Reconnect with nature in the company of your canine explorer as you traverse the lakes of the beautiful Adirondacks with a kayak or canoe rental from **St. Regis Canoe Outfitters** in Saranac Lake. Enjoy a relaxing half-day of paddling, or make it a multi-day adventure combined with hiking. The staff at St. Regis Canoe Outfitters will help you select the appropriate canoe or kayak, as well as the best route for your journey. Set off on your own or book a guided trip. Popular tours include Chubb River, the Seven Carries, Lake Champlain and Valcour Island, and the Middle and Lower Saranac Lakes. Rentals start at $44 per day. Guided trips are available from $59 per person. Man's best friend is welcome on kayak and canoe rentals. Your pup is also free to join you on custom guided tours for no additional charge.

St. Regis Canoe Outfitters
73 Dorsey Street
Saranac Lake, NY 12983
(518) 891-1838
www.canoeoutfitters.com

Seneca Lake Wine Trail

When traveling through the Finger Lakes region of New York with your four-legged friend, be sure to sample some of the first-class vino being produced along the **Seneca Lake Wine Trail**. Many of the member wineries invite your pup to join you as you taste what makes them unique. Visit **Ravines Wine Cellars** for a dry Riesling, **Penguin Bay** for a spicy Gewurztraminer, and **Atwater Estate** for a bubbly Pinot Noir. Throughout the year, you can take in special events on the trail, like the Grapehound Wine Tour, held annually in July. Celebrating greyhounds and other sighthounds, the event is a popular pet-friendly festival filled with wine tastings, art events, vendors, and music. Some of the pet-friendly wineries on the trail welcome dogs off-leash, but others require Fido to be leashed when visiting (so it's best to ask). Most wineries are open for tours throughout the year, but hours vary by season.

Seneca Lake Wine Trail
2 N Franklin Street, Suite 320
Watkins Glen, NY 14891
(877) 536-2717
www.senecalakewine.com

Where to Stay:

After a long day of sightseeing and wine tasting, spend an evening at the **John Morris Manor** in Seneca Falls. Situated on a hilltop with five secluded acres and a swimming pool, this cozy inn is located on the **Cayuga Lake Wine Trail**, which boasts more than a dozen dog-friendly wineries. Up to two dogs of any size are welcome in two of the west wing bedrooms for an additional fee of $15 per night.

John Morris Manor
2138 State Route 89
Seneca Falls, NY 13148
(315) 568-9057
www.johnmorrismanor.com
Rates from $125/night

Where to Stay:

To call **Lake Placid Lodge** warm and inviting would be an understatement. Dogs are welcome in all but one of their spacious cabins at the water's edge. Each is adorned with hand-crafted furniture and stone fireplaces to go along with the unrivaled outdoor scenery. There is a fully stocked refrigerator in each cabin, and a prepared-to-order breakfast is served each morning. One dog of any size is welcome for a fee of $75 per night. Pet beds and treats are provided at check-in.

Lake Placid Lodge
144 Lodge Way
Lake Placid, NY 12946
(518) 523-2700
www.lakeplacidlodge.com
Rates from $450/night

Whiteface Mountain

Become a member of the exclusive Adirondack Forty-Sixers by climbing the 46 Adirondack High Peaks with Fido. Hike up **Whiteface Mountain** to cross the first mountain off your checklist. The main route, along the **Wilmington Trail**, is a 5.2-mile, one-way hike with an elevation gain of nearly 3,700 feet. Spend a day surrounded by the beauty of nature as you hike to the top of New York's fifth-highest peak. At the summit, you'll enjoy spectacular views of the Adirondacks and be on your way to becoming a Forty-Sixer. If you want to view gorgeous scenery without hiking, you can drive up Whiteface Mountain instead. To reach the top, you and Fido will need to climb the last 300 feet by stairs. An elevator is available, but it is not pet-friendly. Entrance to the **Whiteface Veteran's Memorial Highway** is $10 for the driver and $7 for each passenger.

Whiteface Mountain
SR 431 & Whiteface Memorial Highway
Wilmington, NY 12997
(518) 946-2223
www.bringfido.com/attraction/11159

Biltmore Estate

Your dog will love strolling through the hundreds of manicured acres on the **Biltmore Estate** in Asheville. Nestled in the Blue Ridge Mountains, this 8,000-acre property has plenty to offer you and your furry friend, including 22 miles of hiking trails and another 2.5 miles of paths through manicured gardens. Relax with a glass of wine at Biltmore Winery's Bistro or have a bite to eat at Cedric's Tavern (named for George Vanderbilt's Saint Bernard). Dogs must remain leashed at all times and are not allowed in any buildings. Admission fees start at $44 for adults, $22 for youth, and free for dogs and kids under 10. After your day at Biltmore, relax with a good book and a glass of bubbly at the **Battery Park Book Exchange** in downtown Asheville. Fido is welcome to join you inside as you browse thousands of new and used books and sip wine, coffee, or champagne.

Biltmore Estate
1 Lodge Street
Asheville, NC 28803
(828) 225-1333
www.biltmore.com

Where to Stay:

Only five minutes from downtown Asheville, the **Omni Grove Park Inn** has been providing Southern hospitality for over 100 years. And Fido will be happy to know that their legendary service extends to pet guests too! Dogs get a special treat during turndown service and can order items like 'Chicken Pup Pie' and 'Meat Woof' from the in-room dining menu. Up to two dogs under 60 lbs are welcome in the hotel's Vanderbilt wing for an additional fee of $130 per stay.

Omni Grove Park Inn
290 Macon Avenue
Asheville, NC 28804
(828) 252-2711
www.groveparkinn.com
Rates from $200/night

Bald Head Island

For a dog-friendly escape from the mainland, plan a visit to beautiful **Bald Head Island**. Explore 14 miles of beaches, hit the surf for some fun on the water, or take a hike on one of the lovely trails. Start your adventure by driving to the **Deep Point Marina** in Southport, where scheduled ferry service will take you and your pooch on a 20-minute trip to the island. Roundtrip tickets are $25 for adults, $14 for children, and free for dogs. Upon arrival, take a short walk to **Riverside Adventure Company** to rent a golf cart, which will serve as your mode of transportation on this car-free island. Daily cart rentals start at $61. Kayak rentals are available from $35 at **The Sail Shop** if your sea dog would like to explore Bald Head Creek. The company also rents beach chairs, umbrellas, and surfboards from their 'Surf Tent' at Beach Access #42.

Bald Head Island Ferry
Deep Point Marina
1301 Ferry Road
Southport, NC 28461
(910) 269-2380
www.bringfido.com/attraction/11161

Where to Stay:

Extend your visit to Bald Head Island by renting a dog-friendly vacation home from **Bald Head Island Limited**. All of their rentals are fully furnished with expansive living rooms, gourmet kitchens, and luxurious master retreats. Many of them are also oceanfront with screened porches, outdoor showers, and direct beach access. The use of a golf cart is included for free with every vacation rental. Dogs of any size are welcome in select homes for an additional fee of $200 per stay.

Bald Head Island Limited
6 Marina Wynd
Bald Head Island, NC 28461
(910) 457-5002
www.baldheadisland.com
Rates from $450/night

US National Whitewater Center

The **US National Whitewater Center** offers numerous outdoor adventures, whether you're on two legs or four! Dogs aren't allowed on the whitewater rafts or zip lines for safety reasons, but water-loving pups can join you on a kayak, canoe, or stand-up paddleboard trip down the scenic Catawba River. Flatwater trips are $25 with a 'QuickSport' pass, but land lovers can hike, bike, or run with Fido on over 20 miles of trails for free. If your dog has a nose for adventure, you can upgrade your hike to an 'Eco Trek' for $20 and bring him along as you locate hidden cache points around the USN-WC facility with one of their GPS devices. The trails are open daily from dawn to dusk, and dogs are always welcome at special events, festivals, and concerts held on site. Be sure to check their online calendar before your trip!

US National Whitewater Center
5000 Whitewater Center Parkway
Charlotte, NC 28214
(704) 391-3900
www.usnwc.org

Where to Stay:

After tiring your pooch out at the USNWC, check into the **Drury Inn & Suites Northlake** in time for their nightly 'kickback' hour at 5:30 pm. While Fido chills out in the comfortable suite, you'll be treated to some free hot food and cold drinks. Once your furry pal is rested, head to **The Dog Bar**, a unique pub where dogs can run off-leash around a climate-controlled shaded patio. The Drury Inn welcomes dogs of any size for no additional fee.

Drury Inn & Suites Northlake
6920 Northlake Mall Drive
Charlotte, NC 28216
(704) 599-8882
www.tinyurl.com/ruff20
Rates from $113/night

Where to Stay:

Located 40 minutes from Chimney Rock (but totally worth the drive), **Barkwells** is a canine-centric retreat in the heart of the Blue Ridge Mountains. Designed with Fido's comfort in mind, all cabins have doggie doors and fenced yards. And with more than eight acres of meadows and a pond, your best friend will have plenty of room to run, swim, and play during your stay. Two dogs of any size are welcome for no fee. Additional dogs are $25 per stay each.

Barkwells
290 Lance Road
Mills River, NC 28759
(828) 891-8288
www.barkwells.com
Rates from $210/night

Chimney Rock State Park

Whether you have an hour to spare or the entire day to explore, you and Fido will find plenty to do at **Chimney Rock State Park**. Novice and experienced hikers alike will find excellent trails to discover with their pups. Climb to the top for panoramic views, then visit Hickory Nut Falls to enjoy the refreshing waterfall. Once you've worked up an appetite, stop for a bite to eat at the **Old Rock Café**, where you and your pooch can eat a delicious meal on the back deck while admiring the views of the Rocky Broad River and Chimney Rock Mountain. When you've had your fill of hiking, head to Lake Lure and rent a pontoon boat from **Lake Lure Adventure Company** for an afternoon on the water. Fish or swim to your heart's content and then dock at **Larkin's on the Lake** for a scrumptious meal on their pet-friendly patio.

Chimney Rock State Park
431 Main Street
Chimney Rock, NC 28720
(828) 625-9611
www.chimneyrockpark.com

Corolla Outback Adventures

Bring Fido to the Outer Banks of North Carolina to see wild horses on a tour with **Corolla Outback Adventures**. With private access into the Wild Horse Conservation Easement, the company can take you into the refuge areas and sanctuary sites that are home to Colonial Spanish Mustangs. On the two-hour adventure, you're likely to see dozens of horses walking along the beach and maybe even playing in the surf. Tour prices are $50 for adults and $25 for children 12 and under. Well-behaved dogs are welcome for no additional charge. After your tour, head to the dog-friendly **Wild Horse Museum** in Old Corolla Village to learn even more about these amazing wild horses. Admission to the museum is free. Fido can also join you on the back deck of **Steamers** to enjoy a great view of the sunset with a bucket of freshly steamed little neck clams.

Corolla Outback Adventures
1150 Ocean Trail
Corolla, NC 27927
(252) 453-4484
www.corollaoutback.com

Where to Stay:

Less than a mile from Corolla Outback Adventures, you'll find the **Inn at Corolla Light**, a pet-friendly hotel offering waterfront accommodations on the Currituck Sound. The property is located within the renowned Corolla Light Resort. Walk, take the free trolley, borrow a bike to cruise to the ocean, or stroll along the resort's trails to visit the grounds of the **Whalehead Club**. Dogs are welcome for an additional nightly fee of $25 to $40 each, depending on size.

Inn at Corolla Light
1066 Ocean Trail
Corolla, NC 27927
(252) 453-3340
www.innatcorolla.com
Rates from $119/night

Where to Stay:

Following Fido's day of fun in the Outer Banks, retire for the evening at the **Sandbar Bed & Breakfast** in beautiful Nags Head. The inviting three-story cottage offers beachfront convenience paired with Southern hospitality. Complimentary breakfast and evening refreshments are served daily. One dog of any size is welcome for an additional fee of $15 per night. The innkeeper and his dog, Princess, also enjoy guiding guests on backwater boat trips to the moonshine community of Buffalo City.

Sandbar Bed & Breakfast
2508 S Virginia Dare Trail
Nags Head, NC 27959
(252) 489-1868
www.tinyurl.com/ruff21
Rates from $89/night

Wright Brothers Memorial

Aviation and history buffs will enjoy bringing their furry co-pilots to the **Wright Brothers National Memorial** in Kill Devil Hills. Stand on the spot where Orville and Wilbur changed the world with their first flight and view full-scale replicas of their 1902 glider, 1903 flying machine, and first wind tunnel. Take a walk up Big Kill Devil Hill, where the duo conducted their glider experiments. Admission is $4 for adults and free for kids and dogs. If you want to do some flying of your own, head to nearby **Outer Banks Air Charters** for a sightseeing flight. Pilot Charlie Snow will take you and your pooch on an aerial tour of the memorial, Roanoke Island, and Bodie Island Lighthouse. Rates start at $210 per half-hour flight. Once your feet are back on the ground, visit the **Cape Hatteras National Seashore** for some free fun in the sand and surf.

Wright Brothers National Memorial
105 N Croatan Highway
Kill Devil Hills, NC 27948
(252) 473-2111
www.nps.gov/wrbr

Four Paws Kingdom

Enjoy the great American tradition of camping with your pooch at **Four Paws Kingdom** in Rutherfordton. This canine paradise is a full-service campground catering exclusively to adults and their furry friends. Fido will enjoy hours of fun in the kingdom's eight fully-fenced dog parks. He can take a dip in the doggie swimming pond, practice jumps in the Rally-O Obedience Arena, weave through poles in the Agility Fun Playground, or fetch a stick from the stream in Linus Creek Park. Afterwards, clean-up will be a breeze at the grooming station in the doggie bathhouse. Four Paws Kingdom is open seasonally from April through November, and special events are held throughout the year. Whether you come for the Oktoberfest Pawty, Memorial Day Rib Fest, or Agility Beginners Boot Camp, you are sure to have an unforgettable vacation with like-minded humans and their dogs.

Four Paws Kingdom
335 Lazy Creek Drive
Rutherfordton, NC 28139
(828) 287-7324
www.4pawskingdom.com

Where to Stay:

Four Paws Kingdom caters to RV owners by providing full hook-up sites with free cable and wireless internet, along with a bathhouse and laundry facilities. Don't have an RV? Air-conditioned and heated cabin and trailer rentals are also available. Those accommodations include a queen-size bed with futon or sofa sleeper, full kitchen or kitchenette, and an outdoor grill. Linens and bedding are not provided. Up to four dogs are allowed in RV sites for no extra fee (three dog maximum in rental units).

Four Paws Kingdom
335 Lazy Creek Drive
Rutherfordton, NC 28139
(828) 287-7324
www.4pawskingdom.com
Rates from $37/night

International Peace Garden

Lying on the 49th parallel at the Canada–United States border near Dunseith, the **International Peace Garden** is a living tribute to world peace. This 2,339-acre park is accessible to visitors from both countries without the need for a passport. Over 150,000 flowers are planted in the formal garden every spring, but the star attractions are always the American and Canadian flags made out of flowers. The gardens are open year-round, but mid-July through August tends to be the best time to view the colorful floral displays. Entrance to the park is $10 per vehicle; $5 per pedestrian or bicyclist. Your leashed pup is welcome to join you throughout the park for free. As you continue your journey across North Dakota, take a detour to Washburn to visit the **Seaman Overlook**, featuring a 1,400-pound, steel sculpture of the dog that accompanied Lewis and Clark on their expedition across America.

International Peace Garden
10939 Highway 281
Dunseith, ND 58329
(701) 263-4390
www.peacegarden.com

Where to Stay:

The **Hyatt House** in Minot serves as a comfortable overnight stop as you traverse between Dunseith and Washburn. All of the suites in this apartment-style property feature pillow-top beds, fully-equipped kitchens, and free high-speed Internet. Other on-site amenities include a 24-hour fitness center, indoor swimming pool, and convenience store. Bar service is available nightly, and a complimentary breakfast is served each morning. Up to two dogs under 50 lbs are welcome for an additional fee of $75 per stay.

Hyatt House Minot
2301 Landmark Drive NW
Minot, ND 58703
(701) 838-7300
www.tinyurl.com/ruff32
Rates from $110/night

Where to Stay:

After your canoe trip, stay on the river a little longer with an overnight at **Morgan's River-side Campground**. Bring your tent and camping gear along for a gorgeous night under the stars in one of their riverside tent-camping sites, or bunk in an Amish-built cabin. Cabin amenities include a double bed, two single mattresses, charcoal grill, picnic table, fire ring, deck, and outdoor seating. Up to two dogs are welcome at tent sites or in cabins for no additional fee.

Morgan's Riverside Campground
5701 Ohio 350
Oregonia, OH 45054
(513) 932-7658
www.morganscanoe.com
Rates from $23/night

Morgan's Outdoor Adventures

Spend a day floating down the Little Miami River with your canine companion in a canoe rental from **Morgan's Outdoor Adventures** in Oregonia. If you don't have much time, opt for the shortest trip departing from Fort Ancient. The three-mile section boasts beautiful scenery, takes less than 1.5 hours to paddle, and ends at **Morgan's Riverside Campground**, which is a great spot for a picnic or snack break. Go further off the beaten path with the nine-mile trip that takes paddlers to Mount Station, passing by a rookery of great blue herons. For half or full-day trips, start at Deer Creek for 12 to 18 miles of river fun with fantastic wildlife viewing, beaches, swimming spots, and picnic areas. Rates start at $25 per canoe (which can accommodate two adults and one or two dogs). If you have your own canoe, the company will shuttle your equipment for a small fee.

Morgan's Outdoor Adventures
5701 Ohio 350
Oregonia, OH 45054
(513) 932-7658
www.morganscanoe.com

Beavers Bend State Park

With pristine lakes and rivers surrounded by towering pine trees, **Beavers Bend State Park** is a great place to 'ruff it' with your adventure-loving pooch. Located six miles north of Broken Bow in the **Ouachita National Forest**, the park offers numerous outdoor activities year-round. Experienced hikers will enjoy the six-mile Skyline Trail or the more challenging David Boren Trail, but several short hiking trails are available for casual hikers as well. Water-loving dogs might prefer to take a dip in Broken Bow Lake or rent a kayak or canoe to paddle the Class I-II rapids on the Mountain Fork River. The river is stocked with trout on a weekly basis, so anglers should definitely bring their fishing gear along too! For those looking to stay overnight in the park, Beavers Bend State Park offers a number of pet-friendly cabin rentals that can accommodate up to six guests.

Beavers Bend State Park
Highway 259A
Broken Bow, OK 74728
(580) 494-6300
www.beaversbend.com

Where to Stay:

Lago Vista Bed & Breakfast is an adults-only inn located 10 miles from downtown Broken Bow, and just steps from the David Boren Nature Trail. All four of their guest rooms have a luxurious king-size bed, fireplace, hot tub, and private balcony overlooking Broken Bow Lake. Unwind at the nightly beer and wine reception. In the morning, savor a scrumptious breakfast before setting off on more adventures with your pooch. Dogs of any size are welcome for no additional fee.

Lago Vista Bed & Breakfast
489 Bowfin Lane
Broken Bow, OK 74728
(580) 494-7378
www.tinyurl.com/ruff22
Rates from $200/night

Where to Stay:

After a day of adventure in Bend, relax in a luxuriously appointed room at **The Oxford Hotel**. The boutique property features modern, eco-friendly accommodations, nightly turndown service, and a sauna and steam room. The hotel's pet package includes a bed, two pet bowls (one to take home), and organic dog treats. Pet massages, grooming, and walking services can also be arranged. Dogs of any size are welcome for an additional fee of $55 per pet, per stay.

The Oxford Hotel
10 NW Minnesota Avenue
Bend, OR 97701
(541) 382-8436
www.oxfordhotelbend.com
Rates from $209/night

Tumalo Creek Kayak & Canoe

Floating down the slow-moving Deschutes River on an inner tube is one of the best ways to spend a hot summer day in Bend. Fortunately for Fido, dogs are welcome to join in the fun too! If you don't have your own tube, you can rent one from **Tumalo Creek Kayak & Canoe** (which also outfits visitors with kayaks, canoes, stand-up paddleboards, life jackets and other accessories). Conveniently located on the banks of the river near the Old Mill District, the company's rental rates start at $10 for tubes, $40 for kayaks and paddleboards, and $50 for canoes. Doggie life jackets are $10. After your relaxing float down the river with Fido, give him a chance to stretch his legs at **Riverbend Beach Dog Park**. With separate small and large dog areas, pups of any size can enjoy splashing in the water and playing off-leash in this fully-fenced riverfront park.

Tumalo Creek Kayak & Canoe
805 SW Industrial Way
Bend, OR 97702
(541) 317-9407
www.tumalocreek.com

Cannon Beach

Spend a few memorable days discovering the wonderful towns, beaches, and other attractions along the Oregon coast with your dog. When planning your journey, leave plenty of time to explore the pet-friendly seaside town of Cannon Beach. Start your day with an early morning walk along the beach near **Haystack Rock**, a designated bird and marine sanctuary that rises 235 feet above the sand and sea. In the tide pools, you will see a variety of marine life, and the rock itself is home to cormorants, tufted puffins, and seagulls. Dogs are welcome to roam leash-free, provided they remain under voice command. After a mid-day stroll along the streets of downtown, spend an afternoon at **Ecola State Park**. Enjoy miles of hiking along the Oregon Coast Trail, following in the footsteps of Lewis and Clark. Day use admission to the park is $5 per vehicle, and dogs must remain on leash.

Cannon Beach Visitor Center
207 N Spruce Street
Cannon Beach, OR 97110
(503) 436-2623
www.cannonbeach.org

Where to Stay:

The oceanfront **Surfsand Resort** in Cannon Beach offers sweeping views of Haystack Rock and the Tillamook Head Lighthouse. Fido can sneak a biscuit from 'Fred's Cookie Jar' at check-in, and the resort provides a dog bed and basket filled with extra sheets, towels, food bowls, and waste bags for their canine guests. There's even a paw wash station near the beach! Up to two dogs of any size are welcome for an additional fee of $15 per pet, per night.

Surfsand Resort
148 W Gower Avenue
Cannon Beach, OR 97110
(503) 436-2274
www.surfsand.com
Rates from $119/night

Where to Stay:

Nestled on the banks of the Columbia River, the **Best Western Plus Hood River Inn** is the only waterfront hotel in Hood River. The property offers river views, water access, and a private beach, plus a pool, spa, and fitness facility at the river's edge. There is also a large grassy lawn and riverside walking path that Fido will appreciate. Up to two dogs of any size are welcome for an additional fee of $12 per pet, per night.

Best Western Plus Hood River Inn
1108 E Marina Drive
Hood River, OR 97031
(541) 386-2200
www.hoodriverinn.com
Rates from $129/night

Columbia River Gorge

Enjoy breathtaking scenic vistas, abundant wildlife, and a variety of terrains and ecosystems in the picturesque Columbia River Gorge area. Located on the border of Oregon and Washington, this canyon created by the Columbia River offers countless recreational opportunities, including the popular **Dog Mountain Trail**. The 6.9-mile modified loop trail with a 2,800-foot elevation gain is best suited to experienced hikers and well-conditioned dogs, but those reaching the summit are rewarded with amazing views of the gorge below, as well as Mount Saint Helens to the northwest and Mount Hood to the south. Plan a visit in May or June when the wildflowers are in peak bloom. For less experienced hikers, a visit to **Multnomah Falls** is in order. Park near the base of the falls for easy access to the 611-foot cascading waterfall, or hike up the paved trail to Benson Bridge for a closer view of the water.

Columbia River Gorge Visitor Center
404 W 2nd Street
The Dalles, OR 97058
(800) 984-6743
www.crgva.org

Rogue Farms Hopyard

Beer enthusiasts and their canine companions will enjoy spending an afternoon at the **Rogue Farms Hopyard** in Independence. Located on the Willamette River and surrounded by cherry and hazelnut orchards, this beer lover's destination is both a working hop farm and a tasting room for Rogue's delicious offerings. Learn how the brewery's seven varieties of hops are grown and harvested on one of the complimentary hopyard tours. Relax on the Chatoe Rogue tasting room patio to enjoy delicious gastropub fare and sample award-winning brews. Your pup will enjoy frolicking in the open spaces too. Just don't let him chase the chickens! After Fido works up an appetite, treat him to an item or two from Chatoe Rogue's doggie menu. The tasting room is open weekdays from 4:00 pm to 9:00 pm and weekends from 11:00 am to 9:00 pm. Hopyard tours take place every Saturday and Sunday at 3:00 pm.

Rogue Farms Hopyard
3590 Wigrich Road
Independence, OR 97351
(503) 838-9813
www.rogue.com

Where to Stay:

Make Rogue's hopyard your own personal farm for a weekend by renting the **Rogue Hop 'N Bed** farmhouse. This 100-year-old home is located just a few yards from the Chatoe Rogue tasting room. Perfect for family gatherings or parties, the six-bedroom farmhouse can accommodate up to 12 people. Rent a room or the entire house. Either way, dogs are welcome for no extra fee. Breakfast isn't served in the morning, but the refrigerator is stocked with some of Rogue's finest brews.

Rogue Hop N' Bed
3590 Wigrich Road
Independence, OR 97351
(503) 838-9813
www.tinyurl.com/ruff23
Rates from $140/night

Rogue Wilderness Adventures

Bring Fido on the trip of a lifetime with **Rogue Wilderness Adventures** in Merlin. From May to October, the outfitter provides you and your pooch with all the gear and instruction needed for a half-day, full-day, or multi-day self-guided rafting trip along a 13-mile stretch of the Rogue River. In addition to offering kayaks, rafts and paddleboats, the company will equip you with all of your camping needs. You can also purchase put-in and pick-up services, making your adventure as easy as floating down the river. Or, plan ahead and come for the company's 'Paddles and Paws' weekend. Offered just once a year, this three-day adventure lets you and your pup enjoy rafting, hiking, and camping with a small group of like-minded dog lovers. Rental prices vary, depending on the equipment and length of use. The Paddles and Paws rafting trip is $819 per person for all meals, rafting, and accommodations.

Rogue Wilderness Adventures
325 Galice Road
Merlin, OR 97532
(800) 336-1647
www.wildrogue.com

Where to Stay:

Outdoor enthusiasts will feel right at home on the grounds of **Morrison's Rogue River Lodge** in Merlin. Located on the banks of the Rogue River, the property features some of the best fly fishing in the country, as well as rafting, horseback riding, and stand-up paddleboarding. After a day on the river, feast on a four-course gourmet meal at the lodge before retiring to your cabin. Dogs of any size are welcome for a fee of $15 per pet, per night.

Morrison's Rogue River Lodge
8500 Galice Road
Merlin, OR 97532
(541) 476-3825
www.morrisonslodge.com
Rates from $69/night

Where to Stay:

After you ride the Oregon dunes, spend the night with your canine companion in a yurt at **William M. Tugman State Park**. These round tent-like dwellings feature beds, wood flooring, heaters and electricity, but you'll need to bring your own sleeping bags and towels. Shared bathroom facilities are available on-site, and the park is located less than three miles from the John Dellenback Dunes Trail. Up to two dogs of any size are welcome for an optional fee of $10 per night.

William M. Tugman State Park
72549 Oregon Coast Highway
Lakeside, OR 97449
(541) 271-4118
www.tinyurl.com/ruff24
Rates from $39/night

Spinreel Dune Buggy

Bring Fido on an off-road adventure at the Oregon dunes with a dune buggy or ATV rental from **Spinreel Dune Buggy** in North Bend. Located across the street from Oregon's largest dune riding area, the company has two-seater dune buggies with plenty of room in the back for your four-legged friend. After a quick lesson and safety briefing, you're ready to ride. Drive at your own pace as you enjoy panoramic views of the Pacific Ocean from the top of the majestic dunes. Rates start at $110 for a 30-minute ride. If you prefer having someone else at the wheel, visit **Sand Dunes Frontier** for a Big Buggy Tour. Your leashed pup is welcome to join you on guided tours. Rates are $12 for adults, $10 for children, and free for dogs. After your ride, let Fido stretch his legs with a hike along the nearby **John Dellenback Dunes Trail**.

Spinreel Dune Buggy
67045 Spinreel Road
North Bend, OR 97459
(541) 759-3313
www.ridetheoregondunes.com

Portland Food Cart Tour

You and your pooch can lunch like the locals on a **Portland Food Cart Tour** with Brett Burmeister. You might try a fried Spanish anchovy with lemon aioli for the first time at Euro Trash, stuff yourself on a 'Chunky Monkey' waffle at the Gaufre Gourmet, or take a bite of a 'Dude' dog with grilled onions, macaroni and cheese, jalapenos, and bacon at Bro-Dogs. Just be careful—it bites back! Every tour is unique with stops at four different carts. You get a sample-sized portion at each cart, but you definitely won't leave Portland hungry! Tours operate Monday through Saturday from 12:00 pm to 1:30 pm. Tickets are $38 for adults. Dogs and kids under 12 are free. At the end of your tour, rest your tired pups at the **Lucky Lab Brewing Company**, where you can enjoy a craft beer at one of the pet-friendly picnic tables.

Portland Food Cart Tour
Washington Street & 10th Avenue
Portland, OR 97205
tours@foodcartsportland.com
www.foodcartsportland.com/tours

Where to Stay:

Nestled on the banks of the Willamette River in an area known as 'Portland's Front Yard,' the **RiverPlace Hotel** by Kimpton gives Fido easy access to a huge lawn and mile-long riverfront walking trail in downtown Portland. The property also provides complimentary bicycles, a yoga mat in each room, and a hosted wine hour from 5:00 pm to 6:00 pm every evening. There is a pet-friendly restaurant on-site, and dogs of any size are welcome for no additional fee.

RiverPlace Hotel
1510 SW Harbor Way
Portland, OR 97201
(503) 228-3233
www.riverplacehotel.com
Rates from $239/night

Three Sisters Wilderness

With nearly 260 miles of hiking trails, the **Three Sisters Wilderness** area of the Willamette National Forest is a nature lover's delight. Start off your adventure by stocking up on supplies in Sisters, a western-themed town dotted with unique shops. Next, take a scenic hour-long drive to the **Proxy Falls** trailhead, where you and your pooch can enjoy an easy-to-moderate 1.5-mile loop hike. Trek over open lava fields and dense evergreen forests on your way to see two magnificent waterfalls, each offering excellent photo opportunities. After hiking to the falls, make your way back to Sisters, or continue on the McKenzie Highway to hike **Sahalie and Koosah Falls**. Plan a visit in summer to ensure that you won't encounter any road closures due to snow, which can blanket McKenzie Pass for much of the year. Day use access is $5 per vehicle. Dogs should remain leashed in the Three Sisters Wilderness.

Three Sisters Wilderness
McKenzie River Ranger District
57600 McKenzie Highway
McKenzie Bridge, OR 97413
(541) 822-7254
www.bringfido.com/attraction/11233

Where to Stay:

After exploring the Three Sisters Wilderness, enjoy the comforts of home at **FivePine Lodge** in Sisters. Their pet-friendly cabins feature private patios, fireplaces, luxury bedding, and soaker tubs. Unwind at the nightly wine reception, or head next door to share a meal with Fido on the patio at **Three Creeks Brewing**. In the morning, Fido can stretch his legs on the adjacent **Peterson Ridge Trail**. Up to two dogs of any size are welcome for a fee of $25 per pet, per night.

FivePine Lodge
1021 E Desperado Trail
Sisters, OR 97759
(541) 549-5900
www.fivepinelodge.com
Rates from $149/night

Sunriver Resort

Located at the base of the Cascade Mountains in central Oregon, the 3,300-acre resort community of **Sunriver** is a vacation destination that Fido is sure to love. Walk or jog more than 30 miles of paved pathways or cycle around the village with a dog trailer rental from **Village Bike & Ski**. Explore hundreds of off-leash trails in the surrounding **Deschutes National Forest** or drive 30 minutes to **Mount Bachelor Ski Resort**. Experienced hikers can climb all the way to the top of the 9,065-foot summit, or for $16 per person, take a dog-friendly chairlift to the mid-mountain level at 7,775 feet and hike to the top from there. While dogs aren't allowed on Mount Bachelor in the winter, **Wanoga Sno-Park** has a pooch-friendly trail and tubing hill nearby with entry for just $3 per vehicle. And, of course, the dozens of miles of trails back at Sunriver allow dogs year-round!

Sunriver Resort
17600 Center Drive
Sunriver, OR 97707
(800) 801-8765
www.sunriver-resort.com

Where to Stay:

With more than 100 dog-friendly vacation rentals to choose from, **Bennington Properties** is sure to have the perfect Sunriver vacation home for you and your canine companion. With weekly 'Yappy Hours' in July and August, an on-site dog wash, and a fenced off-leash play area for your pups, the company's main office is also a popular gathering spot for dog owners. Dogs of any size are welcome for an additional fee of $12 per pet, per night (treats included).

Bennington Properties
56842 Venture Lane
Sunriver, OR 97707
(541) 593-6300
www.tinyurl.com/ruff25
Rates from $85/night

Where to Stay:

After witnessing the simplicity of Amish life, you and Fido can enjoy a plethora of modern amenities at Best Western Premier's **Eden Resort & Suites**. Relax in oversized guest rooms, swim in the heated indoor and outdoor pools, or practice your swing on the recreation complex's putting green. Historic downtown Lancaster and the famous **Central Market** are both less than three miles away. Up to two dogs under 80 lbs are welcome for an additional fee of $15 per pet, per night.

Eden Resort & Suites
222 Eden Road
Lancaster, PA 17601
(717) 569-6444
www.edenresort.com
Rates from $109/night

Abe's Buggy Rides

Learn about Amish and Mennonite cultures as you and Fido enjoy a ride in an authentic Amish buggy on a private tour with **Abe's Buggy Rides**. Your driver will provide historical facts and stories about the area as you ride along country roads in the horse-drawn buggy. Choose a 20-minute tour for a quick jaunt through the Lancaster County countryside. A leisurely hour-long ride will give you time to see many Amish homes, businesses and attractions, and includes a stop at an Amish home or a Mennonite craft store and bake shop. Custom tours are available, and leashed dogs are welcome on all trips. Hours are Monday through Saturday from 9:00 am to 5:00 pm. Tour prices start at $10 for adults and $5 for children. Accepted payment forms are cash or check only. Plan ahead and bring a picnic lunch to enjoy on the grounds after your tour.

Abe's Buggy Rides
2596 Old Philadelphia Pike
Bird in Hand, PA 17505
(717) 392-1794
www.abesbuggyrides.com

Bushkill Falls

Spanning 300 acres in the scenic Pocono Mountains, Pennsylvania's **Bushkill Falls** is a nature lover's delight. With eight waterfalls accessible from just over two miles of walking trails, the park is an excellent spot to explore with your pup. Open April through November, Bushkill Falls offers four trails of varying degrees of difficulty, making the falls accessible to visitors of all ability levels. Choose the Green Trail for a short 15-minute walk to the Main Falls. Allow at least two hours to hike the Red Trail, which offers a glimpse of all eight waterfalls. Family-friendly attractions, such as miniature golf and paddleboat rides, are also available on-site. Pack a picnic lunch or barbecue on the charcoal grills at the pavilion. Bring your tackle box and fish in one of the ponds. Admission is $13 for adults, $7 for children, and free for dogs. Fido must be leashed in the park.

Bushkill Falls
Route 209 & Bushkill Falls Road
Bushkill, PA 18324
(570) 588-6682
www.visitbushkillfalls.com

Where to Stay:

After exploring Bushkill Falls, join the ranks of famous Americans such as Teddy Roosevelt, Henry Ford, John F. Kennedy and Robert Frost, who have been guests at the luxurious **Hotel Fauchere** in Milford. Relax in the beautifully appointed rooms, wander through the manicured garden, take Fido on a stroll through charming Milford, and enjoy an intimate dinner at the Delmonico Room. Up to two dogs of any size are welcome for an additional fee of $25 per pet, per night.

Hotel Fauchere
401 Broad Street
Milford, PA 18337
(570) 409-1212
www.hotelfauchere.com
Rates from $179/night

On the image: U ARE AS MY T-SQUARE ride any ADULT RIDE / YOU WILL BE TOO TALL FOR MOST KIDDIE RIDES

Knoebels Amusement Resort

A day of family fun at the theme park doesn't have to mean leaving Fido at home. At **Knoebels Amusement Resort** in Elysburg, you can bring your furry family members to enjoy the carnival-like atmosphere of America's largest free amusement park. While the kids are riding the roller coasters, you and your pooch can sample the Pork Chop on a Stick, deep-fried Twinkies, and other confections filling the air with mouth-watering aromas. Test your skills at the carnival games or visit one of three on-site museums, including the famous carousel museum. Your dog will enjoy riding the 1.5-mile Pioneer Train that circles the park, going through the Twister roller coaster and into the woods before returning to the depot. The park features more than 57 rides and attractions. Admission and parking are free, and ride tickets are available for purchase at the gate. Dogs must be leashed at all times.

Knoebels Amusement Resort
391 Knoebels Boulevard
Elysburg, PA 17824
(570) 672-2572
www.knoebels.com

Where to Stay:

RV owners and tent campers can stay overnight with their canine companions at **Knoebels Campground** for no additional fee. Those who prefer a traditional hotel should drive an hour northwest to the **Genetti Hotel & Suites** in Williamsport. Choose from tastefully decorated European-style rooms with city, mountain, or river views. Other amenities include an outdoor swimming pool, fitness center, and picnic area. Up to two dogs under 60 lbs are welcome for an additional fee of $15 per pet, per night.

Genetti Hotel & Suites
200 W Fourth Street
Williamsport, PA 17701
(570)326-6600
www.genettihotel.com
Rates from $107/night

Where to Stay:

The **Battlefield Bed and Breakfast** is a Civil War-era farmhouse located right on the Gettysburg Battlefield with 30 acres for Fido to explore. The B&B is said to be haunted by Confederates, but don't be scared when you see a soldier in the morning—that's just a Civil War reenactor arriving for the daily history program. He'll show you how to fire a musket while the innkeeper prepares a hearty breakfast. Dogs of any size are welcome for no additional fee.

Battlefield Bed and Breakfast
2264 Emmitsburg Road
Gettysburg, PA 17325
(717) 334-8804
www.gettysburgbattlefield.com
Rates from $149/night

Gettysburg Battlefield

American history buffs won't want to miss a visit to the **Gettysburg National Military Park**. You can walk through the battlefield with Fido, take a self-guided auto tour, or hire a licensed battlefield guide from the **Gettysburg Foundation** to accompany you on a private, two-hour tour. Dogs are not permitted in park buildings, but they can join you at all of the outdoor memorials, including the Irish Brigade monument, which depicts a loyal Irish wolfhound mourning the loss of his masters. The park is open year-round from 6:00 am to 7:00 pm, with extended hours from April through October. Admission to the park is free. Private tours are $65 per vehicle. You and your furry friend can also explore Gettysburg by night on a guided walking tour with **Haunted Gettysburg**. Tours depart at 7:30 pm and 9:00 pm each evening. Tickets are $8 for adults, and free for dogs and children under nine.

Gettysburg National Military Park
1195 Baltimore Pike
Gettysburg, PA 17325
(717) 334-1124
www.nps.gov/gett

Lehigh Gorge Scenic Railway

Nicknamed 'The Switzerland of America', Jim Thorpe is a great weekend getaway for you and your canine companion. Walk your pup up and down the streets of the charming downtown village, hike the **Lehigh Gorge Trail** along the Lehigh River, or head straight to the town's main attraction—the **Lehigh Gorge Scenic Railway**. Climb aboard a first-class, enclosed, or open-air coach from the 1920s for a 16-mile roundtrip journey through Lehigh Gorge State Park. On the one-hour narrated train ride, you'll learn about anthracite coal's role in the industrial revolution and enjoy stunning views of the gorge. The train operates on weekends and holidays from late May to late December. Tours typically depart at 11:00 am, 1:00 pm, and 3:00 pm, but additional trips are added in the busy fall foliage and summer seasons. Coach fares start at $12 for adults and $9 for children. Dogs ride for free.

Lehigh Gorge Scenic Railway
1 Susquehanna Street
Jim Thorpe, PA 18229
(570) 325-8485
www.lgsry.com

Where to Stay:

A stay at the **Historic Hotel Bethlehem** is the perfect complement to your train ride through the Lehigh Gorge. The property provides stately rooms with views of Bethlehem's Main Street, nightly turndown treats, and 24-hour room service. Fido will love ordering from the pet menu that includes gourmet meals named after famous dogs of the Roaring 20s, such as Rin Tin Tin and Petey from *Our Gang*. One dog of any size is welcome for an additional fee of $75 per stay.

Historic Hotel Bethlehem
437 Main Street
Bethlehem, PA 18018
(610) 625-5000
www.hotelbethlehem.com
Rates from $149/night

Where to Stay:

Housed in a 1907 landmark building next to Independence Park, the **Hotel Monaco** has incredible rooms overlooking the Liberty Bell, a nightly wine hour, and a wildly popular rooftop bar. The Kimpton property allows pets of any size for no additional fee and welcomes all dogs with a special treat at check-in. A pet bed, leash, bowls, and waste bags are also provided for guests with pets. Sitting, walking and grooming arrangements can be made through the concierge.

Hotel Monaco
433 Chestnut Street
Philadelphia, PA 19106
(215) 925-2111
www.monaco-philadelphia.com
Rates from $206/night

Free Tours by Foot

Bring Fido on a trek around the 'City of Brotherly Love' with **Free Tours by Foot**. Led by a knowledgeable guide, each tour highlights popular historical and cultural attractions around downtown Philadelphia. See the Liberty Bell, Christ Church, Ben Franklin's burial site, the Betsy Ross house, and other famous sites on the Independence Mall Tour. Or travel off the beaten path to Chinatown, Love Park, Antique Row, and South Street on the Real Philadelphia Tour. Rather than charge a standard price for each trip, the company suggests that you pay your guide based on what the tour was worth to you. If all the walking has left you and your pup hungry, head to the corner of 9th Street and Passyunk Avenue, where you can choose a favorite in the longtime cheesesteak war between **Pat's** and **Geno's**. Walk-up windows and outdoor seating make it easy to enjoy the Philly classic with Fido.

Free Tours by Foot
20 N 3rd Street
Philadelphia, PA 19106
(267) 712-9512
www.freetoursbyfoot.com

Block Island

Get away from the mainland for a day or two and visit Block Island with your pooch. Hop on the **Block Island Ferry** for a 55-minute ride from Point Judith to the scenic island. Round-trip rates start at $25 for adults and $13 for children, but dogs ride free of charge. After docking, make your way to **Mohegan Bluffs**, a strip of secluded beach sandwiched between impressive 200-foot cliffs and the Atlantic Ocean. You can walk the four-mile roundtrip distance by foot, or rent a bike and trailer from **Beach Rose Bicycles**. If you want to get there quickly, hail a taxi (both **McAloon's Taxi** and **Mig's Rig Taxi** are dog-friendly). After enjoying your time at the beach, stroll around the Southeast Lighthouse before taking a leisurely walk back to Old Harbor, or head in the opposite direction to complete a 13-mile bike ride around the island.

Block Island Ferry
304 Great Island Road
Narragansett, RI 02882
(401) 783-4613
www.blockislandferry.com

Where to Stay:

Nestled on Crescent Beach, the **Blue Dory Inn** has five pet-friendly cottages with stunning ocean views. Guests are treated to a full buffet breakfast, afternoon wine and hors d'oeuvres, and fresh-baked cookies daily. After a good night's sleep, take Fido for a morning walk on the beach. Dogs can run free on the north and south beaches of Block Island but should remain leashed on the eastern shore. Dogs of any size are welcome for an additional fee of $50 per pet, per stay.

Blue Dory Inn
61 Dodge Street
Block Island, RI 02807
(401) 466-5891
www.blockislandinns.com
Rates from $95/night

Cliff Walk

Visitors to Newport should definitely include a stroll along the majestic **Cliff Walk** on their pet-friendly itinerary. One of the area's most popular attractions, this 3.5-mile oceanfront pathway is a designated National Recreation Trail that stretches from Easton's Beach, just south of Memorial Boulevard, to Bailey's Beach at the south end of Bellevue Avenue. The trek offers you and your pup some of New England's most breathtaking views and a peek into the backyards of stately mansions constructed during the Gilded Age. Most of the path is paved, but navigation over a rocky shoreline is required to reach the trail's end. Cliff Walk is open year-round from sunrise to sunset, and dogs must remain leashed at all times. Afterwards, join **Gansett Cruises** on a 90-minute harbor tour with complimentary Del's Lemonade, Quahog Stuffies, and other Rhode Island state delicacies. Rates start at $26 per person, and dogs ride for free.

Cliff Walk
175 Memorial Boulevard
Newport, RI 02840
(401) 845-5300
www.cliffwalk.com

Where to Stay:

If you want to know what it's like to live in one of the grandiose mansions along the Cliff Walk, reserve a room at the historic **Vanderbilt Grace**, a quintessential Newport mansion built by the Vanderbilt family in 1909. Enjoy a glass of champagne upon arrival, lounge by the mansion's sparkling pool, or treat yourself to a massage at the spa. Dogs of any size are welcome. The fee is $50 for dogs under 25 lbs; $100 for larger canine companions.

Vanderbilt Grace
41 Mary Street
Newport, RI 02840
(401) 846-6200
www.vanderbiltgrace.com
Rates from $495/night

Where to Stay:

After sailing the Charleston Harbor, Fido will be welcomed with gracious hospitality at the elegant **Wentworth Mansion** in Charleston's charming historic district. Guests are treated to a Southern breakfast, afternoon hors d'oeuvres, and evening wine or brandy (which is best enjoyed on the rooftop cupola). Garden Rooms are reserved for guests with pets, so Fido will always have easy access to the courtyard and lawn. Dogs of any size are welcome for an additional fee of $25 per night.

The Wentworth Mansion
149 Wentworth Street
Charleston, SC 29401
(888) 466-1886
www.wentworthmansion.com
Rates from $349/night

Charleston Schooner Pride

Spend a relaxing afternoon on the Charleston Harbor with Fido aboard the *Schooner Pride*, an 84-foot classic tall ship. You can participate in raising and trimming the sails with the crew or just relax with a glass of wine as you enjoy the incredible view. There is no set course, so each cruise is unique, but you're likely to pass by Patriots Point, Fort Sumter, the Cooper River Bridge, and dozens of colorful row houses lining the Battery. Two-hour trips start at $36 for adults and $28 for children. Dogs up to 25 lbs are welcome aboard for free. If your pooch is on the larger side, **Adventure Harbor Tours** and the **Charleston Water Taxi** both welcome dogs of any size for no additional fee. Rates vary from $10 for an all-day pass on the water taxi to $55 for a three-hour 'Shark Tooth Hunting Expedition' with Adventure Harbor Tours.

Charleston Schooner Pride
360 Concord Street
Charleston, SC 29401
(843) 722-1112
www.schoonerpride.com

Magnolia Plantation & Gardens

Step back in time at **Magnolia Plantation & Gardens**, a Charleston estate that survived both the Revolutionary and Civil Wars. You and your dog can take the Nature Train through the plantation's wetlands, forests, and marshes or explore the expansive grounds by foot. Walk along the boardwalks and bridges to discover the Audubon Swamp Garden. If your pup is small enough to be carried, he can join you on a tour inside the gorgeous home as well. Admission prices range from $15 for access to the grounds to $47 for admission to all attractions at the plantation. Dogs are welcome for free. If you and your pooch want to see more historic properties, head to nearby **Drayton Hall Plantation**, where you can observe the oldest surviving example of Georgian Palladian architecture in the country. Or, travel to **Boone Hall Plantation**, where you can view antique roses that are more than 100 years old.

Magnolia Plantation & Gardens
3550 Ashley River Road
Charleston, SC 29414
(843) 571-1266
www.magnoliaplantation.com

Where to Stay:

The Inn at Middleton Place is a marvel of modern architecture in Charleston's plantation district. Take in views of the Ashley River from the floor-to-ceiling windows in your room, or get a closer look with a rental from **Charleston Kayak Company**, located on-site. Enjoy a morning walk through tall pines and live oaks with Fido on the property's 4.5 miles of trails. Up to two dogs under 50 lbs are welcome for an additional fee of $50 per stay.

The Inn at Middleton Place
4290 Ashley River Road
Charleston, SC 29414
(843) 556-0500
www.tinyurl.com/ruff26
Rates from $111/night

Where to Stay:

Enjoy waking up to a view of Hilton Head Island's sugar sand beaches at the **Omni Oceanfront Resort**. Relax on the resort's private beach, order a drink from the poolside swim-up bar, or treat yourself to a massage at the spa. Fido will love exploring the 16 miles of scenic trails and waterways at this tropical oasis by foot (or kayak). Up to two dogs under 50 lbs are welcome for an additional fee of $100 per pet, per stay.

Omni Oceanfront Resort
23 Ocean Lane
Hilton Head Island, SC 29928
(843) 842-8000
www.tinyurl.com/ruff27
Rates from $167/night

Vagabond Cruise

Want to spend a day on the water with your furry first mate? **Vagabond Cruise** offers more than 20 different cruises from their dock at **The Sea Pines Resort** in Hilton Head Island. Choose from a romantic sunset sail, day trip to Savannah, or sightseeing trip to Daufuskie Island, where you can disembark and explore the low country. Tickets range from $30 to $97 per person, and dogs sail for free. There is a $5 fee to enter Sea Pines, but once there, you can also explore the resort's 17 miles of trails with Fido or spend some quality time at the beach. All Hilton Head Island beaches allow dogs after 5:00 pm during summer and anytime in the off-season. If your sea dog begs for more time on the water, you can also search for dolphins aboard **Captain Mark's Dolphin Cruise**, which takes you through Broad Creek into Calibogue Sound.

Vagabond Cruise
149 Lighthouse Road
Hilton Head Island, SC 29928
(843) 363-9026
www.vagabondcruise.com

Custer State Park

If your dog likes to walk on the wild side, he will definitely enjoy hiking the trails carved out by early pioneers at **Custer State Park** in the Black Hills of South Dakota. You're likely to encounter prairie dogs, elk, big horn sheep, mountain goats, and deer on the trails, but the park is most famous for being home to one of the nation's largest free roaming herd of buffalo. The best way to see them is by driving the 18-mile Wildlife Loop Road in the early morning or late evening, just before sunset. The drive usually takes about 45 minutes, but with any luck, you may find yourself stuck in a 'Buffalo Jam' for a while longer. If you do encounter a herd of the 2,000-pound animals on the road, it is important for everyone, including Fido, to remain in the vehicle. Custer State Park is open year-round. Admission is $15 per vehicle.

Custer State Park
Wildlife Loop Road
Custer, SD 57730
(605) 255-4515
www.custerstatepark.com

Where to Stay:

Tucked among the ponderosa pines beside Grace Coolidge Creek, the **State Game Lodge** once served as President Calvin Coolidge's summer residence. Now you can be a guest of the lodge in one of 19 pet-friendly cabins with daily housekeeping service. After a restful night's sleep, take Fido for a morning walk on the adjacent Creekside Trail, then feast on Buffalo Benedict in the lodge's main dining room. Dogs are welcome for an additional fee of $10 per pet, per night.

State Game Lodge
13389 S Dakota 87
Custer, SD 57730
(605) 255-4541
www.custerresorts.com
Rates from $145/night

Reptile Gardens

If you like scales and tails, bring Fido to **Reptile Gardens** in Rapid City. The world's largest reptile zoo welcomes you and your four-legged companion to explore the grounds and observe 225 species of snakes, crocodiles, frogs, lizards, tortoises, and other reptiles. Catch a glimpse of the rare Komodo dragon before visiting the menagerie of cold-blooded creatures in the famous Sky Dome. Need a break from the creepy-crawlies? Visit the park's prairie dog exhibit, where Fido can get up close and personal with these cute critters from an underground bubble. Reptile Gardens is open daily from April through October. Admission starts at $12 for adults; dogs and kids under five are free. For more animal adventures, head to nearby **Bear Country USA**. At this drive-thru wildlife park, you'll see dozens of bears, wolves, sheep, and elk. Admission is $16 per vehicle, and the park is open from May through November.

Reptile Gardens
8955 S Hwy 16
Rapid City, SD 57709
(605) 342-5873
www.reptilegardens.com

Where to Stay:

Located next door to Bear Country USA in Rapid City, **Mystery Mountain Resort** is a dog-friendly campground with 38 acres of shaded RV sites and camping cabins. All cabins are furnished with towels, linens, air conditioning, and satellite televisions. Some also have private bathrooms and kitchenettes. Roast hot dogs on your fire pit in the evening and enjoy all-you-can-eat pancakes for $1 in the morning (summer only). Dogs of any size are welcome for an additional fee of $5 per pet, per night.

Mystery Mountain Resort
13752 S Highway 16
Rapid City, SD 57702
(605) 342-5368
www.blackhillsresorts.com
Rates from $59/night

Where to Stay:

The Hermitage became Nashville's first pet-friendly hotel in 1941 when movie star Gene Autry and his horse, Champion, checked in for a week-long stay. To this day, the hotel continues to welcome four-legged guests with a dose of good old-fashioned Southern hospitality. Fido can sleep on a custom dog bed, order from the pet room service menu, and even enjoy a canine massage during his stay. Dogs up to 100 lbs are welcome for an additional fee of $50 per pet, per night.

The Hermitage Hotel
231 6th Avenue N
Nashville, TN 37219
(615) 244-3121
www.thehermitagehotel.com
Rates from $239/night

Walkin' Nashville

Country music lovers will enjoy learning about the golden era of their favorite genre on a tour with **Walkin' Nashville**. Grammy-nominated music journalist Bill DeMain takes visitors on a 90-minute stroll through downtown Nashville on his Music City Legends Tour. The tour starts at the corner of Fifth Avenue and Union Street and covers approximately one-half mile, visiting sites including the Ernest Tubb Record Shop, Castle Recording Studio, and Sho-Bud Steel Guitar Company. Fans of Dolly Parton, Willie Nelson, Loretta Lynn, and Johnny Cash will hear fascinating stories about their favorite music stars' careers as they walk through the heart of Music City. Tours depart at 10:30 am on Tuesdays, Thursdays, Fridays and Saturdays from April through November. They are only offered on Fridays and Saturdays from December through March. Tickets are $16 for adults and $10 for children 4 and older. Well-behaved dogs can tag along for free.

Walkin' Nashville
5th Avenue & Union Street
Nashville, TN 37203
(615) 499-5159
www.walkinnashville.com

Cades Cove Loop Road

Even though dogs aren't allowed on most trails at **Great Smoky Mountains National Park,** you can still enjoy the park's most popular attraction with Fido in tow. Take a scenic drive on the 11-mile loop around Cades Cove, and you'll easily spot dozens of white-tailed deer, black bears, and other animals roaming the open fields that were once farmed by pioneers. If you'd prefer to take Fido on a walk, be sure to visit on a Wednesday or Saturday morning between May and September. **Cades Cove Loop Road** is closed to motorists until 10:00 am those days to give bicyclists and pedestrians time to enjoy the awe-inspiring scenery. There is no admission fee, but you can purchase a self-guided auto tour booklet for $1 at the entrance. The road is open daily from sunrise to sunset. Allow two to four hours to drive the entire loop, depending on traffic conditions.

Cades Cove Loop Road
Great Smoky Mountains National Park
Townsend, TN 37882
(865) 436-1200
www.bringfido.com/attraction/70

Where to Stay:

After a day of exploring the Smokies, you and your pup can kick back in a cozy cabin at the **Dancing Bear Lodge** in Townsend. All cabins feature luxurious feather beds, wood-burning fireplaces, and private porches with hot tubs. Enjoy a glass of wine and a delicious meal as your pooch sits tableside on the outdoor deck of the Dancing Bear Restaurant. A complimentary breakfast is served daily. Dogs are welcome in cabins for an additional fee of $50 per stay.

Dancing Bear Lodge
137 Apple Valley Way
Townsend, TN 37882
(865) 448-6000
www.dancingbearlodge.com
Rates from $170/night

Where to Stay:

Enjoy world-class dining, accommodations, and service at **Blackberry Farm** in Walland. Delight in a culinary adventure offered by the highly regarded chefs at The Barn, the resort's award-winning restaurant. Relax in a luxurious Estate Room with a feather-topped bed, or opt for one of the tucked-away cottages to give your pup room to explore. The attentive staff at Blackberry Farm will ensure that your trip is not soon forgotten. Dogs of any size are welcome for an additional fee of $250 per stay.

Blackberry Farm
1471 W Millers Cove Road
Walland, TN 37886
(865) 984-8166
www.blackberryfarm.com
Rates from $495/night

Blackberry Farm

Tucked away in the rolling hills of East Tennessee, **Blackberry Farm** offers a relaxing retreat for guests who want to get away from the hustle and bustle of modern life. The estate spans over 9,200 acres in the foothills bordering **Great Smoky Mountains National Park**. Despite its size, the resort has an intimate feel, and you and your pooch may feel as though you have the whole place to yourselves. Explore miles of hiking trails, go fly fishing on Hesse Creek, or wander the lovely gardens together. Fido may even meet one of the farm's Lagotto Romagnolo dogs, a northern Italian breed that's uniquely skilled at hunting truffles. As part of their breeding program, Blackberry Farm hosts a 'Truffle Dog Gathering' annually in February. Lagotto owners (and non-owners alike) are invited to the farm for a weekend of scent detection trials, agility playtime, and chef-prepared meals highlighting the elusive black Périgord truffle.

Blackberry Farm
1471 W Millers Cove Road
Walland, TN 37886
(865) 984-8166
www.blackberryfarm.com

Green River Stables

Saddle up with Fido at **Green River Stables** in Waynesboro. Take a guided horseback ride through forests and fields on a private tour along the Green River. Your canine companion can join in the fun by walking alongside your horse and playing in the river. Trail rides are suitable for children over seven years old, and adults under 250 lbs. One-hour rides cost $35 per person. Two-hour rides are just $15 more. If you and your pooch aren't up for the trail ride, you can still try out horseback riding with an arena ride. Walk, trot, or canter in the safety of an enclosed arena for just $15 per person, per session. To suit the needs of all riders, Green River Stables has horses that range in size from small ponies to large stallions. They also offer boarding facilities, professional lessons, pony parties, horse-drawn wagon rides, and a petting zoo.

Green River Stables
642 Waynesboro Highway
Waynesboro, TN 38485
(931) 722-7002
www.greenriverstables.biz

Where to Stay:

Green River Stables has one pet-friendly cabin on-site that can be rented as part of a weekend riding package. If it's not available, take a 30-minute drive to Clifton to stay in one of 12 uniquely-themed 'Songwriter Cabins' at **The Bear Inn Resort**. After checking in, enjoy a meal with Fido on the deck of the hotel's Backyard Bar & Grill. Dogs up to 50 lbs are welcome in the cabins for an additional fee of $25 per pet, per stay.

The Bear Inn Resort
2250 Billy Nance Highway
Clifton, TN 38425
(931) 676-5552
www.bearinnllc.com
Rates from $89/night

Where to Stay:

After a fun-filled day exploring Austin, recharge at the unique **Hotel Saint Cecilia**. Every suite, studio, and bungalow in this secluded estate pays homage to the great writers, musicians, and artists of the decades. You and your pup can enjoy the sounds of the greats on the in-room Geneva sound systems with turntables. Other amenities include mini-bars stocked with unusual treats, made-to-order breakfasts, and an outdoor pool. Dogs of any size are welcome for an additional fee of $35 per pet, per night.

Hotel Saint Cecilia
112 Academy Drive
Austin, TX 78704
(512) 852-2400
www.hotelsaintcecilia.com
Rates from $295/night

Zilker Park Boat Rentals

On your next visit to Austin, make a bee line for Lady Bird Lake. You and your pup can enjoy the serenity of the water with a canoe or kayak rental from **Zilker Park Boat Rentals**. Located just 10 minutes from downtown, a scenic float on the lake will provide you with magnificent views of the Austin skyline and a glimpse of the famous bat colony that resides under the Congress Avenue Bridge. Rental rates start at $12 per hour. When you're back on dry land, head to **Zilker Botanical Garden** to explore over 30 acres of lush gardens with Fido. The garden is open daily from 7:00 am to 5:30 pm. Admission is $2 for adults and $1 for children. Dogs are free. When you get hungry, check out Austin's amazing food truck scene and track down the **Bow-Wow Chow** truck, which serves fresh-baked pet treats and doggie ice cream.

Zilker Park Boat Rentals
2201 Barton Springs Road
Austin, TX 78746
(512) 478-3852
www.zilkerboats.com

Elkins Ranch

Mosey along with Fido to **Elkins Ranch**—a working cattle ranch in the Texas Panhandle—where you can tour the nation's second largest canyon. Travel back in time to the fascinating Old West as your guide regales you with vivid history and delightful folklore of the area. Enjoy spectacular views of Palo Duro Canyon as you travel over rugged terrain in a customized Jeep that's well-equipped for the trip. Dogs of any size are allowed on the one- or two-hour tours, which are offered daily. Rates start at $25 for adults and $15 for children. Dogs ride for free. After your tour, visit the world-famous **Cadillac Ranch**. At this public art installation, Fido can pose for a photo next to 10 graffiti-covered Cadillacs that have been half-buried into the ground. The public is invited to leave their mark on the vehicles, so be sure to bring a can of spray paint.

Elkins Ranch
11301 E State Highway 217
Canyon, TX 79015
(806) 488-2100
www.theelkinsranch.com

Where to Stay:

If you and your canine companion need a nice place to crash after a long day of exploring **Palo Duro Canyon State Park**, stay in the conveniently located **Holiday Inn Express Canyon**. Enjoy a clean, comfortable room, complimentary daily breakfast, and evening snacks. The hotel also offers many amenities, including a fitness center, indoor pool, hot tub, business center, and free wireless internet. Up to two dogs of any size are welcome for an additional fee of $25 per stay.

Holiday Inn Express Canyon
2901 4th Avenue
Canyon, TX 79015
(806) 655-4445
www.tinyurl.com/ruff28
Rates from $108/night

Where to Stay:

Dog owners looking for upscale accommodations in the 'Big D' should look no further than **Rosewood Mansion on Turtle Creek**. A landmark Dallas property, the hotel offers luxurious guest rooms, complimentary car service, and some of the finest dining available in town. The attentive staff loves dogs and will even walk your pooch upon request. Don't miss having breakfast on the mansion's pet-friendly patio. Dogs of any size are welcome for an additional fee of $100 per pet, per stay.

Rosewood Mansion
2821 Turtle Creek Boulevard
Dallas, TX 75219
(214) 559-2100
www.tinyurl.com/ruff29
Rates from $314/night

Fort Worth Stockyards

Bring your canine compadre to the **Fort Worth Stockyards** for a taste of the Old West. Start your day by watching one of the twice-daily longhorn cattle drives through town. Then, take a GPS-guided walking tour of the historic district with your pup. Capture a memory of the trip with a western-themed portrait of you and your pooch from **Uncle Charlie's Old Time Photo Studio**. Afterwards, grab some grub from one of the popular food trucks at **Fort Worth Food Park**. After getting your fill, drive to Dallas for some budget-friendly sightseeing aboard the **M-Line Trolley**. Fido can ride through Dallas' vibrant Uptown neighborhood with you on the restored vintage streetcars. Hop off at the **Katy Trail**, one of the most popular dog walking routes in Dallas, or visit the pet-friendly **Dallas Farmers Market** to round out your day. There's no charge to ride the trolley, although donations are appreciated.

Fort Worth Stockyards
500 NE 23rd Street
Fort Worth, TX 76164
(817) 624-4741
www.fortworthstockyards.org

Texas Hill Country

Located 75 miles west of Austin, the town of Fredericksburg serves as a central hub for exploring Texas Hill Country's numerous dog-friendly state parks. Start your tour at **Enchanted Rock State Natural Area**. Situated 20 miles north of Fredericksburg, the 1,643-acre park is popular among hikers and rock-climbers. Drive an hour west to **South Llano River State Park**, where you can rent kayaks and canoes or go tubing with your pup down the scenic river. **Pedernales Falls State Park**, in nearby Johnson City, offers excellent family-friendly hiking and wildlife viewing opportunities. Travel north to **Inks Lake State Park** in Burnet to fish for bass or catfish with your four-legged friend. Primitive camping and backpacking are available at the **Hill Country State Natural Area**, located 60 miles away in Bandera. Entrance fees and hours vary by location. As you enjoy the parks, be sure to keep Fido on a leash at all times.

Hill Country State Natural Area
10600 Bandera Creek Road
Bandera, TX 78003
(830) 796-4413
www.bringfido.com/attraction/11177

Where to Stay:

After spending some quality time in the great outdoors, savor the beauty of Texas from the front porch of your cabin at **Spotted Pony Ranch** in Fredericksburg. Watch horses grazing the pasture as you sip a glass of 'Ranch Dog Red' from the nearby **Rancho Ponte Vineyard**. Or take one of their ponies on a trail ride in the backcountry for $115 per person. Dogs of any size are welcome for an additional fee of $35 per stay.

Spotted Pony Ranch
343 Black Bear Lane
Fredericksburg, TX 78624
(830) 443-4520
www.spottedponyranch.com
Rates from $99/night

Boneyard Dog Park & Drinkery

If you'd like to enjoy a cold drink while your pup makes some new four-legged friends in Houston, the **Boneyard Dog Park & Drinkery** is the place to go! The 7,000 square foot, fully fenced dog park offers plenty of room for Fido to run off-leash and have a good time. But this is no ordinary dog park. Humans will appreciate the rotating selection of eight craft beers, plus a wide assortment of local and regional brews. An array of wines from around the world will also satisfy the vino lovers. Order some grub from the food trucks parked out front and enjoy lunch or dinner on the large patio. Dogs must be over 16 weeks old, spayed or neutered, and have proof of current vaccinations in order to enter. The Boneyard is open from 2:00 pm to midnight on weekdays and from noon to midnight on Saturdays and Sundays.

Boneyard Dog Park & Drinkery
8150 Washington Avenue
Houston, TX 77007
(832) 494-1600
www.boneyardhouston.com

Where to Stay:

After an hour or two at the Boneyard, Fido will certainly be dog-tired. Bring him to **Hotel Indigo** in Houston's uptown Galleria area for a relaxing stay in a colorful guest room with hardwood floors and modern amenities. While your pooch is napping on the fluffy, oversized bed, you can get your own run in at the hotel's 24-hour fitness center. Up to two dogs of any size are welcome for an additional fee of $75 per pet, per stay.

Hotel Indigo Houston at the Galleria
5160 Hidalgo Street
Houston, TX 77056
(713) 621-8988
www.bringfido.com/lodging/94761
Rates from $249/night

Where to Stay:

Located on a quiet stretch of the San Antonio River Walk near Travis Park, **Hotel Havana** is a great place to recharge after your 'River City' run. The boutique property features 27 uniquely decorated rooms with original Bastrop pine floors, antique furniture, and vintage Cuban artwork. There is a dog-friendly restaurant on-site, and each room has a retro mini-bar stocked with local and international snacks. Pets of any size are welcome for an additional fee of $25 per night.

Hotel Havana
1015 Navarro Street
San Antonio, TX 78205
(210) 222-2008
www.havanasanantonio.com
Rates from $132/night

River City Run

Put on your running shoes and grab Fido's leash! He's welcome to hit the streets of San Antonio with Tina and Tommy from **River City Run**. The couple offers private guided 5K runs of the 'River City' that combine their love of running with an informative tour about the history of San Antonio. Start your 90-minute adventure at the famed Alamo and enjoy a leisurely jog past 18 city landmarks, including the San Fernando Cathedral, the Spanish Governor's Palace, and the Tower of the Americas. The course also takes you along a portion of the **San Antonio River Walk**, where you can return afterwards to dine on authentic Mexican fare at **Casa Rio** or enjoy a Texas-sized margarita at **Rita's on the River**. Private tours can be arranged seven days a week for $30 per person. Water, action photos, and a commemorative t-shirt are included in the price.

River City Run
300 Alamo Plaza
San Antonio, TX 78205
(210) 201-3786
www.rivercityrunsa.com

Best Friends Animal Sanctuary

Best Friends Animal Sanctuary, located in Kanab's scenic Angel Canyon, is the largest lifetime care animal sanctuary in the nation. Driving through Angel Canyon, you'll immediately feel the peace and tranquility of a place where so many animals have been loved and healed from their hard journeys in life. Any day of the week you can take a free, 90-minute guided tour of the Sanctuary. There are at least four tours offered each day, and dogs are allowed on tour vans. In addition to the tour, you and Fido can relax at the wishing garden, visit Angel's Rest, and hike on ancient Indian trails in and around the beautiful scenery at the Sanctuary. There really is nowhere else like it on earth. If a 90-minute tour just isn't enough, you can also sign up to volunteer at Best Friends for a day, a weekend, or as long as you'd like.

Best Friends Animal Sanctuary
5001 Angel Canyon Road
Kanab, UT 84741
(435) 644-2001
www.bestfriends.org

Where to Stay:

Best Friends Animal Sanctuary has eight cottages, four cabins, and two RV sites available for overnight guests. The buildings are located right in Angel Canyon, so your only neighbors will be horses, deer, squirrels, and other dog-loving volunteers. The cabins sleep up to two people and the cottages can accommodate six. Both have kitchenettes stocked with all of the necessities, and there's a dog door with a private fenced area for each unit. Dogs of any size are welcome for no additional fee.

Best Friends Animal Sanctuary
5001 Angel Canyon Road
Kanab, UT 84741
(435) 644-2001
www.bestfriends.org
Rates from $60/night

Dreamland Safari Tours

With so many natural wonders in the Kanab area, choosing the best way to spend your time there can be challenging. Let the team at **Dreamland Safari Tours** help you plan the best adventure for you and your pup. William James and his crew offer more than 30 different day tour options and can customize a trip that suits your interests. Where else can you hike through a mystical slot canyon, hunt for petroglyphs, and walk in the footsteps of a dinosaur? If you're lucky enough to get your paws on a permit to hike to the famous 'Wave' in the **Paria Canyon Wilderness**, Dreamland Safari Tours can guide you there. If not, your furkids will love playing at **Coral Pink Sand Dunes State Park**. Two-hour tours start at $60 for adults and $30 for children. Well-socialized dogs ride for free and are welcome on all excursions except the Toroweap Tour.

Dreamland Safari Tours
265 N 300 W (Hwy 89)
Kanab, UT 84741
(435) 644-5506
www.dreamlandtours.net

Where to Stay:

Steeped in retro 1960s era charm, the **Quail Park Lodge** in Kanab has the vibe of a traditional roadside motel but offers some upscale amenities you'd only expect in a higher end hotel. All rooms have iPod docking stations, plush bathrobes, spa-quality bath products, and pillow-top mattresses with triple sheeted bedding. One dog of any size is welcome in each guest room for no additional fee. Bowls and treats are provided, and there is an on-site pet relief area.

Quail Park Lodge
125 N 300 W (Highway 89)
Kanab, UT 84741
(435) 215-1447
www.quailparklodge.com
Rates from $89/night

Where to Stay:

Located a few blocks from downtown Moab, **3 Dogs & a Moose Cottages** is the perfect place to wind down after your action-packed adventure on the Colorado River. Up to two dogs of any size are welcome in three of their four cottages (Moosewood, French Quarter, and Bogie's Bungalow) for an additional fee of $10 per pet, per night. Inside, you'll find food and water bowls, pet towels, yummy treats, and a supply of waste bags for your pooch.

3 Dogs & a Moose Cottages
171 W Center Street
Moab, UT 84532
(435) 260-1692
www.tinyurl.com/ruff30
Rates from $165/night

Moab Rafting & Canoe

Let your dog paddle the Colorado River with **Moab Rafting & Canoe Company**. Whether you and your canine compadre plan to paddle the 'Daily' rapids to the edge of Arches National Park in a single afternoon or set off on a multi-day adventure with overnight camping, the staff at Moab Rafting & Canoe Company will help you design the perfect trip. Choose from a variety of self-guided excursions and outfit your canoe with everything you need for the trip. Camping gear rentals include coolers, sleeping bags, tents, dry bags, water jugs, and more. You can even rent a 'Full Kitchen Box' with everything you'll need to prepare meals along the river (except the food). Overnight trips are suitable for humans with moderate wilderness skills, and pups with some camping experience. Rates for self-guided trips vary based on the number of nights. Daily rentals are available from $30, plus a $7 shuttle fee.

Moab Rafting & Canoe Company
805 N Main Street
Moab, UT 84532
(435) 259-7722
www.moab-rafting.com

Zion Adventure Company

Explore Utah's magnificent **Zion National Park** with your canine companion. Start by taking a drive along the scenic Zion-Mount Carmel Highway. Go early in the morning to beat the crowd and have the best chance of spotting area wildlife. Day use access is $25 per vehicle. Following your drive, park the car and take Fido for a walk along the pet-friendly Pa'rus Trail, a two-mile paved path that runs alongside the Virgin River and offers amazing views of the canyon. For an afternoon of excitement, bring you pup on a tour with **Zion Adventure Company**. Depart from the company store in Springdale and buckle your seat belt for a thrilling 2.5-hour Overland Cliffs and Canyons Backcountry Tour. Ride in an open-air 1974 Mercedes-Benz Unimog as you traverse the canyon. Tours operate daily from March through October. Rates are $59 for adults and $45 for children. Dogs ride for free.

Zion Adventure Company
36 Lion Boulevard
Springdale, UT 84767
(435) 772-1001
www.zionadventures.com

Where to Stay:

Complete your tour of Utah with a stay at **Red Mountain Resort**, a top-rated 'adventure spa' on a 55-acre campus in Ivins. Up to two dogs of any size are welcome for an additional fee of $50 per pet, per stay. Dogs receive organic treats at check-in and are invited to tag along on private guided hikes. Those wishing to stay closer to Zion National Park should consider the **Driftwood Lodge in Springdale**, where dogs are welcome for $10 per night.

Red Mountain Resort
1275 Red Mountain Circle
Ivins, UT 84738
(435) 673-4905
www.redmountainresort.com
Rates from $165/night

Dog Mountain

Dog lovers come to St. Johnsbury from all around the world to celebrate and remember their beloved furry friends that have crossed over the Rainbow Bridge in **Dog Mountain**'s chapel. Sit on one of the hand-carved pews inside, surrounded by photos of passed dogs and hand-written messages their owners tacked onto the walls in memoriam. 'You were the best co-pilot, Rocco. I'll always miss you.' Post a message in the Dog Chapel yourself, or hug your canine companion a little tighter and stay awhile. Either way, leave plenty of time to explore the beautiful grounds. Dogs are free to run, play, and swim wherever they'd like in this 150-acre doggie paradise. The only rule is to leave your leash at the door! Dog Mountain was the creation of the late Stephen Huneck, a talented artist whose love for dogs is obvious in his works on display in the on-site gallery.

Dog Mountain
143 Parks Road
St. Johnsbury, VT 05819
(800) 449-2580
www.dogmt.com

Where to Stay:

Located less than 30 minutes from Dog Mountain, the **Wildflower Inn** is situated on 570 acres of bucolic Vermont farmland in Lyndonville. After enjoying the innkeepers' signature buttermilk pancakes topped with fresh-from-the-orchard maple syrup, work off your meal by exploring the vast woods and meadows surrounding the inn with your pooch. Up to two dogs of any size are allowed in ground floor Carriage House rooms, Meadow Building suites, and the School House for a fee of $35 per pet, per stay.

Wildflower Inn
2059 Darling Hill Road
Lyndonville, VT 05851
(802) 626-8310
www.wildflowerinn.com
Rates from $140/night

Where to Stay:

After exploring all that Stowe has to offer, you and your pup can unwind at **Stowe Mountain Lodge**. Located at the base of Mount Mansfield, the alpine-style lodge offers exquisite accommodations with goose-down feather beds, stone fireplaces, and floor-to-ceiling windows in most rooms. Canine guests receive a plush dog bed and assortment of treats at check-in, and there is a 'Dog Sanctuary' on the property for morning walks. Dogs under 100 lbs are welcome for an additional fee of $125 per stay.

Stowe Mountain Lodge
7412 Mountain Road
Stowe, VT 05672
(802) 253-3560
www.stowemountainlodge.com
Rates from $249/night

Gondola SkyRide

Although Stowe is best known for its winter activities, you and Fido will find plenty to do there year-round. In the spring, catch the **Gondola SkyRide** to access pet-friendly hiking trails at the summit of Mount Mansfield. Roundtrip tickets are $25 for adults and $17 for kids. **Smuggler's Notch State Park** is the place to enjoy cool air on a hot summer day. After a quick 20-minute hike to Bingham Falls, Fido can wade in the swimming hole at the base of the 25-foot waterfall. Admission is $3 per person. Finally, zig zag your way to the top of Vermont's highest mountain on the **Mount Mansfield Auto Toll Road** for a brilliant display of New England's famous fall foliage. For $28 per vehicle, you get a 360-degree view of the Adirondack Mountains ablaze in hues of red, orange, gold, and yellow. Dogs are welcome on each of these activities for no extra fee.

Gondola SkyRide
5781 Mountain Road
Stowe, VT 05672
(802) 253-3500
www.gostowe.com/gondola

The Paw House Inn

The Paw House Inn has gone to the dogs, and Fido may never want to leave! This canine-centric inn in West Rutland features a wide variety of activities for you and your pup to enjoy. Fido will get plenty of exercise at Paw House Park, a fully-fenced on-site dog park, but you can also hike along wildflower fields or go berry-picking with your pooch on the property. Plan ahead and visit the Paw House Inn during one of their Doggie Mystery Weekends held at various times throughout the year, or enroll your pooch at Paw House University for some beginning or advanced agility training on the property's recreational agility course. On Saturday nights from June through August, you can even catch a movie under the stars at the Dog-In Theater, a 14-foot screen with surround sound on the back lawn. Just don't forget the 'pupcorn' for your furry friend!

The Paw House Inn
1376 Clarendon Avenue
West Rutland, VT 05777
(802) 558-2661
www.pawhouseinn.com

Where to Stay:

Unwind from your adventures in one of **The Paw House Inn**'s uniquely furnished, dog-themed rooms. Each room offers Fido a comfortable, custom-built dog bed, while also catering to the comfort and enjoyment of the humans. As your pup consumes tasty homemade treats, you are sure to enjoy the delicious country breakfast served every morning. Up to two dogs of any size are welcome for no additional fee. A third dog is permitted for an extra fee of $25 per night.

The Paw House Inn
1376 Clarendon Avenue
West Rutland, VT 05777
(802) 558-2661
www.pawhouseinn.com
Rates from $125/night

Where to Stay:

Located just 15 minutes from Mount Vernon, **Lorien Hotel & Spa** offers elegant accommodations in the heart of Old Town Alexandria. This Kimpton property prides itself on pampering their two- and four-legged guests equally. Relax with a glass of Chardonnay at the nightly hosted wine hour and ask the 'Bath Butler' to have the bubbles ready when you get back. But don't forget about Fido—the concierge can arrange a massage for him too! Dogs of any size are welcome for no additional fee.

Lorien Hotel & Spa
1600 King Street
Alexandria, VA 22314
(703) 894-3434
www.lorienhotelandspa.com
Rates from $239/night

Mount Vernon Estate

During George Washington's lifetime, many beloved dogs lived with him and Martha at the **Mount Vernon Estate & Gardens** in Alexandria. While your dog is not able to venture inside the historic mansion today, there is still plenty to keep both of you busy on this 50-acre plantation. Spend time in the gardens, visit George Washington's tomb, and enjoy breathtaking views of the Potomac River from the piazza. Mount Vernon is open 365 days a year. Tickets are $17 for adults and $8 for children. Dogs are admitted for free, but must remain leashed at all times. In the evening, take your furry friend on a walking tour with **Alexandria's Footsteps to the Past**. Learn about the famous men and women who shaped Alexandria on this entertaining tour with a mix of historical facts, fascinating stories, and a hint of the otherworldly. Tickets are $15 for adults. Dogs and children are free.

Mount Vernon Estate & Gardens
3200 Mount Vernon Memorial Highway
Alexandria, VA 22121
(703) 780-0011
www.mountvernon.org

Torpedo Factory Art Center

Unleash your inner artist at the **Torpedo Factory Art Center** in Alexandria. Take a leisurely stroll along the Potomac River waterfront and wander through this hub of artists' studios with your pooch. See the creative process and resulting artistic works of over 165 vendors in the open studio space. Purchase an original work of art, chat with your favorite artist about their methods and inspiration, or sign up for a class at The Art League School. Six galleries offer exhibition space for photography, fiber arts, enamel work, pottery and ceramic art. The building is open from 10:00 am to 6:00 pm daily, with extended hours on Thursdays. Leashed dogs are always welcome. The Torpedo Factory is located next to Alexandria's City Marina, where the **Potomac Riverboat Company** embarks on a 'Canine Cruise' several times a year. The 40-minute cruise costs $15 for adults and $9 for children. Dogs float for free.

Torpedo Factory Art Center
105 N Union Street
Alexandria, VA 22314
(703) 838-4565
www.torpedofactory.org

Where to Stay:

With unique interior design and vibrant colors throughout the space, the **Hotel Monaco** in Old Town Alexandria resembles a contemporary work of art. Make new friends at the nightly hosted wine hour, or watch a Saturday-night 'Dive In' movie at the indoor pool. Not to be left out—Fido can come, sit, and stay for the 'Doggie Yappy Hour' held on Tuesday and Thursday evenings from April through October. Dogs of any size are welcome for no additional fee.

Hotel Monaco Alexandria
480 King Street
Alexandria, VA 22314
(703) 549-6080
www.monaco-alexandria.com
Rates from $159/night

Where to Stay:

You and your four-legged friend can look forward to incredible waterfront vistas and spectacular sunsets during your stay at **Snug Harbor Marina** on Chincoteague Island. Relax in the beach chairs outside your cottage, plan a family cookout, or take Fido for a stroll down to the beachfront Tiki Bar. You can even rent a skiff or pontoon boat to explore more of the island together. Dogs of any size are welcome for an additional fee of $40 per stay.

Snug Harbor Marina
7536 East Side Road
Chincoteague Island, VA 23336
(757) 336-6176
www.tinyurl.com/ruff31
Rates from $99/night

Assateague Explorer

You and your pup can discover hidden Assateague on a 'Pony Express Nature Cruise' with **Assateague Explorer**. Departing from the Assateague Nature Centre on Chincoteague Island, the two-hour boat tour offers you a glimpse of Virginia's wild pony population, along with the chance to see dolphins, bald eagles, and other wildlife from the 40-foot vessel. Want to really immerse yourself in this wonderful ecosystem? Opt for a kayak rental or join the 3-hour guided kayak tour to get eye to eye with even more of the animals who inhabit these beautiful islands. Tours depart several times a day, but advance reservations are recommended, as they do sell out. Tickets are $43 for the boat tour and $55 for the kayak tour, with a $10 discount for children age 3-11. Kayak rentals start at $39 for a half day. Dogs ride for free on both tours and might even get to meet Captain Mark's beagle.

Assateague Explorer
The Assateague Nature Centre
7512 East Side Road
Chincoteague Island, VA 23336
(757) 336-5956
www.assateagueexplorer.com

Skyline Drive

Spanning the entire length of **Shenandoah National Park** from Front Royal to Waynesboro, the 105-mile **Skyline Drive** National Scenic Byway will give your dog a bird's eye view of the Blue Ridge Mountains in Virginia. This picturesque three-hour drive is wildly popular in the fall when the leaves are changing colors, but roadside rhododendron, trillium, azaleas, and buttercups put on a cheerful show throughout the year. Stop along the way at one of 75 scenic overlooks—most have trailheads that will provide a relatively easy hiking break for your four-legged friend. Of the 500 miles of trails in Shenandoah National Park, all but 20 miles are dog-friendly! The entrance fee is $10 to $15 per vehicle (depending on the season). Dog paddling is also an option with **Downriver Canoe Company**, which allows pets of any size on their paddling, hiking, and camping trips in the park. Short trips start at $49 per canoe.

Skyline Drive
US 340 & Skyline Drive
Front Royal, VA 22630
(540) 999-3500
www.visitskylinedrive.org

Where to Stay:

For a true cabin-in-the-woods getaway with sweeping views and unparalleled serenity, Shenandoah National Park offers a trio of pet-friendly properties: **Big Meadows Lodge, Skyland Resort**, and **Lewis Mountain Cabins**. All three locations allow two dogs of any size for an additional fee of $25 per pet, per night. Guests with pets can choose to 'ruff it' in a rustic cabin at Lewis Mountain or opt for a modern suite at Big Meadows Lodge and Skyland Resort.

Big Meadows Lodge
Shenandoah National Park
Mile 51.2 Skyline Drive
Luray, VA 22851
(801) 559-5070
www.goshenandoah.com
Rates from $132/night

Where to Stay:

Applewood Inn provides cozy rooms, fetching vistas, and a plethora of hiking trails and fishing spots on a 37-acre farm in Lexington. This tranquil paradise overlooking Buffalo Creek is also adjacent to **Douthat State Park** which has an additional 43 miles of dog-friendly hiking trails. Dogs of any size are welcome in the European Room, which has a private enclosed porch and hot tub. The pet fee is $20 for the first night and $10 for additional nights.

Applewood Inn
242 Tarn Beck Lane
Lexington, VA 24450
(800) 463-1902
www.applewoodbb.com
Rates from $145/night

Applewood Inn

Bring your dog to **Applewood Inn & Llama Trekking** in Lexington for a unique experience involving another furry four-legged species. Curious and adventurous llamas will escort you and your pooch on a two-hour trek along the mountain trails of eastern Virginia. The llamas are happy to tote any gear that you bring along, leaving your hands free for a camera or pair of binoculars. Tours take place year-round, with special wildflower and birding treks in the spring. A visit in autumn will inspire you with amazing views of the fall foliage. In winter, you can sip hot chocolate and enjoy the snow-capped mountain scenery. Morning treks depart on Saturdays, Mondays, and Thursdays between 9:30 am and 10:00 am. Tour rates are $30 per person, but overnight guests receive a $10 discount. Lunch is provided for an additional $8 charge. Dogs are welcome to accompany you on the trek for no additional fee.

Applewood Inn & Llama Trekking
242 Tarn Beck Lane
Lexington, VA 24450
(800) 463-1902
www.applewoodbb.com

Colonial Williamsburg

Take Rover on a revolutionary vacation with a visit to **Colonial Williamsburg**. As you explore the nation's largest living history museum, you'll meet dozens of costumed interpreters in period dress. Walk your pooch down the pedestrian-friendly streets lined with nearly 100 original buildings from the 18th century. Grab a bite to eat at the **Cheese Shop** on D.O.G. Street, where your pup can sample some Virginia ham on the outdoor patio. Dogs are welcome in exterior areas of Colonial Williamsburg but may not enter the buildings. If you plan your visit in advance, come for a 'Barkaeology Tour' at **Historic Jamestowne**. During these evening walking tours, held several times a year, an archaeologist will teach you about ongoing excavations at the 1607 James Fort and show you some of the artifacts uncovered there. Your dog will dig it. Tickets are $15 per person. Dogs are free, but reservations are required.

Colonial Williamsburg
101 Visitor Center Drive
Williamsburg, VA 23185
(757) 220-7645
www.colonialwilliamsburg.com

Where to Stay:

Stay in the heart of Colonial Williamsburg at either the opulent **Williamsburg Inn**, where dogs less than 50 lbs are welcome for a fee of $50 per night, or the more economical **Cascades Motel**, which allows dogs up to 70 lbs for no fee. The Cascades is somewhat of a 'secret' hotel in Colonial Williamsburg because it has no website or lobby. Guests (nearly all of whom have pets) are instructed to check in at the front desk of the adjacent Williamsburg Woodlands hotel.

Williamsburg Inn
136 Francis Street E
Williamsburg, VA 23185
(757) 220-7978
www.colonialwilliamsburg.com
Rates from $321/night

Where to Stay:

Give Fido his sea legs with a night on the *Lille Danser*. She'll gently rock him to sleep while moored to the dock at Eagle Harbor Marina in Bainbridge Island. Up to four guests can be accommodated in the boat's three comfortable sleeping berths. There are flush toilets and coin operated showers at the marina, and a light breakfast is provided in the morning. Dogs of any size are welcome for an additional fee of $20 per pet, per night.

Lille Danser Boat & Breakfast
Eagle Harbor Marina
5834 Ward Avenue NE
Bainbridge Island, WA 98110
(206) 786-7627
www.nwboatandbreakfast.com
Rates from $150/night

Lille Danser Boat & Breakfast

Enjoy an exciting twist on the charm of a bed and breakfast with a stay on the *Lille Danser* in Bainbridge Island. This unique 'Boat & Breakfast' package lets you sleep aboard the boat overnight, then try your hand at sailing the 50-foot gaff cutter on a two-hour trip across Puget Sound in the morning. Or, just sit back and enjoy the views of the Seattle skyline, Mount Rainier, and the Olympic Mountains while Fido is busy spotting seals, sea lions, and the occasional whale in the bay. Your host, Tami, is an experienced sailor and the City of Bainbridge Island Harbormaster. She will guide you and up to five other passengers on the trip, regale you with stories of the vessel's history, and provide tips on the best places to play and eat with your pup in the area. The sailing adventure costs $150 in addition to the standard nightly rate.

Lille Danser Boat & Breakfast
Eagle Harbor Marina
5834 Ward Avenue NE
Bainbridge Island, WA 98110
(206) 786-7627
www.nwboatandbreakfast.com

Iron Springs Resort

One of the lasting traditions at **Iron Springs Resort** in Copalis Beach is digging for razor clams with the family. Located in one of the best clam-digging areas along the Washington Coast, the resort offers easy access to these tasty creatures in the fall, winter, and early spring. All you need is a clamming shovel, container, and clamming license for each digger over the age of 15. Pick up all three at the resort's General Store, and let Fido help dig up your quota of these delicious shellfish at the beach. When your buckets are full, the resort's cleaning station and beachside fire pits make it easy to prepare your family's evening clambake. The following day, Fido can paddle through a 'Ghost Forest' at **Griffiths-Priday State Park** in Ocean Shores, or venture a bit farther to see some of the world's largest trees—topping 300 feet—in the **Quinault Rain Forest**.

Iron Springs Resort
3707 Highway 109
Copalis Beach, WA 98536
(360) 276-4230
www.ironspringsresort.com

Where to Stay:

Your overnight stay at **Iron Springs Resort** includes a well-appointed cabin, complete with a kitchen, fireplace or wood-burning stove, grill, deck, and wireless internet. Your pup will receive a tennis ball and special treat at check-in before having his picture snapped for the doggie display in the General Store. Dog bowls, towels, and a washing station are available in each cabin. Up to three dogs of any size are welcome for an additional fee of $20 per pet, per night.

Iron Springs Resort
3707 Highway 109
Copalis Beach, WA 98536
(360) 276-4230
www.ironspringsresort.com
Rates from $149/night

San Juan Island

Hop on board a **Washington State Ferry** in Anacortes for a trip to San Juan Island. When you arrive at Friday Harbor, ditch the car in favor of a 'Scoot Coupe' from **Susie's Mopeds**, which will serve as your transportation for the day. Two miles away, you'll find **Jackson's Beach**, where your dog will enjoy running in the sand. Continue on to **San Juan Island National Historical Park** to learn about the history of the island and the Pig War. Make a pit stop at **Pelindaba Lavender Farm** to let Fido roam the purple fields and try a lavender-flavored dog biscuit. Lastly, head over to **Lime Kiln State Park**—a 36-acre park where whales are commonly spotted between May and September. When you complete your loop around the island, refuel with an 'Amazingly Good Applewood Smoked Ham' sandwich on **The Market Chef's** ocean view deck. There'll be enough to share with your hungry hound!

Anacortes Ferry Terminal
2100 Ferry Terminal Road
Anacortes, WA 98221
(206) 464-6400
www.wsdot.com/ferries/schedule

Where to Stay:

If one day on Friday Harbor isn't enough, spend the night at **Earthbox Inn & Spa**. Located just four blocks from the Friday Harbor Ferry Landing, the property offers clean, modern accommodations in an ideal location. Enjoy complimentary use of the hotel's beach cruiser bikes to explore the charming island, schedule a hot stone massage, or relax in the heated indoor pool. Dogs of any size are welcome for an additional fee of $15 per pet, per night.

Earthbox Inn & Spa
410 Spring Street
Friday Harbor, WA 98250
(360) 378-4000
www.earthboxinn.com
Rates from $162/night

Where to Stay:

Extend your trip to Long Beach with a stay at the **Lighthouse Oceanfront Resort**. The property's one, two, and three bedroom townhouses are just steps from the pet-friendly beach. All units feature separate living areas, full kitchens, fireplaces, and private balconies. On-site amenities include an indoor pool, hot tub, fitness center, grill stations, and indoor tennis courts. Treats and pet towels are available in the lobby. Dogs of any size are welcome for an additional fee of $15 per pet, per night.

Lighthouse Oceanfront Resort
12417 Pacific Way
Long Beach, WA 98631
(360) 642-3622
www.lighthouseresort.net
Rates from $65/night

Discovery Trail

Make the trek to the Long Beach Peninsula for some fun in the sand and surf on over 28 miles of uninterrupted beach. Spend a day walking Fido in the footsteps of Lewis and Clark on the 8.5-mile **Discovery Trail**, a paved oceanfront pathway stretching from North Long Beach to Ilwaco. If you're there during winter, bring your binoculars for some great whale-watching opportunities. The North Head Lighthouse at **Cape Disappointment State Park** is the area's best viewing spot. With over 6.5 miles of hiking trails and a popular dog beach, the park is a great place to play fetch with your furry friend too. Day passes cost $10 per vehicle, and the park is open daily from 6:30 am to dusk. Plan ahead and visit Long Beach during the Doggie Olympic Games or Sand Flea Pet Parade. Both are held during summer and attract thousands of visitors and their pooches each year.

Discovery Trail
210 26th Street NW
Long Beach, WA 98631
(360) 642-2400
www.bringfido.com/attraction/11182

Discovery Bay Golf Course

Play a round of golf with your pup at the pet-friendly **Discovery Bay Golf Course** in Port Townsend. Located on the shores of beautiful Discovery Bay, this 18-hole marvel is Washington's oldest public golf course. Tee off and enjoy the day in the company of your furry friend surrounded by magnificent views of the Olympic and Cascade mountain ranges. Just make sure your well-mannered pooch stays on a leash. Green fees are $28 for adults and $10 for kids under 18. Seniors get a $4 discount. Early-bird and twilight rates are also available. After your round, make your way to **The Resort at Port Ludlow** for a delicious meal on the pet-friendly veranda of The Fireside Restaurant. Stretch your legs on one of the resort's pet-friendly hiking trails or rent a kayak for a day on the water. Dogs must be leashed at all times when exploring the resort's outdoor areas.

Discovery Bay Golf Course
7401 Cape George Road
Port Townsend, WA 98368
(360) 385-0704
www.discoverybaygolfcourse.com

Where to Stay:

The Resort at Port Ludlow is a boutique waterfront inn with 37 rooms and suites overlooking Ludlow Bay. Their staff loves dogs, and Fido is sure to be greeted with a warm welcome (and locally-made biscuit) at check-in. Guests with pets are provided a map of recommended hiking trails in the area, and there is a dog-friendly beach, restaurant, and marina located on site. Up to two dogs of any size are welcome for an additional fee of $35 per room, per stay.

The Resort at Port Ludlow
1 Heron Road
Port Ludlow, WA 98365
(360) 437-7000
www.portludlowresort.com
Rates from $139/night

Where to Stay:

If either you or your pup worked up an appetite at Ewe-topia, you won't go hungry at **Cedarbrook Lodge** in Seattle. The hotel offers around-the-clock complimentary snacks (like yogurt, string cheese, and mini-pints of ice cream) in the communal 'Living Rooms' of each building. There is also a 'Puppy Pantry' room service menu for Fido with dishes like Pasture-Finished Chicken and Chunky Country Meatloaf. One dog up to 50 lbs is welcome for an additional fee of $50 per stay.

Cedarbrook Lodge
18525 36th Avenue S
Seattle, WA 98188
(206) 901-9268
www.cedarbrooklodge.com
Rates from $166/night

Ewe-topia Herd Dog Training

Your dog will think he's died and gone to heaven at **Ewe-topia Herd Dog Training** in Roy. Located near Seattle, Ewe-topia allows dogs of all shapes and sizes to try their paws at sheep herding. The owners, Joe and Linda, are animal behavior experts who can quickly assess your pooch's temperament and match him up to the appropriate livestock—typically three sheep or five ducks. When Fido steps into the ring for the first time, he'll have the time of his life chasing the furry or feathered animals around the ring. But this challenging exercise actually provides an important lesson in socialization as well. You may even notice a difference in your dog's manners after the first visit! All lessons are first-come, first-served on weekends and weekday nights (except Monday and Friday). The price is $11 to $14 per session, and new students are asked to call before their first visit.

Ewe-topia Herd Dog Training
6311 288th Street S
Roy, WA 98580
(253) 843-2929
www.ewe-topia.com

Kenmore Air

For a bird's-eye view of Seattle, take a 'Scenic Flight Tour' with **Kenmore Air**. You and your canine companion will enjoy stunning views of the Seattle skyline, Elliot Bay, and Lake Union's famous houseboat community on a 20-minute flightseeing adventure. Tours start at $99 per person. Lap dogs are welcome for no additional fee, but a seat must be purchased for dogs over 25 lbs. You can also charter the entire airplane and land on a remote island for a gourmet meal catered by **Northwest Floatplane Picnics**. If you are visiting Seattle on a Sunday, bring Fido on **Seattle Ferry Service**'s hourly 'Ice Cream Cruise' for a closer look at Lake Union's houseboats. Tickets are $11 for adults and free for dogs. Should you miss the ferry ride, you can still explore Lake Union in a classic wooden row boat rental from the **Center for Wooden Boats** for $25 per hour.

Kenmore Air
950 Westlake Avenue N
Seattle, WA 98109
(866) 435-9524
www.kenmoreair.com

Where to Stay:

After your aerial adventure, relax at the modern **Hotel 1000**, where your pup will be pampered with treats, toys, and a plush doggie bed. One dog under 50 lbs is welcome for an additional fee of $40 per stay. Guests traveling with larger dogs should opt for a stay at the **Hotel Sorrento**. This historic Seattle icon features luxurious guest suites dripping with European style. Dogs of any size are welcome for an additional fee of $60 per stay.

Hotel 1000
1000 1st Avenue
Seattle, WA 98104
(206) 957-1000
www.hotel1000seattle.com
Rates from $197/night

Where to Stay:

After a full day of cross-country skiing, Fido can relax in one of three dog-friendly **Rendez-vous Huts**. Located along the groomed trails, these huts offer ski-in, ski-out access along with full kitchens, cooking utensils, wood stove heaters, sleeping pads, propane lights, and out-houses. Freight haulers will sup-ply your hut with personal items for an additional $85 fee. Each hut can accommodate up to eight people. Dogs are welcome for no extra cost and even get their own bed!

Rendezvous Huts
Cub Creek Road
Winthrop, WA 98862
(509) 996-8100
www.rendezvoushuts.com
Rates from $100/night

Methow Valley Sports Trails

If you and your pup are avid outdoor adven-turers, you will love a trip to **Methow Valley Sports Trails** near Winthrop at any time of year. In spring, summer and fall, you can hike the trail system for breathtaking scenery, bird-watching, and wildlife viewing. But the real fun starts with the winter's first snow! Fido is wel-come to join you off-leash as you explore 25 miles of superb Nordic ski trails. Practice your skills to prepare for the 'Doggie Dash' event held every February, where dogs and their humans ski a short loop together in costume. Come to the trails for a day, or stay overnight in one of three dog-friendly **Rendezvous Huts**. All Rendezvous ski trails require the purchase of a day-use pass at the MVSTA office. Passes cost $22 for adults and $5 for dogs. No pass is needed for the Lunachick and Big Valley trails, which are also dog-friendly.

Methow Valley Sports Trails
309 Riverside Avenue
Winthrop, WA 98862
(509) 996-3287
www.mvsta.com

Warehouse Wine District

Located just 30 minutes from Seattle, the town of Woodinville is home to more than 90 wineries and tasting rooms that showcase the fine wines produced in Washington's Columbia Valley—and most of them are dog-friendly! Though you won't find any picturesque vineyards near the **Warehouse Wine District**, this industrial area has the largest concentration of tasting rooms in the state. Most are open on weekends from noon to 5:00 pm. On the third Thursday of each month, the vitners also roll up their bay doors for a 'Wine Walk' from 4:00 pm to 8:00 pm. For $25 per person, dog-loving vinophiles get 15 tasting tickets and a souvenir glass to sample the evening's featured small-batch wines. Monthly themes such as 'Spring Barrel Tasting' or 'Chocolate and Cheese' make each walk unique. It's always free to B.Y.O.D. (Bring Your Own Dog), and you can save $5 if you bring your own glass.

Warehouse Wine District
144th Avenue NE
Woodinville, WA 98072
(425) 208-2770
www.woodwarewine.com

Where to Stay:

Foodies and vinophiles will love spending a relaxing weekend at the **Willows Lodge**. Located a stone's throw from some of Washington's finest vineyards, this luxurious Woodinville hotel also features world-class fine dining. In the morning, you'll see chefs from the Barking Frog restaurant harvesting ingredients from the herb garden for their evening tasting menu. For a special treat, let Fido choose a 'Yappatizer' from the doggie room service menu. Dogs of any size are welcome for an additional fee of $35 per stay.

Willows Lodge
14580 NE 145th Street
Woodinville, WA 98072
(425) 424-3900
www.willowslodge.com
Rates from $197/night

Where to Stay:

Located on the shores of Stonewall Jackson Lake, **Stonewall Resort** is a charming Adirondack-style lodge in Roanoke. Enjoy spectacular lake, mountain, or golf course views as you relax in your oversized room, or head outdoors to explore 1,900 acres of woodlands with your pooch. The surrounding state park has 16 miles of dog-friendly hiking trails, and kayak rentals are always complimentary for resort guests (and their pets). Up to two dogs under 25 lbs are welcome for no additional fee.

Stonewall Resort
940 Resort Drive
Roanoke, WV 26447
(304) 269-7400
www.stonewallresort.com
Rates from $159/night

Trans-Allegheny Lunatic Asylum

You'll be glad to have Fido by your side as you take a spine-chilling tour of the historic **Trans-Allegheny Lunatic Asylum** in Weston. A working facility from 1864 to 1994, the asylum was intended as a sanctuary for those suffering from mental illness. However, ever-changing definitions of 'humane treatment' led to a number of experimental procedures being performed here over the years. A costumed tour guide will tell you all about them as she escorts your group around the expansive building. Small dogs that can be carried are permitted to join you on tours at any time. Larger, well-behaved dogs are permitted with prior management approval. The asylum is open annually from late March to early November. Tours are offered several times daily (except Mondays). Rates start at $10 per person for first floor tours. If you want to tour all four floors, the admission fee is $30 per person.

Trans-Allegheny Lunatic Asylum
71 Asylum Drive
Weston, WV 26452
(304) 269-5070
www.talawv.com

American Folklore Theatre

Door County's **American Folklore Theatre** brings original musical theatre to the dogs! All summer long, the professional non-profit theatre company performs a variety of Wisconsin-centric, family-friendly musicals in the outdoor amphitheater at Peninsula State Park in Fish Creek. Your pup is welcome to take in one of the shows, which are offered nightly except Sundays, from mid-June through August. Dogs aren't allowed to sing along with the show, so guests with pets are simply asked to find a spot for Spot at the back of the amphitheater (in case you need to make a quick exit). Bring a picnic to enjoy during the show, or purchase snacks and beverages at the concession stand. Average temperatures can dip into the 50s at night, so wear layers and bring a blanket for your pooch. Ticket prices are $19 for adults, $9 for teens, $6 for children ages 3-12, and free for dogs.

American Folklore Theatre
Peninsula State Park
10169 Shore Road
Fish Creek, WI 54212
(920) 854-6117
www.folkloretheatre.com

Where to Stay:

Located just a short drive from Peninsula State Park, the **Edgewater Resort** is nestled on a private shoreline overlooking Wisconsin's beautiful Eagle Harbor in Ephraim. Choose a one or two bedroom cottage with a kitchenette, gas fireplace, and private entry for a cozy and relaxing stay. When the sun goes down, bring Fido to the nightly 'Fish Boil' at the resort's **Old Post Office Restaurant**. Dogs of any size are welcome for an additional fee of $15 per pet, per night.

Edgewater Resort
10040 Water Street
Ephraim, WI 54211
(920) 854-2734
www.edge-waterresort.com
Rates from $139/night

Where to Stay:

Motorcycle enthusiasts will be in hog heaven at the **Iron Horse Hotel**, a boutique property geared toward bikers and their furry friends. Guests arriving in Milwaukee on two wheels will appreciate the covered motorcycle parking, self-service bike wash, and industrial loft-style guest rooms designed with boot benches and custom hooks for hanging leathers. Dogs of any size are welcome for an additional $50 fee. Fido can join you for dinner at The Yard or order a meal from the doggie room service menu.

The Iron Horse Hotel
500 W Florida Street
Milwaukee, WI 53204
(888) 543-4766
www.theironhorsehotel.com
Rates from $188/night

Milwaukee Boat Line

The **Milwaukee Boat Line** invites canines to join their crew for a 90-minute cruise down the Milwaukee River to Lake Michigan. Departing from the **Milwaukee RiverWalk** in the historic Third Ward district, the company's popular sightseeing tour combines history and trivia with gorgeous views of the city. Live narration is provided by a certified Historic Milwaukee Guide and snacks, soft drinks, beer, and cocktails are available for purchase. Tours are offered several times a day from early May through the end of September. There's also a 'Happy Hour' cruise at sundown with lively music and drink specials on the menu. Prices start at $15 for adults and $8 for children. Well-behaved dogs are welcome aboard for no additional fee. After the tour, enjoy a leisurely walk on the scenic three-mile RiverWalk with your pooch or head straight to **Estabrook Beer Garden** to wash down a bratwurst with a pint of Milwaukee's Best.

Milwaukee Boat Line
101 W Michigan Street
Milwaukee, WI 53203
(414) 294-9450
www.mkeboat.com

Justin Trails Resort

With over 200 acres of open fields and forests, your pooch will have plenty of space for off-leash frolicking at the **Justin Trails Resort** in Sparta. Fido can fetch Frisbees on the 18-basket championship disc golf course or go for a hike on the property's 10-mile trail system with resident Siberian huskies, Heidi and George. In the winter, the same trails can be enjoyed on a snowshoeing or skijoring adventure. Not sure how to skijor? The owners, Don and Donna Justin, can give your dog a private lesson. In less than an hour, he'll be pulling you along the 3/4-mile groomed 'Dog Loop' on skis! Sparta is also home to the nation's first Rails-to-Trails bicycle path. To ride the 32-mile **Elroy-Sparta Trail** with your pup, rent a bike and dog cart from the **Kendall Depot** for $38 per day. A $4 trail pass is also required for all bikers over 16 years old.

Justin Trails Resort
7452 Kathryn Avenue
Sparta, WI 54656
(608) 269-4522
www.justintrails.com

Where to Stay:

With accommodations ranging from primitive campsites to deluxe cabins with full kitchens, **Justin Trails Resort** offers a lodging option for everyone's budget. Rates include most on-site activities and a hearty four-course breakfast featuring organic eggs, pancakes, and Donna's famous homemade granola. Dogs of any size are welcome for an additional fee of $15 per pet, per night. Your pups are free to explore the resort's fields and forests off-leash, but they must be leashed around the main lodge and cabins.

Justin Trails Resort
7452 Kathryn Avenue
Sparta, WI 54656
(608) 269-4522
www.justintrails.com
Rates from $115/night

Where to Stay:

After watching a fellow dog leap through the air at Standing Rock, Fido will be glad to have all four paws on the ground at **Baker's Sunset Bay Resort** in Wisconsin Dells. This family-friendly resort on Lake Delton features a sandy beach, indoor and outdoor pools, and a nightly bonfire. Rowboats and kayaks are available free of charge. Up to two dogs of any size are welcome for an additional fee of $10 per pet, per night. Treats are provided at check-in.

Baker's Sunset Bay Resort
921 Canyon Road
Wisconsin Dells, WI 53965
(608) 254-8406
www.sunsetbayresort.com
Rates from $78/night

Dells Boat Tours

Shaped by an ancient glacier, the Wisconsin Dells is a five-mile-long gorge on the Wisconsin River with incredible sandstone cliffs towering as high as 100 feet in the air. These magnificent rock formations are best seen from the water on a two-hour scenic river cruise with **Dells Boat Tours**. The company offers tours of both the Upper and Lower Dells, but dog lovers should definitely choose the Upper Dells Boat Tour. Fido will have a chance to stretch his legs at the mysterious Witches Gulch and witness a specially trained dog leap over a five-foot chasm between two cliffs at Stand Rock. The demonstration is a tribute to the world's first stop-action photo taken by famous Dells photographer H.H. Bennett in 1888. Tickets are $25 for adults and $13 for children. Dogs of all sizes ride for free, provided there is room on the boat. Tours depart several times daily from April through October.

Dells Boat Tours
107 Broadway Avenue
Wisconsin Dells, WI 53965
(608) 254-8555
www.dellsboats.com

Cody Wyoming Adventures

The folks at **Cody Wyoming Adventures** have been rafting the Shoshone River, just outside of Yellowstone National Park, for more than thirty years. If you'd like to introduce your furry family member to whitewater rafting, the two-hour Shoshone Canyon trip is a good place to start. Fido will get to run four rapids and float through a golden eagle nesting area before completing the seven-mile course. Half-day and full-day trips are available for more experienced paddlers. Landlubbers will love the company's Red Canyon Wild Mustang Tour. On this two-hour guided bus trip, you'll venture deep into the McCullough Peaks area, where wild mustangs still run free. Rates start at $33 per person for both tours. Top off your day in the Wild West by sharing a prime rib with your pup at **Buffalo Bill's Restaurant & Saloon**, located at the famous Irma Hotel, which was built by Buffalo Bill Cody in 1902.

Cody Wyoming Adventures
1119 12th Street
Cody, WY 82414
(307) 587-6988
www.codywyomingadventures.com

Where to Stay:

After a full day of activities in cowboy country, **The Cody** is a great place to unwind. The hotel's friendly staff will welcome both you and Fido with cookies upon arrival. Enjoy them by the fireplace, or retreat to the Jacuzzi in your guest room. Want s'more? You'll find marshmallows, chocolate bars, and graham crackers outside by the fire pit too! Up to two dogs of any size are welcome for an additional fee of $18 per pet, per night.

The Cody Hotel
232 W Yellowstone Avenue
Cody, WY 82414
(307) 587-5915
www.thecody.com
Rates from $110/night

DIRECTORY

ALABAMA
ATTRACTIONS
Hudson Marina at Skull Harbor
4575 S Wilson Boulevard
Orange Beach, AL 36561
(251) 981-4127
www.hudsonmarina.net
pg. 12

Russell Cave National Monument
3729 County Road 98
Bridgeport, AL 35740
(256) 495-2672
www.nps.gov/ruca
pg. 11

HOTELS
Staybridge Suites Gulf Shores
3947 State Highway 59
Gulf Shores, AL 36542
(251) 975-1030
www.tinyurl.com/ruff01
pg. 12

ALASKA
HOTELS
3 Dog Night Hostel
5972 Richardson Highway
Fairbanks, AK 99714
(907) 590-8207
www.3dognighthostel.com
pg. 13

ARIZONA
ATTRACTIONS
A Day in the West
252 N Highway 89-A
Sedona, AZ 86336
(928) 282-4320
www.adayinthewest.com
pg. 16

Glen Canyon National Recreation Area
PO Box 1507
Page, AZ 86040
(928) 608-6200
www.nps.gov/glca
pg. 14

Ken's Creekside Restaurant
251 Highway 179
Sedona, AZ 86336
(928) 282-1705
www.kenscreekside.com
pg. 16

McCormick-Stillman Railroad Park
7301 E Indian Bend Road
Scottsdale, AZ 85250
(480) 312-2312
www.therailroadpark.com
pg. 15

McDowell Sonoran Preserve
18333 N Thompson Peak Parkway
Scottsdale, AZ 85259
(480) 998-7971
www.mcdowellsonoran.org
pg. 15

HOTELS
El Portal Sedona
95 Portal Lane
Sedona, AZ 86336
(800) 313-0017
www.elportalsedona.com
pg. 16

FireSky Resort & Spa
4925 N Scottsdale Road
Scottsdale, AZ 85251
(480) 945-7666
www.fireskyresort.com
pg. 15

Lake Powell Resort & Marina
100 Lake Shore Drive
Page, AZ 86040
(928) 645-2433
www.lakepowell.com
pg. 14

ARKANSAS
ATTRACTIONS
Belle of Hot Springs Riverboat
5200 Central Highway 7 S
Hot Springs, AR 71913
(501) 525-4438
www.belleriverboat.com
pg. 17

Garvan Woodland Gardens
550 Arkridge Road
Hot Springs, AR 71913
(501) 262-9300
www.garvangardens.org
pg. 17

HOTELS
Lookout Point Lakeside Inn
104 Lookout Circle
Hot Springs, AR 71913
(501) 525-6155
www.lookoutpointinn.com
pg. 17

CALIFORNIA
ATTRACTIONS
17-Mile Drive
Highway 1 & Highway 68
Carmel, CA 93923
(800) 654-9300
www.bringfido.com/attraction/49
pg. 22

Abalonetti's Seafood Trattoria
57 Fisherman's Wharf
Monterey, CA 93940
(831) 373-1851
www.abalonettimonterey.com
pg. 37

Adventure Center
10001 Minaret Road
Mammoth Lakes, CA 93546
(800) 626-6684
www.bringfido.com/attraction/11344
pg. 35

Aqua Adventures Kayak Center
1548 Quivira Way
San Diego, CA 92109
(619) 523-9577
www.aqua-adventures.com
pg. 42

Arroyo Burro Beach
2981 Cliff Drive
Santa Barbara, CA 93109
(805) 687-3714
www.bringfido.com/attraction/574
pg. 45

Asilomar State Park
800 Asilomar Avenue
Pacific Grove, CA 93950
(831) 372-8016
www.visitasilomar.com
pg. 22

Avila Valley Barn
560 Avila Beach Drive
San Luis Obispo, CA 93405
(805) 595-2816
www.avilavalleybarn.com
pg. 44

Baker Beach
1504 Pershing Drive
San Francisco, CA 94129
(415) 561-4323
www.bringfido.com/attraction/542
pg. 43

Balboa Island Ferry
410 S Bay Front
Balboa Island, CA 92662
(949) 673-1070
www.balboaislandferry.com
pg. 19

Blue Angel Café
1132 Ski Run Boulevard
South Lake Tahoe, CA 96150
(530) 544-6544
www.theblueangelcafe.com
pg. 49

Bluerush Boardsports
400 Harbor Drive
Sausalito, CA 94965
(415) 339-9112
www.bluerushboardsports.com
pg. 48

Bouchon Bakery
6528 Washington Street
Yountville, CA 94599
(707) 944-2253
www.bouchonbakery.com/yountville
pg. 39

Bronson Canyon Trail at Griffith Park
3200 Canyon Drive
Los Angeles, CA 90068
(323) 666-5046
www.bringfido.com/attraction/11146
pg. 33

Bungee America
Bridge to Nowhere Trailhead
Camp Bonita Road
Azusa, CA 91702
(310) 322-8892
www.bungeeamerica.com
pg. 18

Cannery Row
649 Cannery Row
Monterey, CA 93940
(831) 649-6690
www.canneryrow.com
pg. 37

Carmel Beach
Ocean Avenue & Scenic Road
Carmel, CA 93921
(831)620-2020
www.bringfido.com/attraction/206
pg. 23

Catch a Canoe & Bicycles Too
1 S Big River Road
Mendocino, CA 95460
(707) 937-0273
www.catchacanoe.com
pg. 36

City to the Sea Trail
7001 Ontario Road
San Luis Obispo, CA 93405
(805) 781-5930
www.bringfido.com/attraction/11145
pg. 44

Coronado Dog Beach
200 Ocean Boulevard
Coronado, CA 92118
(619) 522-7300
www.bringfido.com/attraction/508
pg. 25

Coronado Surfing Academy
116 B Avenue
Coronado, CA 92118
(619) 293-3883
www.coronadosurfing.com
pg. 25

Crissy Field
1199 East Beach
San Francisco, CA 94129
(415) 561-4323
www.bringfido.com/attraction/2237
pg. 43

DeeTours of Santa Barbara
1 Garden Street
Santa Barbara, CA 93101
(805) 448-8425
www.deetoursofsb.com
pg. 47

Devils Postpile National Monument
Ranger Station & Trailhead
1 Reds Circle
Mammoth Lakes, CA 93546
(760) 934-2289
www.nps.gov/depo
pg. 35

Dirty Dog Wash
504 Main Street
Huntington Beach, CA 92648
(714) 960-7002
www.dirtydogwash.com
pg. 31

Dog Beach Dog Wash
4933 Voltaire Street
San Diego, CA 92107
(619) 523-1700
www.dogwash.com
pg. 25

Douglas Family Preserve
Medcliff Road & Selrose Lane
Santa Barbara, CA 93101
(805) 564-5418
www.bringfido.com/attraction/573
pg. 45

Fiesta Island Park
1590 E Mission Bay Drive
San Diego, CA 92109
(619) 525-8213
www.bringfido.com/attraction/104
pg. 42

Fish
350 Harbor Drive
Sausalito, CA 94965
(415) 331-3474
www.331fish.com
pg. 48

Fisherman's Beach
3915 Avila Beach Drive
Avila Beach, CA 93424
(805) 595-5400
www.bringfido.com/attraction/11031
pg. 44

Forge in the Forest
Junipero Street & 5th Avenue
Carmel, CA 93921
(831) 624-2233
www.forgeintheforest.com
pg. 23

Fountain of Woof
Carmel Plaza
Ocean Avenue & Mission Street
Carmel, CA 93921
(831) 624-1385
www.carmelplaza.com
pg. 23

Fun Zone Boat Company
600 E Edgewater Avenue
Balboa Island, CA 92661
(949) 673-0240
www.funzoneboats.com
pg. 19

Garland Ranch Regional Park
700 W Carmel Valley Road
Carmel, CA 93923
(831) 372-3196
www.bringfido.com/attraction/205
pg. 24

Golden Gate National Park
Marin Headlands Visitor Center
948 Fort Barry
Mill Valley, CA 94941
(415) 331-1540
www.nps.gov/goga
pg. 48

Hollywood Walk of Fame
7018 Hollywood Boulevard
Los Angeles, CA 90028
(323) 469-8311
www.walkoffame.com
pg. 34

Huntington Dog Beach
100 Goldenwest Street
Huntington Beach, CA 92647
(714) 841-8644
www.dogbeach.org
pg. 31

Knight Wine Tours
1436 2nd Street
Napa, CA 94558
(707) 738-4500
www.knightwinetours.com
pg. 39

Lake Hollywood Park
3204 Canyon Lake Drive
Los Angeles, CA 90068
(323) 913-4688
www.bringfido.com/attraction/11147
pg. 33

MacDuff's Public House
1041 Fremont Avenue
South Lake Tahoe, CA 96150
(530) 542-8777
www.macduffspub.com
pg. 49

Mammoth Mountain Scenic Gondola
10001 Minaret Road
Mammoth Lakes, CA 93546
(760) 934-2571
www.bringfido.com/attraction/10593
pg. 35

Mendocino Coast Botanical Gardens
18220 N Highway One
Fort Bragg, CA 95437
(707) 964-4352
www.gardenbythesea.org
pg. 27

Monterey Bay Whale Watch
84 Fisherman's Wharf
Monterey, CA 93940
(831) 375-4658
www.montereybaywhalewatch.com
pg. 37

Original Dog Beach
5199 Brighton Avenue
San Diego, CA 92167
(619) 515-4400
www.originaldogbeachsandiego.com
pg. 25

The Patio on Lamont Street
4445 Lamont Street
San Diego, CA 92109
(858) 412-4648
www.thepatioonlamont.com
pg. 42

Presidio of San Francisco
103 Montgomery Street
San Francisco, CA 94129
(415) 561-4323
www.nos.gov/prsf
pg. 43

Pussy & Pooch
4818 E 2nd Street
Long Beach, CA 90803
(562) 434-7700
www.pussyandpooch.com
pg. 32

Roaring Camp Railroads
5401 Graham Hill Road
Felton, CA 95018
(831) 335-4484
www.roaringcamp.com
pg. 26

Rosie's Dog Beach
5000 E Ocean Boulevard
Long Beach, CA 90802
(562) 570-3100
www.hautedogs.org/beach.html
pg. 32

Runyon Canyon Park
2000 N Fuller Avenue
Los Angeles, CA 90046
(323) 666-5046
www.bringfido.com/attraction/50
pg. 34

Russian River Adventures
20 Healdsburg Avenue
Healdsburg, CA 95448
(707) 433-5599
www.russianriveradventures.com
pg. 29

Skunk Train
100 W Laurel Street
Fort Bragg, CA 95437
(707) 964-6371
www.skunktrain.com
pg. 28

Squaw Valley Aerial Tram
1960 Squaw Valley Road
Olympic Valley, CA 96146
(800) 403-0206
www.bringfido.com/attraction/10404
pg. 40

Tahoe Sport Fishing
900 Ski Run Boulevard
South Lake Tahoe, CA 96150
(530) 541-5448
www.tahoesportfishing.com
pg. 49

Top of the Sierra Café
Gondola Building on Summit
Mammoth Lakes, CA 93546
(760) 934-2571
www.bringfido.com/restaurant/11922
pg. 35

Truckee River Rafting
175 River Road
Tahoe City, CA 96145
(530) 583-1111
www.truckeeriverrafting.com
pg. 40

Zimzala Restaurant
500 E Pacific Coast Highway
Huntington Beach, CA 92648
(714) 960-5050
www.restaurantzimzala.com
pg. 31

HOTELS

Ace Hotel & Swim Club
701 E Palm Canyon Drive
Palm Springs, CA 92264
(760) 325-9900
www.acehotel.com/palmsprings
pg. 41

Balboa Bay Resort
1221 West Coast Highway
Newport Beach, CA 92663
(949) 645-5000
www.balboabayresort.com
pg. 19

Bardessono
6526 Yount Street
Yountville, CA 94599
(707) 204-6000
www.bardessono.com
pg. 39

Beach House Inn
320 W Yanonali Street
Santa Barbara, CA 93101
(805) 966-1126
www.thebeachhouseinn.com
pg. 45

Big Basin Redwoods State Park
21600 Big Basin Way
Boulder Creek, CA 95006
(831) 338-4745
www.bigbasintentcabins.com
pg. 26

Calistoga Ranch
580 Lommel Road
Calistoga, CA 94515
(707) 254-2800
www.calistogaranch.com
pg. 21

Carmel Valley Ranch
1 Old Ranch Road
Carmel, CA 93923
(831) 625-9500
www.carmelvalleyranch.com
pg. 24

Cavallo Point
601 Murray Circle
Sausalito, CA 94965
(415) 339-4700
www.cavallopoint.com
pg. 48

Cypress Inn
Lincoln Street & 7th Avenue
Carmel, CA 93921
(831) 624-3871
www.cypress-inn.com
pg. 23

El Encanto by Orient-Express
800 Alvarado Place
Santa Barbara, CA 93103
(805) 845-5800
www.elencanto.com
pg. 47

Fireside Lodge
515 Emerald Bay Road
South Lake Tahoe, CA 96150
(530) 544-5515
www.tahoefiresidelodge.com
pg. 49

h2hotel Healdsburg
219 Healdsburg Avenue
Healdsburg, CA 95448
(707) 431-2202
www.h2hotel.com
pg. 29

Healdsburg Inn on the Plaza
112 Matheson Street
Healdsburg, CA 95448
(707) 433-6991
www.healdsburginn.com
pg. 29

Hotel Indigo Gaslamp Quarter
509 9th Avenue
San Diego, CA 92101
(619) 727-4000
www.hotelinsd.com
pg. 25

The Inn at Schoolhouse Creek
7051 N Highway One
Little River, CA 95456
(707) 937-5525
www.schoolhousecreek.com
pg. 28

Inn at the Presidio
42 Moraga Avenue
San Francisco, CA 94129
(415) 800-7356
www.innatthepresidio.com
pg. 43

Little River Inn
7901 N Highway One
Little River, CA 95456
(707) 937-5942
www.littleriverinn.com
pg. 27

Loews Coronado Bay Resort
4000 Coronado Bay Road
Coronado, CA 92118
(619) 424-4000
www.tinyurl.com/ruff03
pg. 25

Loews Hollywood Hotel
1755 N Highland Avenue
Hollywood, CA 90028
(323) 856-1200
www.tinyurl.com/ruff04
pg. 34

Luv San Diego Surf
4439 Lamont Street
San Diego, CA 92109
(858) 230-6682
www.luv-surf.com
pg. 42

Pacific Edge Hotel
647 S Coast Highway
Laguna Beach, CA 92651
(949) 281-5709
www.pacificedgehotel.com
pg. 19

Pacific Gardens Inn
701 Asilomar Boulevard
Pacific Grove, CA 93950
(831) 646-9414
www.pacificgardensinn.com
pg. 22

Pismo Lighthouse Suites
2411 Price Street
Pismo Beach, CA 93449
(805) 773-2411
www.pismolighthousesuites.com
pg. 44

PlumpJack Squaw Valley Inn
1920 Squaw Valley Road
Olympic Valley, CA 96146
(530) 583-1576
www.tinyurl.com/ruff05
pg. 40

PodShare Hollywood Lofts
1617 Cosmo Street
Los Angeles, CA 90028
(310) 800-6696
www.thehollywoodloft.com
pg. 33

Portola Hotel & Spa
2 Portola Plaza
Monterey, CA 93940
(800) 342-4295
www.portolahotel.com
pg. 37

The Queen Mary
1126 Queens Highway
Long Beach, CA 90802
(800) 437-2934
www.queenmary.com
pg. 32

SeaCrest OceanFront Hotel
2241 Price Street
Pismo Beach, CA 93449
(805) 773-4608
www.seacrestpismo.com
pg. 44

Shorebreak Hotel
500 E Pacific Coast Highway
Huntington Beach, CA 92648
(714) 861-4470
www.shorebreakhotel.com
pg. 31

Stanford Inn
44850 Comptche Ukiah Road
Mendocino, CA 95460
(707) 937-5615
www.stanfordinn.com
pg. 36

Westin Monache Resort
50 Hillside Drive
Mammoth Lakes, CA 93546
(760) 934-0400
www.westinmammoth.com
pg. 35

Wigwam Motel
2728 Foothill Boulevard
San Bernardino, CA 92410
(909) 875-3005
www.wigwammotel.com
pg. 18

COLORADO
ATTRACTIONS

Crazy Mountain Brewing Company
439 Edwards Access Road
Edwards, CO 81632
(970) 926-3009
www.crazymountainbrewery.com
pg. 55

Garden of the Gods
1805 N 30th Street
Colorado Springs, CO 80904
(719) 634-6666
www.gardenofgods.com
pg. 50

Mountain Tails
307 E Colorado Avenue
Telluride, CO 81435
(970) 369-4240
www.mountaintails.com
pg. 54

Skijor-n-More
PO Box 1875
Silverthorne, CO 80498
(970) 406-0158
www.skijornmore.com
pg. 53

The Steaming Bean
221 W Colorado Avenue
Telluride, CO 81435
(970) 369-5575
www.thesteamingbean.com
pg. 54

Telluride Gondola
W San Juan Avenue & S Oak Street
Telluride, CO 81435
(970) 728-3041
www.bringfido.com/attraction/10277
pg. 54

Vail Farmers' Market & Art Show
141 E Meadow Drive
Vail, CO 81657
(970) 401-3320
www.vailfarmersmarket.com
pg. 55

Vail Nature Center
601 Vail Valley Drive
Vail, CO 81657
(970) 479-2291
www.vailrec.com/nature.cfm
pg. 55

HOTELS
The Broadmoor
1 Lake Avenue
Colorado Springs, CO 80906
(719) 577-5775
www.broadmoor.com
pg. 50

Devils Thumb Ranch
3530 County Highway 83
Tabernash, CO 80478
(970) 726-5632
www.devilsthumbranch.com
pg. 53

Mountain Lodge at Telluride
457 Mountain Village Boulevard
Telluride, CO 81435
(970) 369-5000
www.tinyurl.com/ruff06
pg. 54

Ritz-Carlton Bachelor Gulch
130 Daybreak Ridge
Avon, CO 81620
(970) 748-6200
www.tinyurl.com/ruff07
pg. 55

Sundance Trail Guest Ranch
17931 Red Feather Lakes Road
Red Feather Lakes, CO 80545
(970) 224-1222
www.sundancetrail.com
pg. 51

CONNECTICUT
ATTRACTIONS
Mystic Seaport
75 Greenmanville Avenue
Mystic, CT 06355
(860) 572-5302
www.mysticseaport.org
pg. 57

HOTELS
Harbour Inne & Cottages
15 Edgemont Street
Mystic, CT 06355
(860) 572-9253
www.harbourinne-cottage.com
pg. 57

Saybrook Point Inn & Spa
2 Bridge Street
Old Saybrook, CT 06475
(860) 395-2000
www.saybrook.com
pg. 57

DELAWARE
ATTRACTIONS
Delaware Family Fishing
Anglers Marina
400 Anglers Road
Lewes, DE 19958
(302) 430-3414
www.delawarefamilyfishing.com
pg. 58

HOTELS
Homestead at Rehoboth
35060 Warrington Road
Rehoboth Beach, DE 19971
(302) 226-7625
www.homesteadrehoboth.com
pg. 58

DISTRICT OF COLUMBIA
ATTRACTIONS
DC by Foot
15th & Constitution Avenue NW
Washington, DC 20560
(202) 370-1830
www.freetoursbyfoot/dc
pg. 59

Discover DC Pedicab Tours
3 Washington Circle NW
Washington, DC 20037
(202) 656-3593
www.discoverdctours.com
pg. 59

HOTELS
The Jefferson
1200 16th Street NW
Washington, DC 20036
(202) 448-2300
www.jeffersondc.com
pg. 59

FLORIDA
ATTRACTIONS
Airboat Nature Tours
14400 Reese Drive
Lake Wales, FL 33898
(863) 696-0313
www.airboatnaturetours.com
pg. 66

Art Deco Tours
Collins Avenue & 10th Street
Miami Beach, FL 33139
(305) 218-9952
www.artdecotours.com
pg. 67

Captain Gill's River Cruises
501 Bay City Road
Apalachicola, FL 32320
(850) 370-0075
www.captgill.com
pg. 60

Crab Island Cruises
US 98 at Destin Bridge
Destin, FL 32541
(850) 685-7027
www.crabislandcruises.com
pg. 62

Dockside Watersports
288 Harbor Boulevard
Destin, FL 32541
(850) 428-3313
www.boatrentalsindestin.com
pg. 62

Florida Manatee Adventures
2880 N Seabreeze Point
Crystal River, FL 34429
(352) 476-7556
www.floridamanateeadventures.com
pg. 61

Fountain of Youth Archaeological Park
11 Magnolia Avenue
St. Augustine, FL 32084
(904) 829-3168
www.fountainofyouthflorida.com
pg. 71

Gulfside Beach
2001 Algiers Lane
Sanibel, FL 33957
(239) 472-6477
www.bringfido.com/attraction/45
pg. 70

Henderson Beach State Park
17000 Emerald Coast Parkway
Destin, FL 32541
(850) 837-7550
www.bringfido.com/attraction/11199
pg. 62

Hurricane Hole Bar & Grill
5130 Overseas Highway
Key West, FL 33040
(305) 294-8025
www.hurricaneholekeywest.com
pg. 65

The Island Cow
2163 Periwinkle Way
Sanibel, FL 33957
(239) 472-0606
www.sanibelislandcow.com
pg. 70

J.N. Ding Darling NWR
1 Wildlife Drive
Sanibel, FL 33957
(239) 472-1100
www.fws.gov/dingdarling
pg. 70

Jupiter Dog Beach
2188 Marcinski Road
Jupiter, FL 33477
(561) 748-8140
www.bringfido.com/attraction/290
pg. 69

Jupiter Outdoor Center
1116 Love Street
Jupiter, FL 33477
(561) 316-6203
www.jupiteroutdoorcenter.com
pg. 69

Keewaydin Island
Boat Rentals at Naples Bay Resort
1500 5th Avenue S
Naples, FL 34102
(239) 530-5134
www.nbrboatrental.com
pg. 68

Key West Aquarium
1 Whitehead Street
Key West, FL 33040
(305) 296-2051
www.keywestaquarium.com
pg. 63

Lake Kissimmee State Park
14248 Camp Mack Road
Lake Wales, FL 33898
(863) 696-1112
www.bringfido.com/attraction/11016
pg. 66

Lazy Dog Kayak
Hurricane Hole Marina
5114 Overseas Highway
Key West, FL 33040
(305) 295-9898
www.lazydog.com
pg. 65

Lee County Dog Beach
8600 Estero Boulevard
Fort Myers Beach, FL 33931
(239) 533-7275
www.bringfido.com/attraction/293
pg. 68

Lincoln Road Mall
1610 Lenox Avenue
Miami Beach, FL 33139
(305) 535-1111
www.lincolnroadmall.com
pg. 67

Palm Beach Bicycle Trail Shop
223 Sunrise Avenue
Palm Beach, FL 33480
(561) 659-4583
www.palmbeachbicycle.com
pg. 69

Palm Beach Lake Trail
Flagler Museum Parking
1 Whitehall Way
Palm Beach, FL 33480
(800) 554-7256
www.bringfido.com/attraction/11022
pg. 69

St. Augustine Eco Tours
111 Avenida Menendez
St. Augustine, FL 32084
(904) 377-7245
www.staugustineecotours.com
pg. 72

Tarpon Bay Explorers
900 Tarpon Bay Road
Sanibel, FL 33957
(239) 472-8900
www.tarponbayexplorers.com
pg. 70

HOTELS

Ambrosia Key West
622 Fleming Street
Key West, FL 33040
(305) 296-9838
www.ambrosiakeywest.com
pg. 63

Banana Bay Resort & Marina
2319 N Roosevelt Boulevard
Key West, FL 33040
(305) 296-6925
www.bananabayresortkeywest.com
pg. 65

Bayfront Marin House
142 Avenida Menendez
St. Augustine, FL 32084
(904) 824-4301
www.bayfrontmarinhouse.com
pg. 72

Beachside Inn
2931 Scenic Highway 98
Destin, FL 32541
(888) 232-2498
www.destinbeachsideinn.com
pg. 62

Chalet Suzanne
3800 Chalet Suzanne Drive
Lake Wales, FL 33859
(863)-676-6011
www.chaletsuzanne.com
pg. 66

The Chesterfield Palm Beach
363 Cocoanut Row
Palm Beach, FL 33480
(561) 659-5800
www.chesterfieldpb.com
pg. 69

Naples Bay Resort
1500 5th Avenue S
Naples, FL 34102
(239) 530-1199
www.naplesbayresort.com
pg. 68

Plantation on Crystal River
9301 W Fort Island Trail
Crystal River, FL 34429
(352) 795-4211
www.tinyurl.com/ruff08
pg. 61

Saint Augustine Beach House
10 Vilano Road
St. Augustine, FL 32084
(904) 217-3765
www.sabhonline.com
pg. 71

Signal Inn
1811 Olde Middle Gulf Drive
Sanibel, FL 33957
(239) 472-4690
www.signalinn.com
pg. 70

Speakeasy Inn and Rum Bar
1117 Duval Street
Key West, FL 33040
(305) 296-2680
www.speakeasyinn.com
pg. 63

Surfcomber Hotel
1717 Collins Avenue
Miami Beach, FL 33139
(305) 532-7715
www.surfcomber.com
pg. 67

Tropical Winds Motel & Cottages
4819 Tradewinds Drive
Sanibel, FL 33957
(239) 472-1765
www.sanibeltropicalwinds.com
pg. 70

Water Street Hotel and Marina
329 Water Street
Apalachicola, FL 32320
(850) 653-3700
www.waterstreethotel.com
pg. 60

GEORGIA
ATTRACTIONS

Barnsley Gardens
597 Barnsley Gardens Road
Adairsville, GA 30103
(770) 773-7480
www.barnsleyresort.com
pg. 73

Bonaventure Cemetery
330 Bonaventure Road
Savannah, GA 31401
(912) 651-6843
www.bonaventurehistorical.org
pg. 77

Captain Mike's Dolphin Tours
180 Old Tybee Road
Tybee Island, GA 31328
(912) 786-5848
www.tybeedolphins.com
pg. 79

The Crab Shack
40 Estill Hammock Road
Tybee Island, GA 31328
(912) 786-9857
www.thecrabshack.com
pg. 79

Ghost City Tours
Johnson Square
Bull Street & Congress Street
Savannah, GA 31401
(912) 660-9539
www.ghosttoursinsavannah.com
pg. 77

Hearse Ghost Tours
412 E Duffy Street
Savannah, GA 31401
(912) 695-1578
www.hearseghosttours.com
pg. 77

Oglethorpe Tours
526 Turner Boulevard
Savannah, GA 31401
(912) 233-8380
www.oglethorpetours.com
pg. 78

Oliver Bentleys
13 W York Street
Savannah, GA 31401
(912) 201-1688
www.oliverbentleys.com/tour
pg. 78

Rock City Gardens
1400 Patten Road
Lookout Mountain, GA 30750
(706) 820-2531
www.seerockcity.com
pg. 76

Savannah Movie Tour
Savannah Visitor Information Center
301 Martin Luther King Jr. Boulevard
Savannah, GA 31401
(912) 234-3440
www.savannahmovietours.com
pg. 78

Tybee Jet Ski & Watersports
1 Old Tybee Road
Tybee Island, GA 31328
(912) 786-8062
www.tybeejetski.com
pg. 79

HOTELS

Barnsley Resort
597 Barnsley Gardens Road
Adairsville, GA 30103
(770) 773-7480
www.barnsleyresort.com
pg. 73

Foley House Inn
14 W Hull Street
Savannah, GA 31401
(912) 232-6622
www.foleyinn.com
pg. 78

Mermaid Cottages
1517 Chatham Avenue
Tybee Island, GA 31328
(912) 313-0784
www.mermaidcottages.com
pg. 79

Olde Harbour Inn
508 E Factors Walk
Savannah, GA 31401
(912) 234-4100
www.oldeharbourinn.com
pg. 77

Seventy-Four Ranch
9205 Highway 53 W
Jasper, GA 30143
(706) 692-0123
www.seventyfourranch.com
pg. 75

HAWAII
ATTRACTIONS

Gone Surfing Hawaii
330 Saratoga Road
Honolulu, HI 98615
(808) 429-6404
www.gonesurfinghawaii.com
pg. 80

HOTELS

Aqua Waikiki Wave
2299 Kuhio Avenue
Honolulu, HI 96815
(808) 922-1262
www.aquawaikikiwave.com
pg. 80

IDAHO
ATTRACTIONS
Brooks Sea Plane
Independence Point City Dock
Coeur d'Alene, ID 83814
(208) 664-2842
www.brooks-seaplane.com
pg. 81

Tubbs Hill
210 S 3rd Street
Coeur d'Alene, ID 83814
(208) 769-2252
www.bringfido.com/attraction/10487
pg. 81

HOTELS
The Coeur d'Alene Resort
115 S 2nd Street
Coeur d'Alene, ID 83814
(208) 765-4000
www.cdaresort.com
pg. 81

Dog Bark Park Inn
2421 Business Highway 95
Cottonwood, ID 83522
(208) 983-1236
www.dogbarkparkinn.com
pg. 83

ILLINOIS
ATTRACTIONS
Allerton Park & Retreat Center
515 Old Timber Road
Monticello, IL 61856
(217) 333-3287
www.allerton.illinois.edu
pg. 86

Garden of the Gods Recreation Area
Garden of the Gods Road
Herod, IL 62947
(618) 253-7114
www.bringfido.com/attraction/849
pg. 85

Houlihan's Restaurant
1902 S 1st Street
Champaign, IL 61820
(217) 819-5005
www.houlihans.com
pg. 86

Mercury Cruises
112 E Wacker Drive
Chicago, IL 60601
(312) 332-1353
www.mercurycruises.com
pg. 84

Rim Rock Recreation Area
Karbers Ridge Road
Junction, IL 62954
(618) 253-7114
www.bringfido.com/attraction/11148
pg. 85

Seadog Cruises
600 E Grand Avenue
Chicago, IL 60611
(877) 902-6216
www.seadogcruises.com
pg. 84

Shawnee National Forest
Illinois 34
Harrisburg, IL 62946
(618) 253-7114
www.fs.usda.gov/shawnee
pg. 85

HOTELS
I Hotel & Conference Center
1900 S 1st Street
Champaign, IL 61820
(217) 819-5000
www.stayatthei.com
pg. 86

Hotel Palomar
505 N State Street
Chicago, IL 60654
(312) 755-9703
www.tinyurl.com/ruff09
pg. 84

Rim Rock's Dogwood Cabins
3900 Pounds Hollow Blacktop
Elizabethtown, IL 62931
(618) 264-6036
www.tinyurl.com/ruff10
pg. 85

INDIANA
100 Acres Art and Nature Park
4000 N Michigan Road
Indianapolis, IN 46208
(317) 923-1331
www.imamuseum.org/visit/100acres
pg. 89

French Lick Scenic Railway
1 Monon Drive
French Lick, IN 47432
(812) 936-2405
www.frenchlickscenicrailway.org
pg. 87

Indianapolis Art Center Artspark
820 E 67th Street
Indianapolis, IN 46220
(317) 255-2464
www.indplsartcenter.org
pg. 89

The Alexander
333 S Delaware Street
Indianapolis, IN 46204
(317) 624-8200
www.thealexander.com
pg. 89

Artist's Inn & Cottages
592 S Summit Street
French Lick, IN 47432
(812) 936-7333
www.artistsinnandcottages.com
pg. 87

French Lick Resort
8670 W State Road 56
French Lick, IN 47432
(812) 936-9300
www.frenchlick.com
pg. 87

Residence Inn on the Canal
350 W New York Street
Indianapolis, IN 46202
(317) 822-0840
www.bringfido.com/lodging/77808
pg. 89

IOWA
Living History Farms
11121 Hickman Road
Urbandale, IA 50322
(515) 278-5286
www.lhf.org
pg. 90

Stoney Creek Inn
5291 Stoney Creek Court
Johnston, IA 50131
(515) 334-9000
www.stoneycreekinn.com
pg. 90

KANSAS
Greyhound Hall of Fame
407 S Buckeye Avenue
Abilene, KS 67410
(785) 263-3000
www.greyhoundhalloffame.com
pg. 91

Holiday Inn Express Abilene
110 E Lafayette Avenue
Abilene, KS 67410
(785) 263-4049
www.tinyurl.com/ruff11
pg. 91

KENTUCKY
Dinosaur World
711 Mammoth Cave Road
Cave City, KY 42127
(270) 773-4345
www.dinosaurworld.com
pg. 93

Green River Lake State Park
179 Park Office Road
Campbellsville, KY 42718
(270) 465-8255
www.bringfido.com/attraction/11149
pg. 92

Kentucky Horse Park
4089 Iron Works Parkway
Lexington, KY 40511
(800) 678-8813
www.kyhorsepark.com
pg. 94

Mega Cavern
1841 Taylor Avenue
Louisville, KY 40213
(877) 614-6342
www.louisvillemegacavern.com
pg. 95

HOTELS
21c Museum Hotel
700 W Main Street
Louisville, KY 40202
(502) 217-6300
www.21cmuseumhotels.com
pg. 95

Green River Marina
2892 Lone Valley Road
Campbellsville, KY 42718
(270) 465-2512
www.greenrivermarina.com
pg. 92

Jellystone Park
1002 Mammoth Cave Road
Cave City, KY 42127
(270) 773-3840
www.tinyurl.com/ruff13
pg. 93

Rose Hill Inn
233 Rose Hill Avenue
Versailles, KY 40383
(859) 873-5957
www.rosehillinn.com
pg. 94

LOUISIANA
ATTRACTIONS
The Algiers Ferry
1 Canal Street
New Orleans, LA 70130
(504) 376-8100
www.dotd.la.gov/ferry
pg. 97

Atchafalaya Experience
338 N Sterling Street
Lafayette, LA 70501
(337) 277-4726
www.theatchafalayaexperience.com
pg. 96

Avery Island
Louisiana 329
Avery Island, LA 70513
(337) 369-6243
www.tabasco.com/avery-island
pg. 96

Bloody Mary's Tours
4905 Canal Street
New Orleans, LA 70119
(504) 523-7684
www.bloodymarystours.com
pg. 97

Blue Dog Café
1211 W Pinhook Road
Lafayette, LA 70503
(337) 237-0005
www.bluedogcafe.com
pg. 96

HOTELS
Bois de Chenes Bed & Breakfast
338 N Sterling Street
Lafayette, LA 70501
(337) 233-7816
www.boisdechenes.com
pg. 96

Windsor Court Hotel
300 Gravier Street
New Orleans, LA 70130
(504)523-6000
www.windsorcourthotel.com
pg. 97

MAINE
ATTRACTIONS
Acadia National Park
20 McFarland Hill Drive
Bar Harbor, ME 04609
(207) 288-3338
www.nps.gov/acad
pg. 99

Belgrade Lakes Golf Club
46 Clubhouse Drive
Belgrade Lakes, ME 04918
(207) 495-4653
www.belgradelakesgolf.com
pg. 100

Camden Hills State Park
80 Belfast Road
Camden, ME 04843
(207) 236-3109
www.bringfido.com/attraction/11150
pg. 103

Cap'n Fish's Boat Trips
1 Wharf Street
Boothbay Harbor, ME 04538
(207) 633-3244
www.boothbayboattrips.com
pg. 101

Captain Jack Lobster Tours
Middle Pier
1 Park Drive
Rockland, ME 04841
(207) 542-6852
www.captainjacklobstertours.com
pg. 103

Carriages of Acadia
21 Dane Farm Road
Seal Harbor, ME 04730
(877) 276-3622
www.carriagesofacadia.com
pg. 99

Casco Bay Lines
56 Commercial Street
Portland, ME 04112
(207) 774-7871
www.cascobaylines.com
pg. 102

Island Explorer
19 Firefly Lane
Bar Harbor, ME 04609
(207) 288-4573
www.exploreacadia.com
pg. 99

Jordan Pond House
1 Park Loop Road
Seal Harbor, ME 04675
(207) 276-3316
www.thejordanpondhouse.com
pg. 99

Portland Lobster Company
180 Commercial Street
Portland, ME 04101
(207) 775-2112
www.portlandlobstercompany.com
pg. 102

Sea Princess Cruises
41 Harbor Drive
Mount Desert, ME 04660
(207) 276-5352
www.barharborcruises.com
pg. 99

HOTELS

Canterbury Cottage Bed & Breakfast
12 Roberts Avenue
Bar Harbor, ME 04069
(207) 288-2112
www.canterburycottage.com
pg. 99

Inn by the Sea
40 Bowery Beach Road
Cape Elizabeth, ME 04107
(207) 799-3134
www.innbythesea.com
pg. 102

Lakeside Motel & Cabins
77 Turtle Run Road
East Winthrop, ME 04343
(207) 395-6741
www.lakesidelodging.com
pg. 100

Lord Camden Inn
24 Main Street
Camden, ME 04843
(207) 236-4325
www.lordcamdeninn.com
pg. 103

Spruce Point Inn Resort & Spa
88 Grandview Avenue
Boothbay Harbor, ME 04538
(207) 633-4152
www.sprucepointinn.com
pg. 101

MARYLAND
ATTRACTIONS

Ayers Creek Adventures
8628 Grey Fox Lane
Berlin, MD 21811
(888) 602-6288
www.ayerscreekadventures.com
pg. 105

Crampton's Gap Trailhead
Gathland State Park
900 Arnoldstown Road
Jefferson, MD 21718
(301) 791-4767
www.bringfido.com/attraction/11151
pg. 107

Quiet Waters Park
600 Quiet Waters Park Road
Annapolis, MD 21403
(410) 222-1777
www.bringfido.com/attraction/494
pg. 104

River & Trail Outfitters
604 Valley Road
Knoxville, MD 21758
(301) 695-5177
www.rivertrail.com
pg. 107

Savage River State Forest
127 Headquarters Lane
Grantsville, MD 21536
(301) 895-5759
www.bringfido.com/attraction/11152
pg. 106

Watermark Cruises
1 Dock Street
Annapolis, MD 21401
(410) 268-7601
www.watermarkcruises.com
pg. 104

HOTELS

Castaways Campground
12550 Eagles Nest Road
Berlin, MD 21811
(410) 213-0097
www.castawaysrvoc.com
pg. 105

Loews Annapolis Hotel
126 West Street
Annapolis, MD 21401
(410) 263-7777
www.tinyurl.com/ruff14
pg. 104

Savage River Lodge
1600 Mount Aetna Road
Frostburg, MD 21532
(301) 689-3200
www.savageriverlodge.com
pg. 106

The Treehouse Camp
20716 Townsend Road
Rohrersville, MD 21779
(301) 432-5585
www.thetreehousecamp.com
pg. 107

MASSACHUSETTS
ATTRACTIONS

Blue Bellies
Nobadeer Beach
Nantucket, MA 02554
(443) 797-9524
www.blue-bellies.com
pg. 113

Boston Common
139 Tremont Street
Boston, MA 02111
(617) 536-4100 x88
www.bringfido.com/attraction/2007
pg. 109

Cisco Brewers
5 Bartlett Farm Road
Nantucket, MA 02554
(508) 325-5929
www.ciscobrewers.com
pg. 113

City Water Taxi
300 Congress Street
Boston, MA 02210
(617) 633-9240
www.citywatertaxi.com
pg. 109

deCordova Sculpture Park
51 Sandy Pond Road
Lincoln, MA 01773
(781) 259-8355
www.decordova.org
pg. 111

Dog Gone Sailing Charters
8 Macmillan Wharf
Provincetown, MA 02657
(508) 566-0410
www.doggonesailingcharters.com
pg. 114

Dolphin Fleet of Provincetown
307 Commercial Street
Provincetown, MA 02657
(508) 240-3636
www.whalewatch.com
pg. 114

The Freedom Trail
139 Tremont Street
Boston, MA 02111
(617) 357-8300
www.thefreedomtrail.org
pg. 109

Joe's American Bar & Grill
100 Atlantic Avenue
Boston, MA 02110
(617) 367-8700
www.joesamerican.com
pg. 109

Nantucket Airlines
Barnstable Municipal Airport
660 Barnstable Road
Hyannis, MA 02601
(508) 228-6234
www.nantucketairlines.com
pg. 113

Nobadeer Beach
Nobadeer Avenue
Nantucket, MA 02554
(508) 228-0925
www.nantucket.net/beaches/fat.php
pg. 113

Public Garden
Charles Street & Beacon Street
Boston, MA 02116
(617) 723-8144
www.friendsofthepublicgarden.org
pg. 109

Sanford Farm
115 Madaket Road
Nantucket, MA 02554
(508) 228-2884
www.nantucketconservation.org
pg. 113

The Steamship Authority
141 School Street
Hyannis, MA 02601
(508) 477-8600
www.steamshipauthority.com
pg. 113

The T
10 Park Plaza
Boston, MA 02116
(617) 222-3200
www.mbta.com
pg. 109

Tupancy Links
173 Cliff Road
Nantucket, MA 02554
(508) 228-2884
www.nantucketconservation.org
pg. 113

The Wave
3 E Chestnut Street
Nantucket, MA 02554
(508) 228-7025
www.nrtawave.com
pg. 113

HOTELS

Aloft Lexington
727 Marrett Road
Lexington, MA 02421
(781) 761-1700
www.aloftlexington.com
pg. 111

Birchwood Inn
7 Hubbard Street
Lenox, MA 01240
(413) 637-2600
www.birchwood-inn.com
pg. 110

The Cottages & Lofts at the Boat Basin
24 Old South Wharf
Nantucket, MA 02554
(508) 325-1499
www.thecottagesnantucket.com
pg. 113

Provincetown Hotel at Gabriel's
102 Bradford Street
Provincetown, MA 02657
(508) 487-3232
www.provincetownhotel.com
pg. 114

XV Beacon Hotel
15 Beacon Street
Boston, MA 02108
(617) 670-1500
www.xvbeacon.com
pg. 109

MICHIGAN
ATTRACTIONS

Argo Canoe Livery
1055 Longshore Drive
Ann Arbor, MI 48105
(734) 794-6241
www.a2gov.org/canoe
pg. 115

Bavarian Belle Riverboat
925 S Main Street
Frankenmuth, MI 48734
(866) 808-2628
www.bavarianbelle.com
pg. 116

Fort Mackinac
7127 Huron Road
Mackinac Island, MI 49757
(906) 847-6330
www.mackinacparks.com
pg. 119

Gilmore Car Museum
6865 W Hickory Road
Hickory Corners, MI 49060
(269) 671-5089
www.gilmorecarmuseum.org
pg. 117

Grandpa Tiny's Farm
7775 Weiss Street
Frankenmuth, MI 48734
(989) 652-5437
www.grandpatinysfarm.com
pg. 116

Hart-Montague Trail State Park
Dowling Street & Water Street
Montague, MI 49437
(231) 873-3083
www.bringfido.com/attraction/7002
pg. 120

Mackinac Island Carriage Tours
7278 Main Street
Mackinac Island, MI 49757
(906) 847-3325
www.mict.com
pg. 119

Nichols Arboretum
1800 N Dixboro Road
Ann Arbor, MI 48105
(734) 647-7600
www.lsa.umich.edu/mbg
pg. 115

Seney National Wildlife Refuge
1674 Refuge Entrance Road
Seney, MI 49883
(906) 586-9851
www.fws.gov/midwest/seney
pg. 121

Shepler's Ferry
556 E Central Avenue
Mackinaw City, MI 49701
(800) 828-6157
www.sheplersferry.com
pg. 119

Silver Lake Buggy Rentals
8288 W Hazel Road
Mears, MI 49436
(231) 873-8833
www.silverlakebuggys.com
pg. 120

South Higgins Lake State Park
106 State Park Drive
Roscommon, MI 48653
(989) 821-6374
www.bringfido.com/attraction/9918
pg. 118

Toonerville Trolley
7195 Soo Junction Road
Soo Junction, MI 49000
(888) 778-7246
www.trainandboattours.com
pg. 121

White Lake Excursions
4464 Dowling Street
Montague, MI 49437
(231) 740-5673
www.whitelakeexcursions.com
pg. 120

HOTELS

Beachfront Hotel
4990 W Houghton Lake Drive
Houghton Lake, MI 48629
(855) 235-9709
www.beachfronthl.com
pg. 118

Drury Inn & Suites Frankenmuth
260 S Main Street
Frankenmuth, MI 48734
(989) 652-2800
www.tinyurl.com/ruff16
pg. 116

Kara's Kottages
837 W Main Street
Kalamazoo, MI 49006
(269) 491-0765
www.karaskottages.com
pg. 117

Mission Point Resort
6633 Main Street
Mackinac Island, MI 49757
(906) 847-3312
www.missionpoint.com
pg. 119

Northland Outfitters
8174 Highway M-77
Germfask, MI 49836
(906) 586-9801
www.northoutfitters.com
pg. 121

TownePlace Suites Ann Arbor
1301 Briarwood Circle Drive
Ann Arbor, MI 48108
(734) 327-5900
www.tinyurl.com/ruff15
pg. 115

The Weathervane Inn
4527 Dowling Street
Montague, MI 49437
(231) 893-8931
www.theweathervaneinn.net
pg. 120

MINNESOTA
ATTRACTIONS

Sky Dan Air Tours
80 Skyport Lane
Grand Marais, MN 55604
(218) 370-0645
www.skydanairtours.com
pg. 123

HOTELS

Gunflint Lodge
143 S Gunflint Lake Road
Grand Marais, MN 55604
(218) 388-2296
www.gunflint.com
pg. 123

MISSISSIPPI
ATTRACTIONS

Biloxi Shrimping Trip
693 Beach Boulevard
Biloxi, MS 39530
(228) 392-8645
www.biloxishrimpingtrip.com
pg. 124

Shaggy's Beach Bar & Grill
1763 Beach Boulevard
Biloxi, MS 39531
(228) 432-5005
www.shaggys.biz
pg. 124

HOTELS

Hard Rock Hotel & Casino Biloxi
777 Beach Boulevard
Biloxi, MS 39530
(228) 374-7625
www.hardrockbiloxi.com
pg. 124

MISSOURI
ATTRACTIONS

AKC Museum of the Dog
1721 S Mason Road
Ballwin, MO 63011
(314) 821-3647
www.museumofthedog.org
pg. 125

The Boathouse in Forest Park
6101 Government Drive
St. Louis, MO 63110
(314) 367-2224
www.boathouseforestpark.com
pg. 125

Fantastic Caverns
4872 N Farm Road 125
Springfield, MO 65803
(417) 833-2010
www.fantasticcaverns.com
pg. 127

National Tiger Sanctuary
518 State Highway BB
Saddlebrooke, MO 65630
(417) 587-3633
www.nationaltigersanctuary.org
pg. 126

Purina Farms
200 Checkerboard Drive
Gray Summit, MO 63039
(314) 982-3232
www.purinafarms.com
pg. 125

HOTELS

The Cheshire
6300 Clayton Road
St. Louis, MO 63117
(314) 647-7300
www.cheshirestl.com
pg. 125

Drury Inn & Suites Springfield
2715 N Glenstone Avenue
Springfield, MO 65803
(417) 863-8400
www.tinyurl.com/ruff17
pg. 127

Lilley's Landing Resort & Marina
367 River Lane
Branson, MO 65616
(417) 334-6380
www.lilleyslanding.com
pg. 126

MONTANA
ATTRACTIONS

Lava Creek Adventures
433 Targhee Pass Highway
West Yellowstone, MT 59758
(406) 646-5145
www.lavacreekadventures.com
pg. 129

Paradise Adventure Company
1 Old Chico Road
Pray, MT 59065
(406) 333-7183
www.paradiserafting.com
pg. 128

HOTELS

Chico Hot Springs Resort
1 Old Chico Road
Pray, MT 59065
(406) 333-4933
www.chicohotsprings.com
pg. 128

Yellowstone Under Canvas
3111 Targhee Highway
West Yellowstone, MT 59758
(406) 219-0441
www.mtundercanvas.com
pg. 129

NEBRASKA
ATTRACTIONS

Bryson's Airboat Tours
839 County Road 19
Fremont, NE 68025
(402) 968-8534
www.brysonsairboattours.com
pg. 130

Little Outlaw Canoe
1005 E Highway 20
Valentine, NE 69201
(402) 376-1822
www.outlawcanoe.com
pg. 131

Three Dog Bakery
17151 Davenport Street #105
Omaha, NE 68118
(402) 614-3647
www.threedogomaha.com
pg. 130

HOTELS

Element by Westin
3253 Dodge Street
Omaha, NE 68131
(402) 614-8080
www.tinyurl.com/ruff18
pg. 130

Trade Winds Motel
1009 E Highway 20
Valentine, NE 69201
(402) 376-1600
www.tradewindslodge.com
pg. 131

NEVADA
ATTRACTIONS

Bernard's Bistro by the Lake
15 Via Bel Canto
Henderson, NV 89011
(702) 565-1155
www.bernardsbistro.com
pg. 132

Gondola Adventures
41 Costa Di Lago
Henderson, NV 89011
(949) 646-2067
www.gondola.com
pg. 132

Mount Charleston
Foxtail Picnic Area
Lee Canyon Rd & Forest Road 106
Las Vegas, NV 89124
(702) 872-5486
www.gomtcharleston.com
pg. 133

Omni Limousine
1401 Helm Drive
Las Vegas, NV 89119
(702) 703-6840
www.omnilimo.com
pg. 135

Paddle to the Core
Westin Lake Las Vegas Resort
101 Montelago Boulevard
Henderson, NV 89011
(702) 567-6128
www.suplv.com
pg. 132

Red Rock Canyon
1000 Scenic Loop Drive
Las Vegas, NV 89161
(702) 515-5367
www.redrockcanyonlv.org
pg. 135

TNT Stagelines
F Street
Virginia City, NV 89440
(775) 721-1496
www.tntstagelines.com
pg. 136

Virginia & Truckee Railroad
F Street
Virginia City, NV 89440
(775) 847-0380
www.virginiatruckee.com
pg. 136

Wedding Bells Chapel
375 E Harmon Avenue
Las Vegas, NV 89169
(702) 731-2355
www.weddingbellschapel.com
pg. 135

HOTELS

Caesars Palace
3570 S Las Vegas Boulevard
Las Vegas, NV 89109
(702) 731-7110
www.caesarspalace.com
pg. 135

Mount Charleston Lodge
5375 Kyle Canyon Road
Las Vegas, NV 89124
(702) 872-5408
www.mtcharlestonlodge.com
pg. 133

Silver Queen Hotel
28 North C Street
Virginia City, NV 89440
(775) 847-0440
www.silverqueenhotel.net
pg. 136

Westin Lake Las Vegas Resort
101 Montelago Boulevard
Henderson, NV 89011
(702) 567-6000
www.westinlakelasvegas.com
pg. 132

NEW HAMPSHIRE

NEW JERSEY

NEW MEXICO

HOTELS

Casa Gallina
613 Callejon
Taos, NM 87571
(575) 758-2306
www.casagallina.net
pg. 141

Hotel Andaluz
125 2nd Street NW
Albuquerque, NM 87102
(505) 242-9090
www.hotelandaluz.com
pg. 140

The Inn of the Five Graces
150 E De Vargas Street
Santa Fe, NM 87501
(505) 992-0957
www.fivegraces.com
pg. 143

NEW YORK

ATTRACTIONS

Atwater Estate Vineyards
5055 New York 414
Burdett, NY 14818
(800) 331-7323
www.atwatervineyards.com
pg. 151

Buttermilk Falls State Park
116 E Buttermilk Falls Road
Ithaca, NY 14850
(607) 273-3440
www.nysparks.com/parks/151
pg. 146

Cayuga Lake Wine Trail
2770 County Road 128
Romulus, NY 14541
(607) 869-4281
www.cayugawinetrail.com
pg. 151

Cedar Point County Park
5 Cedar Point Road
East Hampton, NY 11937
(631) 852-7620
www.bringfido.com/attraction/9373
pg. 144

The Classy Canine
468 County Road 39
Southampton, NY 11968
(631) 283-1306
www.classycaninehamptons.com
pg. 144

Coindre Hall
101 Browns Road
Huntington, NY 11743
(631) 854-4410
www.bringfido.com/attraction/11156
pg. 145

Main Beach
101 Ocean Avenue
East Hampton, NY 11937
(631) 324-0074
www.bringfido.com/attraction/11157
pg. 144

Penguin Bay Winery
6075 New York 414
Hector, NY 14841
(607) 546-5115
www.penguinbaywinery.com
pg. 151

Ravines Wine Cellars
14630 New York 54
Hammondsport, NY 14840
(607) 292-7007
www.ravineswine.com
pg. 151

Robert H. Treman State Park
105 Enfield Falls Road
Ithaca, NY 14850
(607) 273-3440
www.nysparks.com/parks/135
pg. 146

Sagamore Hill
20 Sagamore Hill Road
Oyster Bay, NY 11771
(516) 922-4788
www.nps.gov/sahi
pg. 145

Sands Point Preserve at Falaise
127 Middleneck Road
Port Washington, NY 11050
(516) 571-7900
www.sandspointpreserve.org
pg. 145

Seneca Lake Wine Trail
2 N Franklin Street, Suite 320
Watkins Glen, NY 14891
(877) 536-2717
www.senecalakewine.com
pg. 151

Shake Shack
366 Columbus Avenue
New York, NY 10024
(646) 747-8770
www.shakeshack.com
pg. 149

Sprinkles Cupcakes
780 Lexington Avenue
New York, NY 10065
(212) 207-8375
www.sprinkles.com
pg. 149

St. Regis Canoe Outfitters
73 Dorsey Street
Saranac Lake, NY 12983
(518) 891-1838
www.canoeoutfitters.com
pg. 150

Whiteface Mountain
SR 431 & Whiteface Memorial Hwy
Wilmington, NY 12997
(518) 946-2223
www.bringfido.com/attraction/11159
pg. 152

William Secord Gallery
52 E 76th Street #3
New York, NY 10021
(212) 249-0075
www.dogpainting.com
pg. 149

Wilmington Trail
Whiteface Memorial Hwy & Reservoir Rd
Wilmington, NY 12941
(518) 946-2223
www.bringfido.com/attraction/11160
pg. 152

Z-Travel and Leisure Tours
81 Van Etten Boulevard
New Rochelle, NY 10804
(914) 633-6658
www.ztravelandleisure.com
pg. 149

HOTELS
Adirondack Motel
248 Lake Flower Avenue
Saranac Lake, NY 12983
(518) 891-2116
www.adirondackmotel.com
pg. 150

c/o The Maidstone
207 Main Street
East Hampton, NY 11937
(631) 324-5006
www.careofhotels.com/maidstone
pg. 144

Glen Highland Farm
217 Pegg Road
Morris, NY 13808
(607) 263-5416
www.highlandvue.com
pg. 147

John Morris Manor
2138 State Route 89
Seneca Falls, NY 13148
(315) 568-9057
www.johnmorrismanor.com
pg. 151

La Tourelle Resort & Spa
1150 Danby Road
Ithaca, NY 14850
(607) 273-2734
www.latourelle.com
pg. 146

Lake Placid Lodge
144 Lodge Way
Lake Placid, NY 12946
(518) 523-2700
www.lakeplacidlodge.com
pg. 152

Mill House Inn
31 N Main Street
East Hampton, NY 11937
(631) 324-9766
www.millhouseinn.com
pg. 144

Oheka Castle
135 W Gate Drive
Huntington, NY 11743
(631) 659-1400
www.oheka.com
pg. 145

The Surrey
20 E 76th Street
New York, NY 10021
(212) 288-3700
www.thesurrey.com
pg. 149

NORTH CAROLINA
ATTRACTIONS

Bald Head Island Ferry
Deep Point Marina
1301 Ferry Road
Southport, NC 28461
(910) 269-2380
www.bringfido.com/attraction/11161
pg. 154

Battery Park Book Exchange
1 Page Avenue
Asheville, NC 28801
(828) 252-0020
www.batteryparkbookexchange.com
pg. 153

Biltmore Estate
1 Lodge Street
Asheville, NC 28803
(828) 225-1333
www.biltmore.com
pg. 153

Cape Hatteras National Seashore
1401 National Park Drive
Manteo, NC 27954
(252) 473-2111
www.nps.gov/caha
pg. 158

Chimney Rock State Park
431 Main Street
Chimney Rock, NC 28720
(828) 625-9611
www.chimneyrockpark.com
pg. 156

Corolla Outback Adventures
1150 Ocean Trail
Corolla, NC 27927
(252) 453-4484
www.corollaoutback.com
pg. 157

The Dog Bar
3307 N Davidson Street
Charlotte, NC 28205
(704) 370-3595
www.dogbarcharlotte.com
pg. 155

Lake Lure Adventure Company
480 Memorial Highway
Lake Lure, NC 28746
(828) 625-8066
www.lakelureadventurecompany.com
pg. 156

Larkin's on the Lake
1020 Memorial Highway
Lake Lure, NC 28746
(828) 625-4075
www.larkinsonthelake.com
pg. 156

Old Rock Café
431 Main Street
Chimney Rock, NC 28720
(828) 625-2329
www.bringfido.com/restaurant/12062
pg. 156

Outer Banks Air Charters
410 Airport Road
Manteo, NC 27954
(252) 256-2322
www.outerbanksaircharters.com
pg. 158

Riverside Adventure Company
14 Marina Wynd
Bald Head Island, NC 28461
(910) 457-4944
www.riversideadventure.com
pg. 154

The Sail Shop
96 Keelson Row
Bald Head Island, NC 28461
(910) 457-6844
www.thesailshop.com
pg. 154

Steamers
798-B Sunset Boulevard
Corolla, NC 27927
(252) 453-3305
www.steamerstogo.com
pg. 157

US National Whitewater Center
5000 Whitewater Center Parkway
Charlotte, NC 28214
(704) 391-3900
www.usnwc.org
pg. 155

Whalehead Club
1100 Club Road
Corolla, NC 27927
(252) 453-9040
www.visitwhalehead.com
pg. 157

Wild Horse Museum
1129 Corolla Village Road
Corolla, NC 27927
(252) 453-8002
www.corollawildhorses.com
pg. 157

Wright Brothers National Memorial
105 N Croatan Highway
Kill Devil Hills, NC 27948
(252) 473-2111
www.nps.gov/wrbr
pg. 158

HOTELS

Bald Head Island Limited
6 Marina Wynd
Bald Head Island, NC 28461
(910) 457-5002
www.baldheadisland.com
pg. 154

Barkwell's
290 Lance Road
Mills River, NC 28759
(828) 891-8288
www.barkwells.com
pg. 156

Drury Inn & Suites Northlake
6920 Northlake Mall Drive
Charlotte, NC 28216
(704) 599-8882
www.tinyurl.com/ruff20
pg. 155

Four Paws Kingdom
335 Lazy Creek Drive
Rutherfordton, NC 28139
(828) 287-7324
www.4pawskingdom.com
pg. 159

Omni Grove Park Inn
290 Macon Avenue
Asheville, NC 28804
(828) 252-2711
www.groveparkinn.com
pg. 153

Inn at Corolla Light
1066 Ocean Trail
Corolla, NC 27927
(252) 453-3340
www.innatcorolla.com
pg. 157

Sandbar Bed & Breakfast
2508 S Virginia Dare Trail
Nags Head, NC 27959
(252) 489-1868
www.tinyurl.com/ruff21
pg. 158

NORTH DAKOTA
ATTRACTIONS

International Peace Garden
10939 Highway 281
Dunseith, ND 58329
(701) 263-4390
www.peacegarden.com
pg. 161

Seaman Overlook
Lewis & Clark Interpretive Center
2576 8th Street SW
Washburn, ND 58577
(701) 462-8535
www.fortmandan.com
pg. 161

HOTELS

Hyatt House Minot
2301 Landmark Drive NW
Minot, ND 58703
(701) 838-7300
www.tinyurl.com/ruff32
Rates from $110/night
page. 161

OHIO
ATTRACTIONS

Morgan's Outdoor Adventures
5701 Ohio 350
Oregonia, OH 45054
(513) 932-7658
www.morganscanoe.com
pg. 162

OKLAHOMA
ATTRACTIONS
Beavers Bend State Park
Highway 259A
Broken Bow, OK 74728
(580) 494-6300
www.beaversbend.com
pg. 163

Ouachita National Forest
52175 Highway 59
Hodgen, OK 74939
(918) 653-2991
www.fs.usda.gov/ouachita
pg. 163

HOTELS
Lago Vista Bed & Breakfast
489 Bowfin Lane
Broken Bow, OK 74728
(580) 494-7378
www.tinyurl.com/ruff22
pg. 163

OREGON
ATTRACTIONS
Cannon Beach Visitor Center
207 N Spruce Street
Cannon Beach, OR 97110
(503) 436-2623
www.cannonbeach.org
pg. 165

Columbia River Gorge Visitor Center
404 W 2nd Street
The Dalles, OR 97058
(800) 984-6743
www.crgva.org
pg. 166

Deschutes National Forest
63095 Deschutes Market Road
Bend, OR 97701
(541) 383-5300
www.fs.usda.gov/centraloregon
pg. 173

Ecola State Park
84318 Ecola State Park Road
Cannon Beach, OR 97110
(503) 436-2844
www.bringfido.com/attraction/11162
pg. 165

Haystack Rock
Midtown Parking Area
S Hemlock Street & W Gower Avenue
Cannon Beach, OR 97110
(503) 436-2623
www.friendsofhaystackrock.org
pg. 165

John Dellenback Dunes Trail
Eel Creek Campground
72044 Oregon Coast Highway
Lakeside, OR 97449
(541) 750-7000
www.bringfido.com/attraction/11163
pg. 170

Lucky Lab Brewing Company
915 SE Hawthorne Boulevard
Portland, OR 97214
(503) 236-3555
www.luckylab.com
pg. 171

Mount Bachelor Ski Resort
13000 Century Drive
Bend, OR 97702
(541) 382-2442
www.bringfido.com/attraction/11164
pg. 173

Multnomah Falls
50000 E Historic Columbia River Hwy
Bridal Veil, OR 97019
(503) 695-2372
www.bringfido.com/attraction/11166
pg. 166

Peterson Ridge Trail
800 Buckaroo Trail
Sisters, OR 97759
(541) 549-2091
www.sisterstrails.com
pg. 172

Portland Food Cart Tour
Washington Street & 10th Avenue
Portland, OR 97205
tours@foodcartsportland.com
www.foodcartsportland.com/tours
pg. 171

Proxy Falls
OR-242 W (McKenzie Highway)
Sisters, OR 97759
(304) 636-1800
www.bringfido.com/attraction/10496
pg. 172

Riverbend Beach Dog Park
799 SW Columbia Street
Bend, OR 97702
(541) 389-7275
www.bringfido.com/attraction/10420
pg. 164

Rogue Farms Hopyard
3590 Wigrich Road
Independence, OR 97351
(503) 838-9813
www.rogue.com
pg. 167

Rogue Wilderness Adventures
325 Galice Road
Merlin, OR 97532
(800) 336-1647
www.wildrogue.com
pg. 169

Sahalie and Koosah Falls
OR-126 W (McKenzie Highway)
Sisters, OR 97759
(541) 225-6300
www.bringfido.com/attraction/11167
pg. 172

Sand Dunes Frontier
83960 Oregon Coast Highway
Florence, OR 97439
(541) 997-3544
www.sanddunesfrontier.com
pg. 170

Spinreel Dune Buggy
67045 Spinreel Road
North Bend, OR 97459
(541) 759-3313
www.ridetheoregondunes.com
pg. 170

Three Creeks Brewing
721 S Desperado Court
Sisters, OR 97759
(541) 549-1963
www.threecreeksbrewing.com
pg. 172

Three Sisters Wilderness
McKenzie River Ranger District
57600 McKenzie Highway
McKenzie Bridge, OR 97413
(541) 822-7254
www.bringfido.com/attraction/11233
pg. 172

Tumalo Creek Kayak & Canoe
805 SW Industrial Way
Bend, OR 97702
(541) 317-9407
www.tumalocreek.com
pg. 164

Village Bike & Ski
57100 Beaver Drive, Building 21
Sunriver, OR 97707
(541) 593-2453
www.villagebikeandski.com
pg. 173

Wanoga Sno-Park
OR-46 & Forest Service Road 45
Bend, OR 97701
(541) 383-4000
www.bringfido.com/attraction/11165
pg. 173

HOTELS
Bennington Properties
56842 Venture Lane
Sunriver, OR 97707
(541) 593-6300
www.tinyurl.com/ruff25
pg. 173

Best Western Plus Hood River Inn
1108 E Marina Drive
Hood River, OR 97031
(541) 386-2200
www.hoodriverinn.com
pg. 166

FivePine Lodge
1021 E Desperado Trail
Sisters, OR 97759
(541) 549-5900
www.fivepinelodge.com
pg. 172

Morrison's Rogue River Lodge
8500 Galice Road
Merlin, OR 97532
(541) 476-3825
www.morrisonslodge.com
pg. 169

The Oxford Hotel
10 NW Minnesota Avenue
Bend, OR 97701
(541) 382-8436
www.oxfordhotelbend.com
pg. 164

RiverPlace Hotel
1510 SW Harbor Way
Portland, OR 97201
(503) 228-3233
www.riverplacehotel.com
pg. 171

Rogue Hop N' Bed
3590 Wigrich Road
Independence, OR 97351
(503) 838-9813
www.tinyurl.com/ruff23
pg. 167

Sunriver Resort
17600 Center Drive
Sunriver, OR 97707
(800) 801-8765
www.sunriver-resort.com
pg. 173

Surfsand Resort
148 W Gower Avenue
Cannon Beach, OR 97110
(503) 436-2274
www.surfsand.com
pg. 165

William M. Tugman State Park
72549 Oregon Coast Highway
Lakeside, OR 97449
(541) 271-4118
www.tinyurl.com/ruff24
pg. 170

PENNSYLVANIA

ATTRACTIONS

Abe's Buggy Rides
2596 Old Philadelphia Pike
Bird in Hand, PA 17505
(717) 392-1794
www.abesbuggyrides.com
pg. 174

Bushkill Falls
Route 209 & Bushkill Falls Road
Bushkill, PA 18324
(570) 588-6682
www.visitbushkillfalls.com
pg. 175

Central Market
23 N Market Street
Lancaster, PA 17603
(717) 735-6890
www.centralmarketlancaster.com
pg. 174

Free Tours by Foot
20 N 3rd Street
Philadelphia, PA 19106
(267) 712-9512
www.freetoursbyfoot.com
pg. 180

Geno's Steaks
1219 S 9th Steet
Philadelphia, PA 19147
(215) 389-0659
www.genosteaks.com
pg. 180

Gettysburg Foundation
1195 Baltimore Pike
Gettysburg, PA 17325
(717) 334-2436
www.gettysburgfoundation.org
pg. 178

Gettysburg National Military Park
1195 Baltimore Pike
Gettysburg, PA 17325
(717) 334-1124
www.nps.gov/gett
pg. 178

Haunted Gettysburg
27 Steinwehr Avenue
Gettysburg, PA 17325
(717) 334-1200
www.hauntedgettysburgtour.com
pg. 178

Knoebels Amusement Resort
391 Knoebels Boulevard
Elysburg, PA 17824
(570) 672-2572
www.knoebels.com
pg. 177

Lehigh Gorge Scenic Railway
1 Susquehanna Street
Jim Thorpe, PA 18229
(570) 325-8485
www.lgsry.com
pg. 179

Lehigh Gorge Trail
Packer Hill Road & Lehigh Avenue
Jim Thorpe, PA 18229
(570) 443-0400
www.bringfido.com/attraction/11170
pg. 179

Pat's King of Steaks
1237 E Passyunk Avenue
Philadelphia, PA 19147
(215) 468-1546
www.patskingofsteaks.com
pg. 180

HOTELS
Battlefield Bed and Breakfast
2264 Emmitsburg Road
Gettysburg, PA 17325
(717) 334-8804
www.gettysburgbattlefield.com
pg. 178

Eden Resort & Suites
222 Eden Road
Lancaster, PA 17601
(717) 569-6444
www.edenresort.com
pg. 174

Genetti Hotel & Suites
200 W Fourth Street
Williamsport, PA 17701
(570)326-6600
www.genettihotel.com
pg. 177

Historic Hotel Bethlehem
437 Main Street
Bethlehem, PA 18018
(610) 625-5000
www.hotelbethlehem.com
pg. 179

Hotel Fauchere
401 Broad Street
Milford, PA 18337
(570) 409-1212
www.hotelfauchere.com
pg. 175

Hotel Monaco
433 Chestnut Street
Philadelphia, PA 19106
(215) 925-2111
www.monaco-philadelphia.com
pg. 180

Knoebels Campground
391 Knoebels Boulevard
Elysburg, PA 17824
(570) 672-9555
www.bringfido.com/lodging/172436
pg. 177

RHODE ISLAND
ATTRACTIONS
Beach Rose Bicycles
1622 Roslyn Road
Block Island, RI 02807
(401) 466-5925
www.beachrosebicycles.com
pg. 181

Block Island Ferry
304 Great Island Road
Narragansett, RI 02882
(401) 783-4613
www.blockislandferry.com
pg. 181

Cliff Walk
175 Memorial Boulevard
Newport, RI 02840
(401) 845-5300
www.cliffwalk.com
pg. 183

Gansett Cruises
Bowens Wharf
150 Bowens Landing
Newport, RI 02840
(401) 787-4438
www.gansettcruises.com
pg. 183

McAloon's Taxi
Water Street
Block Island, RI 02807
(401) 741-1410
www.bringfido.com/attraction/11172
pg. 181

Mig's Rig Taxi
Water Street
Block Island, RI 02807
(401) 480-0493
www.migsrigtaxi.com
pg. 181

Mohegan Bluffs
Spring Street & Mohegan Trail
Block Island, RI 02807
(800) 383-2474
www.bringfido.com/attraction/11175
pg. 181

HOTELS
Blue Dory Inn
61 Dodge Street
Block Island, RI 02807
(401) 466-5891
www.blockislandinns.com
pg. 181

Vanderbilt Grace
41 Mary Street
Newport, RI 02840
(401) 846-6200
www.vanderbiltgrace.com
pg. 183

SOUTH CAROLINA
ATTRACTIONS
Adventure Harbor Tours
20 Patriot's Point Road
Mount Pleasant, SC 29464
(843) 442-9455
www.adventureharbortours.com
pg. 184

Boone Hall Plantation
1235 Long Pond Road
Mount Pleasant, SC 29464
(843) 884-4371
www.boonehallplantation.com
pg. 185

Captain Mark's Dolphin Cruise
Shelter Cove Harbour, Dock C
9 Harbourside Lane
Hilton Head Island, SC 29928
(843) 785-4558
www.captmarksdolphincruises.com
pg. 186

Charleston Kayak Company
4290 Ashley River Road
Charleston, SC 29414
(843) 628-2879
www.charlestonkayakcompany.com
pg. 185

Charleston Schooner Pride
360 Concord Street
Charleston, SC 29401
(843) 722-1112
www.schoonerpride.com
pg. 184

Charleston Water Taxi
10 Wharfside Street
Charleston, SC 29403
(843) 330-2989
www.charlestonwatertaxi.com
pg. 184

Drayton Hall Plantation
3380 Ashley River Road
Charleston, SC 29414
(843) 769-2600
www.draytonhall.org
pg. 185

Magnolia Plantation & Gardens
3550 Ashley River Road
Charleston, SC 29414
(843) 571-1266
www.magnoliaplantation.com
pg. 185

Vagabond Cruise
149 Lighthouse Road
Hilton Head Island, SC 29928
(843) 363-9026
www.vagabondcruise.com
pg. 186

HOTELS
The Inn at Middleton Place
4290 Ashley River Road
Charleston, SC 29414
(843) 556-0500
www.tinyurl.com/ruff26
pg. 185

Omni Oceanfront Resort
23 Ocean Lane
Hilton Head Island, SC 29928
(843) 842-8000
www.tinyurl.com/ruff27
pg. 186

The Sea Pines Resort
32 Greenwood Drive
Hilton Head Island, SC 29928
(843) 842-1872
www.seapines.com
pg. 186

The Wentworth Mansion
149 Wentworth Street
Charleston, SC 29401
(888) 466-1886
www.wentworthmansion.com
pg. 184

SOUTH DAKOTA
ATTRACTIONS
Bear Country USA
13820 S Highway 16
Rapid City, SD 57702
(605) 343-2290
www.bearcountryusa.com
pg. 189

Custer State Park
Wildlife Loop Road
Custer, SD 57730
(605) 255-4515
www.custerstatepark.com
pg. 187

Reptile Gardens
8955 S Highway 16
Rapid City, SD 57709
(605) 342-5873
www.reptilegardens.com
pg. 189

HOTELS
Mystery Mountain Resort
13752 S Highway 16
Rapid City, SD 57702
(605) 342-5368
www.blackhillsresorts.com
pg. 189

State Game Lodge
13389 S Dakota 87
Custer, SD 57730
(605) 255-4541
www.custerresorts.com
pg. 187

TENNESSEE
ATTRACTIONS
Great Smoky Mountains National Park
Cades Cove Loop Road
Townsend, TN 37882
(865) 436-1200
www.bringfido.com/attraction/70
pg. 191

Green River Stables
642 Waynesboro Highway
Waynesboro, TN 38485
(931) 722-7002
www.greenriverstables.biz
pg. 193

Walkin' Nashville
5th Avenue & Union Street
Nashville, TN 37203
(615) 499-5159
www.walkinnashville.com
pg. 190

HOTELS
The Bear Inn Resort
2250 Billy Nance Highway
Clifton, TN 38425
(931) 676-5552
www.bearinnllc.com
pg. 193

Blackberry Farm
1471 W Millers Cove Road
Walland, TN 37886
(865) 984-8166
www.blackberryfarm.com
pg. 192

Chattanooga Choo Choo Hotel
1400 Market Street
Chattanooga, TN 37402
(800) 872-2529
www.choochoo.com
pg. 76

Dancing Bear Lodge
137 Apple Valley Way
Townsend, TN 37882
(865) 448-6000
www.dancingbearlodge.com
pg. 191

Hales Bar Marina Floating Cabins
1265 Hales Bar Road
Guild, TN 37340
(423) 942-9000
www.halesbarmarina.com
pg. 11

The Hermitage Hotel
231 6th Avenue N
Nashville, TN 37219
(615) 244-3121
www.thehermitagehotel.com
pg. 190

TEXAS
ATTRACTIONS

Boneyard Dog Park & Drinkery
8150 Washington Avenue
Houston, TX 77007
(832) 494-1600
www.boneyardhouston.com
pg. 199

Bow-Wow Chow
Mobile Food Truck
Austin, TX 78704
www.bow-wowchow.com
pg. 194

Cadillac Ranch
I-40 Frontage Road (Exit 60)
Amarillo, TX 79124
(800) 692-1338
www.bringfido.com/attraction/10468
pg. 195

Casa Rio
430 E Commerce Street
San Antonio, TX 78205
(210) 225-6718
www.casa-rio.com
pg. 200

Dallas Farmers Market
1010 S Pearl Expressway
Dallas, TX 75201
(214) 939-2808
www.dallasfarmersmarket.org
pg. 196

Elkins Ranch
11301 E State Highway 217
Canyon, TX 79015
(806) 488-2100
www.theelkinsranch.com
pg. 195

Enchanted Rock State Natural Area
16710 Ranch Road 965
Fredericksburg, TX 78624
(830) 685-3636
www.bringfido.com/attraction/11176
pg. 197

Fort Worth Food Park
2509 Weisenberger Street
Fort Worth, TX 76107
(972) 850-8736
www.fwfoodpark.com
pg. 196

Fort Worth Stockyards
500 NE 23rd Street
Fort Worth, TX 76164
(817) 624-4741
www.fortworthstockyards.org
pg. 196

Hill Country State Natural Area
10600 Bandera Creek Road
Bandera, TX 78003
(830) 796-4413
www.bringfido.com/attraction/11177
pg. 197

Inks Lake State Park
3630 Park Road 4 W
Burnet, TX 78611
(512) 793-2223
www.bringfido.com/attraction/11178
pg. 197

Katy Trail
American Airlines Center (Lot F)
2500 Victory Avenue
Dallas, TX 75201
(214) 303-1180
www.katytraildallas.org
pg. 196

McKinney Avenue Trolley
3153 Oak Grove Avenue
Dallas, TX 75204
(214) 855-0006
www.mata.org
pg. 196

Palo Duro Canyon State Park
11450 Park Road 5
Canyon, TX 79015
(806) 488-2227
www.bringfido.com/attraction/10904
pg. 195

Pedernales Falls State Park
2585 Park Road 6026
Johnson City, TX 78636
(830) 868-7304
www.bringfido.com/attraction/11179
pg. 197

Rancho Ponte Vineyard
315 Ranch Road 1376
Fredericksburg, TX 78624
(830) 990-8555
www.ranchoponte.com
pg. 197

Rita's on the River
245 E Commerce Street
San Antonio, TX 78205
(210) 227-7482
www.ritasontheriver.com
pg. 200

River City Run
300 Alamo Plaza
San Antonio, TX 78205
(210) 201-3786
www.rivercityrunsa.com
pg. 200

San Antonio River Walk
849 E Commerce Street
San Antonio, TX 78205
(210) 227-4262
www.thesanantonioriverwalk.com
pg. 200

South Llano River State Park
1927 Park Road 73
Junction, TX 76849
(325) 446-3994
www.bringfido.com/attraction/11180
pg. 197

Uncle Charlie's Old Time Photo Studio
2400 N Main Street
Fort Worth, TX 76164
(817) 714-6648
www.unclecharliesphotos.com
pg. 196

Zilker Botanical Gardens
2220 Barton Springs Road
Austin, TX 78746
(512) 477-8672
www.zilkergarden.org
pg. 194

Zilker Park Boat Rentals
2201 Barton Springs Road
Austin, TX 78746
(512) 478-3852
www.zilkerboats.com
pg. 194

HOTELS
Holiday Inn Express Canyon
2901 4th Avenue
Canyon, TX 79015
(806) 655-4445
www.tinyurl.com/ruff28
pg. 195

Hotel Havana
1015 Navarro Street
San Antonio, TX 78205
(210) 222-2008
www.havanasanantonio.com
pg. 200

Hotel Indigo Houston at the Galleria
5160 Hidalgo Street
Houston, TX 77056
(713) 621-8988
www.bringfido.com/lodging/94761
pg. 199

Hotel Saint Cecilia
112 Academy Drive
Austin, TX 78704
(512) 852-2400
www.hotelsaintcecilia.com
pg. 194

Rosewood Mansion
2821 Turtle Creek Boulevard
Dallas, TX 75219
(214) 559-2100
www.tinyurl.com/ruff29
pg. 196

Spotted Pony Ranch
343 Black Bear Lane
Fredericksburg, TX 78624
(830) 443-4520
www.spottedponyranch.com
pg. 197

UTAH
ATTRACTIONS
Best Friends Animal Sanctuary
5001 Angel Canyon Road
Kanab, UT 84741
(435) 644-2001
www.bestfriends.org
pg. 201

Coral Pink Sand Dunes State Park
Coral Pink Sand Dunes Road
Kanab, UT 84741
(435) 648-2800
www.bringfido.com/attraction/11243
pg. 203

Dreamland Safari Tours
265 N 300 W (Hwy 89)
Kanab, UT 84741
(435) 644-5506
www.dreamlandtours.net
pg. 203

Moab Rafting & Canoe Company
805 N Main Street
Moab, UT 84532
(435) 259-7722
www.moab-rafting.com
pg. 204

Paria Canyon Wilderness
Wire Pass Trailhead
US 89 & House Rock Valley Road
Kanab, UT 84741
(435) 644-4600
www.bringfido.com/attraction/11242
pg. 203

Zion Adventure Company
36 Lion Boulevard
Springdale, UT 84767
(435) 772-1001
www.zionadventures.com
pg. 205

Zion National Park
Utah 9
Springdale, UT 84767
(435) 772-3256
www.nps.gov/zion
pg. 205

HOTELS

3 Dogs & a Moose Cottages
171 W Center Street
Moab, UT 84532
(435) 260-1692
www.tinyurl.com/ruff30
pg. 204

Driftwood Lodge
1515 Zion Park Boulevard
Springdale, UT 84767
(435) 772-3262
www.driftwoodlodge.net
pg. 205

Quail Park Lodge
125 N 300 W (Hwy 89)
Kanab, UT 84741
(435) 215-1447
www.quailparklodge.com
pg. 203

Red Mountain Resort
1275 Red Mountain Circle
Ivins, UT 84738
(435) 673-4905
www.redmountainresort.com
pg. 205

VERMONT
ATTRACTIONS

Dog Mountain
143 Parks Road
St. Johnsbury, VT 05819
(800) 449-2580
www.dogmt.com
pg. 207

Gondola SkyRide
5781 Mountain Road
Stowe, VT 05672
(802) 253-3500
www.gostowe.com/gondola
pg. 208

Mount Mansfield Auto Toll Road
5837 Mountain Road
Stowe, VT 05672
(802) 253-3500
www.gostowe.com/auto-toll-road
pg. 208

Smugglers' Notch State Park
6443 Mountain Road
Stowe, VT 05672
(802) 253-4014
www.bringfido.com/attraction/10531
pg. 208

HOTELS

The Paw House Inn
1376 Clarendon Avenue
West Rutland, VT 05777
(802) 558-2661
www.pawhouseinn.com
pg. 209

Stowe Mountain Lodge
7412 Mountain Road
Stowe, VT 05672
(802) 253-3560
www.stowemountainlodge.com
pg. 208

Wildflower Inn
2059 Darling Hill Road
Lyndonville, VT 05851
(802) 626-8310
www.wildflowerinn.com
pg. 207

VIRGINIA
ATTRACTIONS
Alexandria's Footsteps to the Past
Ramsay House Visitor Center
221 King Street
Alexandria, VA 22314
(703) 683-3451
www.footstepstothepast.com
pg. 210

Assateague Explorer
The Assateague Nature Centre
7512 East Side Road
Chincoteague Island, VA 23336
(757) 336-5956
www.assateagueexplorer.com
pg. 212

The Cheese Shop
410 W Duke of Gloucester Street
Williamsburg, VA 23185
(757) 220-0298
www.cheeseshopwilliamsburg.com
pg. 215

Colonial Williamsburg
101 Visitor Center Drive
Williamsburg, VA 23185
(757) 220-7645
www.colonialwilliamsburg.com
pg. 215

Douthat State Park
14239 Douthat State Park Road
Millboro, VA 24460
(540) 862-8100
www.bringfido.com/attraction/11253
pg. 214

Downriver Canoe Company
884 Indian Hollow Road
Bentonville, VA 22610
(540) 635-5526
www.downriver.com
pg. 213

Historic Jamestowne
2110 Jamestown Road
Williamsburg, VA 23185
(757) 253-4838
www.historicjamestowne.org
pg. 215

Mount Vernon Estate & Gardens
3200 Mount Vernon Memorial Highway
Alexandria, VA 22121
(703) 780-0011
www.mountvernon.org
pg. 210

Potomac Riverboat Company
205 The Strand
Alexandria, VA 22314
(703) 684-0580
www.potomacriverboatco.com
pg. 211

Shenandoah National Park
3655 Highway 211 E
Luray, VA 22835
(540) 999-3500
www.nps.gov/shen
pg. 213

Torpedo Factory Art Center
105 N Union Street
Alexandria, VA 22314
(703) 838-4565
www.torpedofactory.org
pg. 211

HOTELS
Applewood Inn & Llama Trekking
242 Tarn Beck Lane
Lexington, VA 24450
(800) 463-1902
www.applewoodbb.com
pg. 214

Big Meadows Lodge
Shenandoah National Park
Mile 51.2 Skyline Drive
Luray, VA 22851
(801) 559-5070
www.goshenandoah.com
pg. 213

Cascades Motel
102 Visitor Center Drive
Williamsburg, VA 23185
(800) 447-8679
www.colonialwilliamsburg.com
pg. 215

Hotel Monaco Alexandria
480 King Street
Alexandria, VA 22314
(703) 549-6080
www.monaco-alexandria.com
pg. 211

Lewis Mountain Cabins
Shenandoah National Park
Mile 57.5 Skyline Drive
Luray, VA 22835
(801) 559-5070
www.goshenandoah.com
pg. 213

Lorien Hotel & Spa
1600 King Street
Alexandria, VA 22314
(703) 894-3434
www.lorienhotelandspa.com
pg. 210

Skyland Resort
Shenandoah National Park
Mile 41.7 Skyline Drive
Luray, VA 22835
(801) 559-5070
www.goshenandoah.com
pg. 213

Snug Harbor Marina
7536 East Side Road
Chincoteague Island, VA 23336
(757) 336-6176
www.tinyurl.com/ruff31
pg. 212

Williamsburg Inn
136 Francis Street E
Williamsburg, VA 23185
(757) 220-7978
www.colonialwilliamsburg.com
pg. 215

WASHINGTON

ATTRACTIONS

Anacortes Ferry Terminal
2100 Ferry Terminal Road
Anacortes, WA 98221
(206) 464-6400
www.wsdot.com/ferries/schedule
pg. 219

Cape Disappointment State Park
N Head Road & Robert Gray Drive
Ilwaco, WA 98624
(360) 642-3078
www.bringfido.com/attraction/1519
pg. 220

Center for Wooden Boats
1010 Valley Street
Seattle, WA 98109
(206) 382-2628
www.cwb.org/rent
pg. 223

Discovery Bay Golf Course
7401 Cape George Road
Port Townsend, WA 98368
(360) 385-0704
www.discoverybaygolfcourse.com
pg. 221

Discovery Trail
210 26th Street NW
Long Beach, WA 98631
(360) 642-2400
www.bringfido.com/attraction/11182
pg. 220

Dog Mountain Trail
Lewis and Clark Hwy (Milepost 53)
Stevenson, WA 98648
(800) 989-9178
www.bringfido.com/attraction/11183
pg. 166

Ewe-topia Herd Dog Training
6311 288th Street S
Roy, WA 98580
(253) 843-2929
www.ewe-topia.com
pg. 222

Griffiths-Priday State Park
Benner Road
Ocean Shores, WA 98569
(360) 289-5353
www.bringfido.com/attraction/1594
pg. 217

Jackson's Beach
Jackson Beach Road
Friday Harbor, WA 98250
(360) 378-2688
www.bringfido.com/attraction/10411
pg. 219

Kenmore Air
950 Westlake Avenue N
Seattle, WA 98109
(866) 435-9524
www.kenmoreair.com
pg. 223

Lime Kiln State Park
1567 West Side Road
Friday Harbor, WA 98250
(360) 902-8844
www.bringfido.com/attraction/10414
pg. 219

The Market Chef
225 A Street
Friday Harbor, WA 98250
(360) 378-4546
www.bringfido.com/restaurant/10710
pg. 219

Methow Valley Sports Trails
309 Riverside Avenue
Winthrop, WA 98862
(509) 996-3287
www.mvsta.com
pg. 224

Northwest Floatplane Picnics
PO Box 63
Medina, WA 98039
(425) 765-9204
www.nwfloatplanepicnics.com
pg. 223

Pelindaba Lavender Farms
45 Hawthorne Lane
Friday Harbor, WA 98250
(360) 378-4248
www.pelindabalavender.com
pg. 219

Quinault Rain Forest
Information Center
353 South Shore Road
Quinault, WA 98575
(360) 288-2525
www.quinaultrainforest.com
pg. 217

San Juan Island National Historical Park
4668 Cattle Point Road
Friday Harbor, WA 98250
(360) 378-224
www.nps.gov/sajh
pg. 219

Seattle Ferry Service
Valley Street & Terry Avenue N
Seattle, WA 98109
(206) 713-8446
www.seattleferryservice.com
pg. 223

Susie's Mopeds
125 Nichols Street
Friday Harbor, WA 98250
(360) 378-5244
www.susiesmopeds.com
pg. 219

Warehouse Wine District
144th Avenue NE
Woodinville, WA 98072
(425) 208-2770
www.woodwarewine.com
pg. 225

HOTELS

Cedarbrook Lodge
18525 36th Avenue S
Seattle, WA 98188
(206) 901-9268
www.cedarbrooklodge.com
pg. 222

Earthbox Inn & Spa
410 Spring Street
Friday Harbor, WA 98250
(360) 378-4000
www.earthboxinn.com
pg. 219

Hotel 1000
1000 1st Avenue
Seattle, WA 98104
(206) 957-1000
www.hotel1000seattle.com
pg. 223

Hotel Sorrento
900 Madison Street
Seattle, WA 98104
(206) 622-6400
www.hotelsorrento.com
pg. 223

Iron Springs Resort
3707 Highway 109
Copalis Beach, WA 98536
(360) 276-4230
www.ironspringsresort.com
pg. 217

Lighthouse Oceanfront Resort
12417 Pacific Way
Long Beach, WA 98631
(360) 642-3622
www.lighthouseresort.net
pg. 220

Lille Danser Boat & Breakfast
Eagle Harbor Marina
5834 Ward Avenue NE
Bainbridge Island, WA 98110
(206) 786-7627
www.nwboatandbreakfast.com
pg. 216

Rendezvous Huts
Cub Creek Road
Winthrop, WA 98862
(509) 996-8100
www.rendezvoushuts.com
pg. 224

The Resort at Port Ludlow
1 Heron Road
Port Ludlow, WA 98365
(360) 437-7000
www.portludlowresort.com
pg. 221

Willows Lodge
14580 NE 145th Street
Woodinville, WA 98072
(425) 424-3900
www.willowslodge.com
pg. 225

WEST VIRGINIA
ATTRACTIONS

Trans-Allegheny Lunatic Asylum
71 Asylum Drive
Weston, WV 26452
(304) 269-5070
www.talawv.com
pg. 226

HOTELS

Stonewall Resort
940 Resort Drive
Roanoke, WV 26447
(304) 269-7400
www.stonewallresort.com
pg. 226

WISCONSIN
ATTRACTIONS

American Folklore Theatre
Peninsula State Park
10169 Shore Road
Fish Creek, WI 54212
(920) 854-6117
www.folkloretheatre.com
pg. 227

Dells Boat Tours
107 Broadway Avenue
Wisconsin Dells, WI 53965
(608) 254-8555
www.dellsboats.com
pg. 230

Elroy-Sparta Trail
111 Milwaukee Street
Sparta, WI 54656
(608) 269-4123 chamber
www.elroy-sparta-trail.com
pg. 229

Estabrook Beer Garden
4600 Estabrook Parkway
Milwaukee, WI 53217
(414) 226-2728
www.oldgermanbeerhall.com
pg. 228

Kendall Depot
113 White Street
Kendall, WI 54638
(608) 463-7109
www.kendalldepot.com
pg. 229

Milwaukee Boat Line
101 W Michigan Street
Milwaukee, WI 53203
(414) 294-9450
www.mkeboat.com
pg. 228

Milwaukee RiverWalk
1555 N RiverCenter Drive
Milwaukee, WI 53212
(414) 273-3950
www.visitmilwaukee.org/riverwalk
pg. 228

Old Post Office Restaurant
10040 Water Street
Ephraim, WI 54211
(920) 854-4034
www.bringfido.com/restaurant/8484
pg. 227

HOTELS
Baker's Sunset Bay Resort
921 Canyon Road
Wisconsin Dells, WI 53965
(608) 254-8406
www.sunsetbayresort.com
pg. 230

Edgewater Resort
10040 Water Street
Ephraim, WI 54211
(920) 854-2734
www.edge-waterresort.com
pg. 227

The Iron Horse Hotel
500 W Florida Street
Milwaukee, WI 53204
(888) 543-4766
www.theironhorsehotel.com
pg. 228

Justin Trails Resort
7452 Kathryn Avenue
Sparta, WI 54656
(608) 269-4522
www.justintrails.com
pg. 229

WYOMING
ATTRACTIONS
Buffalo Bill's Restaurant & Saloon
The Irma Hotel
1192 Sheridan Avenue
Cody, WY 82414
(307) 587-4221
www.irmahotel.com
pg. 231

Cody Wyoming Adventures
1119 12th Street
Cody, WY 82414
(307) 587-6988
www.codywyomingadventures.com
pg. 231

Yellowstone National Park
Old Faithful Viewing Area
1 Grand Loop Road
Yellowstone National Park, WY 82190
(307) 344-7381
www.nps.gov/yell
pg. 129

HOTELS
The Cody Hotel
232 W Yellowstone Avenue
Cody, WY 82414
(307) 587-5915
www.thecody.com
pg. 231

INDEX

ACKNOWLEDGEMENTS

Dog people are a friendly and helpful breed. In doing research for this book, we asked dog owners around the country to share their favorite spots to spend a day with their pooch. And share they did! We received literally thousands of suggestions, tips, and photos from dog families coast to coast. We were touched by the passion, kindness, and generosity of everyone who responded to our call. Several of the contributors became so involved in our project that it is only fitting to display their names below, alongside our employees who worked so tirelessly on the book this year.

And, of course, we need to thank the people who inspired us to write the book in the first place. The thing is—they're not people at all! They are the dogs who begged to come along on our road trip, posed for the camera so effortlessly, and made each and every hotel room feel like home. Thanks for sharing the road with us! It wouldn't have been the same without you.

Ace, Ann Allums, Annabelle, Sara Argue, Gerilyn Attebery, Biscuit, Bunter, Anna Braunscheidel, Alyssa Buecker, Camden, Chloe Polka Dot, Clara, Cooper, Elizabeth Clinard, Dali, DaVinci, Django, Doughall, Brenda Ernst, Ashleigh & Chase Finch, Frederick, Beth & Hunter Freeman, Erin Gregory, Samantha Gromoll, Gus, Hairy Putter, Jackson Halliburton, Jason & Melissa Halliburton, Hazel, Nancy Heinonen, Brian Howard, Huckleberry, Humphrey, Isabelle, Izzi, Jackson, Peggy Jammer, Little Jerry, Josie, Candice Katayama, Kathy & Robert Kendall, Kris Kendall, Courtney Kotowski, Julie Jameson Leaver, Linus, Lucy, Candilynn & Michael Lockhart, Maddie, Marabelle, Eve Memmer, Kate Mendez, Mona, Elizabeth Morrisey, Jennifer Most, Rene Nedelkoff, Odo, Oddi, Jennifer Ott, Pablo, Parker, Mr. Peabody, Picaso, Brandon Rhodes, Larry Rich, Ringo, Rocco, Roxy, Shonda Rutland, Sammy, Lorena Sanchez, Renee Sartell Sanchez, Sarge, Alison Seidenberg, Leah Senona, Shamus, Eric Stevens, Sylvie, Sugar Booger, Tank, Thomas, Tito, Scott Tunstall, Vegas, Katie & Tom Whitfield, Wishbone

PHOTOGRAPHERS

Ruff Guide to the United States

Editor Melissa Halliburton
Contributing Writers Ann Allums, Jason Halliburton, Melissa Halliburton, Elizabeth Morrisey, Leah Senona, Scott Tunstall
Art Directors Brenda Ernst, Eric Stevens
Cover Design Gerilyn Attebery
Photo Editors Brenda Ernst, Candilynn Lockhart
Copy Editors Elizabeth Clinard, Jason Halliburton
Researchers Erin Gregory, Samantha Gromoll, Julie Jameson Leaver, Jennifer Ott, Brandon Rhodes, Shonda Rutland

Published by Kendall Media, Inc.
PO Box 1489, Travelers Rest, SC 29690

Library of Congress Control Number 2014900188

ISBN 978-1-939726-00-1

Printed in the United States of America.
First printed in 2014

10 9 8 7 6 5 4 3 2 1